100,000 HEARTS

Denton A. Cooley MD

100,000 Hearts

A Surgeon's Memoir

Denton A. Cooley, M.D.

A Bag of Tools

Isn't it strange
That princes and kings,
And clowns that caper
In sawdust rings,
And common people
Like you and me
Are builders for eternity?

Each is given a bag of tools,
A shapeless mass
A book of rules;
And each must make
Ere life has flown
A stumbling block
Or a stepping stone.

R. L. Sharpe

To my wife, Louise, and my five daughters, who have balanced my life.

IT WAS THE MOST BEAUTIFUL SURGERY I HAD EVER SEEN IN MY LIFE. Every movement had a purpose and achieved its aim. Where most surgeons would take three hours, he could do the same operation in one hour. It went forward like a broad river—never fast, never in obvious haste, yet never going back. Some surgeons drove themselves, their hands groping for a solution to the imbalance before them. Dr. Cooley's hands moved effortlessly, as though he was simply putting everything back in place. This allowed him to make direct and often dramatic entries which would seem daring if done by anyone else. In dissecting the femoral artery, for example, one normally would make a small cut, then another and another, until it was exposed. Dr. Cooley simply made one slit, and the femoral artery lay open. No one in the world, I knew, could equal it . . . Dr. Cooley's skill was matched by his grace and kindness towards me.

—*Christiaan Barnard*
One Life, George G. Harrap & Co., London, 1969

DR. COOLEY HAS ALWAYS PLAYED AT THE TOP OF HIS GAME, WHETHER as a basketball star at the University of Texas or as a world-class heart surgeon. How he accomplished all that is a must read.

—*Tom Brokaw*

EVEN WERE HE NOT AN EXTRAORDINARY SURGEON, DENTON COOLEY would still be considered a great human being because of his intelligence, optimistic nature, and determination to be the very best. But when one combines those qualities with his contributions to medicine, it becomes crystal clear that Denton Cooley is a once-in-a-generation figure. *100,000 Hearts* is a must read for anyone who has a heart—not just because of Denton's contributions to medicine but also because he is the gold standard for all who wish to live life to its fullest.

—*James A. Baker III*

DR. COOLEY'S MEMOIR SERVES AS AN ENTHRALLING HISTORY OF THE innovative spirit that forged our heart surgery specialty, and the broad reach of his influence is reflected in the brilliant healers he trained, including my greatest teacher (and father-in-law) Gerald Lemole, M.D.

—*Mehmet Oz, M.D.*

DENTON COOLEY IS NOT ONLY A NATIONAL TREASURE FOR HIS pioneering work in heart transplants and artificial hearts but also a great personal friend of George's and mine. Denton's own caring heart has earned him a Presidential Medal of Freedom from Ronald Reagan, and we feel he is a true Point of Light.

—*Barbara Bush*

THE MEMOIR OF DENTON COOLEY SHARES WITH US THE EXCITEMENT of his monumental accomplishments. His prodigious talents allowed him to guide the next generation of pioneering heart surgeons. To attain his enormous success, he stepped lightly or charged vigorously, depending on the nature of the situation. History will remember him as the world's most versatile and masterful heart surgeon. As his protégé and intimate friend, I know this to be true.

—*John Ochsner, M.D.*

PIONEERING SURGEON, INVENTOR, FAMILY MAN, ATHLETE, RANCHER, world traveler, businessman, philanthropist, peacemaker . . . these are some of the faces of Denton Cooley you will meet in the pages of this book. I am proud to call Denton my friend.

—*Gene Cernan*

WHEN WE THINK OF AMERICA'S BEGINNINGS, WE THINK OF Columbus. When we think of planet earth's moon, we think of Neil Armstrong. When we think of the incredible feat of a human heart transplant, we think of Dr. Denton Cooley.

—*Tom Watson*

Contents

Foreword

D<small>R. DENTON COOLEY AND I FIRST MET</small> when I was a young
astronaut and when he was already a legendary cardiovascular surgeon. Our friendship grew over the years, possibly
because we were both pioneers in our respective professions and he
had an intense interest in the space program. My passion led me to
reach for the stars, leading to the day I could call the moon my home.
Denton Cooley's passion led him to reach into the human heart and
heal it. A common bond between us was the nature of the territories
we explored: the moon was an "almost mythical land" that had long
been regarded as a religious icon and a romantic symbol; likewise, the
human heart was traditionally viewed as the seat of the soul and emotions. In venturing into these unexplored territories, both of us chal-
lenged long-held beliefs and attitudes. We took risks that few others
would have dared to consider.

Such exploration is fueled by curiosity, which is the essence of
human existence. Denton has always had a restless curiosity that never
lets him accept things as they are but drives him to seek better, newer
alternatives. He is well known for pioneering heart transplants and
many other surgical procedures, including the first implant of a total
artificial heart in man. But he has done numerous other things that are
equally important—as you will learn from reading this book.

Denton's scientific bent has never eclipsed his warm bedside manner. A few years ago, his warmth and friendship were especially com-
forting when I became a heart patient. In 2005 I began to have trouble
breathing and soon had difficulty doing almost anything. As a naval
aviator and later space voyager, I was used to moving confidently into
the unknown, but illness was a different kind of unknown for me.
From an "invincible" moonwalker I felt transformed into an ordinary

mortal. A stress test showed a triple blockage of my coronary arteries. Bypass surgery offered my only hope for avoiding an eventual heart attack and returning to a normal life. My mind was eased because my operation would be performed by Dr. J. Michael Duncan, a member of the Cooley team at the Texas Heart Institute at St. Luke's Episcopal Hospital. This team comprises undoubtedly the finest heart surgeons in the country. Although Denton would not personally wield the scalpel on me, I was greatly relieved to know that my old friend would be in the game. After the operation, I awakened in the intensive care unit. I was wired like a robot, and plastic tubes seemed to fill every vacancy in my body. Through the dimness of anesthesia, I became aware of a tall man in a white coat standing beside my bed. It was Denton, there when I needed him most. "Gene," he said gently, "everything turned out great. You're going to be fine." At that moment, I thought Denton Cooley stood one step short of God. He was right, of course, as always. I recovered fully, and my flight surgeon cleared me to fly again.

In my own memoirs, *The Last Man on the Moon*, I described how—once the race to the moon was over—the rivalry between the United States and the Soviet Union was set aside. After being bitter enemies, the American astronauts and Soviet cosmonauts finally became colleagues and friends. I was surprised and pleased to learn that my description of that rapprochement influenced Denton to seek reconciliation with Dr. Michael DeBakey after forty years of rivalry. To my mind, that peacemaking overture showed Denton Cooley's true greatness of soul.

In reading *100,000 Hearts*, you will have an opportunity to look more closely at the man behind the Cooley legend. This book could have been written like a scientific treatise, but instead it is a warm look at a rare person who has explored life to its fullest in a profession where "good" is never "good enough." Pioneering surgeon, inventor, family man, athlete, rancher, world traveler, businessman, philanthropist, peacemaker . . . these are some of the faces of Denton Cooley you will meet in the pages of this book. Above all, he is a man committed to being the very best at whatever he does. Because of that commitment, his surgical skill and innovation have given thousands of patients back their lives. I am thankful that mine is among the 100,000 hearts reflected in the title of this book.

Thank you, Denton. I am proud to call you my friend.

GENE CERNAN

Preface

FOR NEARLY A DECADE, my colleagues and trainees have been urging me to write about my long career in heart surgery and what led up to it. I myself have long wanted to set the record straight about various episodes in my career, particularly the first implant of the total artificial heart and my subsequent feud with Dr. Michael E. DeBakey. As I approached my ninetieth birthday, I realized that if I were going to write my memoirs, I needed to get on with it.

One of the first things I had to decide was what audience to aim for in this book. Should I write primarily for doctors and give all the complicated details of surgical procedures, or should I write mainly for lay people and keep medical details to a minimum? It would have been hard to do both. The surgical details have already been published in my collected papers, some of which are listed in Appendix D. After much thought, I decided to make this book informal and conversational, aiming it mainly at a lay audience. In describing the surgical procedures, a certain amount of technical material was unavoidable. Wherever possible, I put this material in a footnote. At the end of the book is a glossary that defines all the medical terms mentioned in the text. There are also drawings of the heart, the great vessels, and several medical conditions described in the book. In addition, there is a list of my surgical firsts and some other brief biographical information in the back of the book. Anyone who wants to learn more or see pictures we couldn't fit into this book can visit the Texas Heart Institute website, www.texasheart.org/cooley.

These memoirs reflect my personality, in that I've tried to tell the story simply and truthfully, letting the events speak for themselves. I've also tried to be respectful and considerate, to avoid gossip, and to omit surgical details that might ruin your lunch. Other people have written sensationalized accounts of my life that may be more entertaining than this one. What you will read here is *my* version, and I know it well. In writing these memoirs, I relied on a series of oral interviews that I did at the Texas Heart Institute a number of years ago. I also depended extensively on my collected medical papers. To the degree possible, I carefully checked each fact, although I sometimes had to rely on memory alone. My colleagues tell me that, for someone my age, I have an amazing memory still. However, if there are mistakes, I apologize in advance. It's too bad I didn't have the time or foresight to keep a diary!

Another decision I had to make was whose names to mention in the book. I hope you won't be disappointed if you don't find your name here. If I had mentioned too many people who didn't figure in the stories, other people might feel that they had been left out. Where would I have drawn the line? So I decided to mention names and details based mainly on how they furthered the story line.

This book couldn't have been completed without the help of several people at the Texas Heart Institute who have worked with me closely for at least thirty years: Marianne Mallia and Virginia Fairchild, who edited these memoirs and assisted with fact-checking; Joan Miller, my administrative assistant, who dredged up many letters, photos, and historical records from her files; Dena Houchin, my clinical coordinator, who critiqued the manuscript and helped jog my memory; Ken Hoge and his staff in Visual Communications, who prepared the photographs and illustrations used in the text; and the staff of the Department of Biostatistics, who supplied crucial numbers. I owe special thanks to my surgical associate Bud Frazier, who critiqued the manuscript and offered valuable suggestions. I've known Bud since the mid-1960s, when he was a medical student at Baylor, and he's been an integral part of my program since his days as a resident with me.

I also had help from outside the Texas Heart Institute. My wife, Louise, and daughters—Mary, Susan, "Weezie," and Helen—reminded me of a few stories I had forgotten and dipped into the "archives" for photographs and historical documents. Luckily, my nephew Talbot Cooley preserved many early family photos and was happy to share them for this project. I am also very grateful to my friend Eugene Cernan for writing the foreword for this book. I thank the Dolph Briscoe Center for American History and the University of Texas Press for their work in getting this manuscript published, especially Holly Taylor and Erin Purdy at the Briscoe Center. I also want to thank Briscoe Center Executive Director Dr. Don Carleton, whose work made this book possible.

Finally, I owe a sincere debt of gratitude to my entire team at the Texas Heart Institute—my surgical associates and the other medical staff, as well as nurses, technicians, perfusionists, researchers, support personnel, and administrators—for their assistance over the years. By doing their jobs, they freed me to do mine.

DENTON A. COOLEY, M.D.
OCTOBER 2011

THE CONVENTIONAL THINKING ABOUT CARDIAC SURGERY AT THE
BEGINNING OF THE TWENTIETH CENTURY:

"Any surgeon who would attempt an operation on the heart should
lose the respect of his colleagues."

—Theodor Billroth, intrepid Viennese surgeon
General Surgery . . . A Handbook for Students and Physicians, 1893

"Surgery of the heart has probably reached the limits set by
nature to all surgery."

—Stephen Paget, prominent English surgeon
The Surgery of the Chest, 1896

"In a large proportion of the cases [of congenital heart disease], the
anomaly is not compatible with life, and in others nothing can be
done to remedy the defect or even to relieve the symptoms. . . .
The child should be [kept] warmly clad . . ."

—Sir William Osler, renowned North American physician
The Principles and Practice of Medicine, 1912

Introduction

"**O**KAY, DOMINGO, let's see how well this thing works in a human being." Dr. Domingo Liotta gave me a quick thumbs-up as a nurse placed the artificial heart in my hands. The date was April 4, 1969, and the setting was Operating Room 1 at St. Luke's Episcopal Hospital, in Houston, Texas. Domingo and I were standing over the anesthetized form of Haskell Karp, a forty-seven-year-old man whose heart I had just removed. Scarred and useless, it reminded me of a deflated basketball. I was ready to replace this failed heart with a plastic pump that Domingo and I had designed and tested in calves. We hoped that the artificial heart would keep Mr. Karp alive until a suitable donor heart could be found for transplantation. As he lay before us on the operating table, he had no respiration or pulse of his own. His circulation was being supported by a heart-lung machine.

Nobody had ever tried to use an artificial heart in a human being before. This would be a supreme test not only of my skill as a surgeon but also of my judgment as a physician. I would soon be trading the bright lights of the operating room for the glare of public opinion. My critics would be eager to pounce, seeing this operation not as an attempt to save my patient but as a bid for the surgical limelight.

At the end of the procedure, however, I felt optimistic. The plastic pump took over Mr. Karp's circulation without any problems. His condition immediately began to improve. Before long, he was conscious and able to move his fingers and toes. I could hardly believe how smoothly everything had gone.

The first implant of a total artificial heart is probably the operation for which I am best known. But there's much more to my story than that one procedure. I am very fortunate to have taken part in the renowned 1944 "blue baby" operation at Johns Hopkins Hospital, which marked the dawn of heart surgery, and in most of the subsequent major developments in the field. As of 2001, I and my team at the Texas Heart Institute had operated on more than 100,000 human hearts. Many of those procedures also involved surgical breakthroughs, and we're still making them—thousands of hearts later.

What formative influences and twists of fate led me to achieve what I did? How would I like to be remembered by future generations? Over the years, there have been many stories about me in the news media, but they may not necessarily reflect the way things actually happened. Some of my closest associates are familiar with those stories and even took part in them. They urged me to write my memoirs and set the record straight to the best of my recollection. They also thought that others might be inspired by learning how a shy young man became a famous heart surgeon.

I'll start with my birth more than ninety years ago.

100,000 HEARTS

My mother, Mary Fraley Cooley, and me.

CHAPTER 1

My Roots

I AM ONE OF THOSE RARITIES, a native Houstonian. Born at Baptist Hospital on Sunday, August 22, 1920, I was delivered by a friend of my parents, Dr. Ernst William Bertner, who would later help found the Texas Medical Center. My birth was a breech delivery. That means I arrived seat first, which was good for me because it paved the way for my oversized head. Poor mother! Even now, I wear a size 8-plus hat and have trouble finding a golf cap that fits. According to family legend, my difficult birth encouraged Dr. Bertner to consider retiring from obstetrics and concentrating on surgery.

My roots in the "Bayou City" go back to the 1890s, the Gilded Age in American history. At that time, the nation was undergoing massive industrialization. Large numbers of people were moving from rural to urban areas in search of new opportunities. The population growth in cities such as Houston attracted developers eager to buy land and build houses. It was because of the enterprising spirit of the Gilded Age that my story began in Houston.

I am proud that my paternal grandfather, Daniel Denton Cooley, was one of the developers who ended up here. Grandfather Cooley was born in 1850, at the beginning of the tumultuous decade that led up to the Civil War. He grew up in Binghamton, New York, where he attended business college. A true pioneer, he moved west as a young man. He eventually landed as treasurer and general manager of the Omaha and South Texas Land Company in Ashland, Nebraska. In 1891 the company purchased 1,765 unincorporated acres on the northwest outskirts of what is now downtown Houston. Being some twenty-three feet higher than Houston's swampy downtown area, this bare tract was optimistically christened Houston Heights.

Two years after the company bought the site, Granddad was sent to Houston to organize and develop what became known as "The Heights." He set to work laying out the street plan and building the new town's infrastructure. Granddad also helped design its impressive main street, Heights Boulevard, which was comparable to Commonwealth Boulevard in Boston. For several decades, Heights Boulevard was considered the most beautiful street in Houston. Granddad insisted on having twin bridges built on the boulevard across White Oak Bayou to connect the Heights to downtown. Because the boulevard had an elaborately landscaped esplanade, my grandfather wanted to build a separate bridge for each lane to maintain the boulevard's symmetry. Most of the other land company members thought that this would be an extravagance and that a single bridge would suffice. Granddad won that argument. As a result of his hard work, history now regards him as the "father" of the Heights. In 1919 the Heights was incorporated into the city of Houston.

When Granddad came to Houston, he brought his wife, Helen Grace Winfield, and their three small boys: Denton, Arthur, and Ralph. The first dwelling in the Heights, and for many decades the most impressive, was their house, which was built at 1802 Heights Boulevard in 1893. It was meant to set the tone for all the other homes in the neighborhood. A three-story frame mansion, Granddad's house had the typical cupola and ornate gingerbread trim of the Victorian era. It had eight bedrooms, hot and cold running water, and an arrangement of speaking tubes that served as an intercom. The house also was the first residence in the Heights to have electricity. The Houston Electric Company's trolley travelled to and from downtown Houston on a rail line that ran up and down the esplanade in the middle of Heights Boulevard. The story was that Granddad, like other residents near the streetcar line, lit his house by hooking a line onto the trolley wire. Whenever a streetcar passed, the house's lights would grow dim. Despite its Victorian splendor, the area long remained enough of a wilderness that prowling wolves were considered a threat. At times, my grandmother even kept her children indoors for fear of wolves.

My grandparents both believed in giving back to the community, and their example has always inspired me. I never met Grandmother Cooley because she died in 1916, before I was born, but I know that, like Granddad, she believed in civic service. She worked tirelessly to beautify the Heights and plant gardens along the esplanade. In 1911 she and Granddad donated a parcel of land for the Houston Heights Woman's Club. Grandmother and the other women quickly raised money to build a clubhouse. The club was responsible for a variety of community programs and social activities. During World Wars I and II, the American Red Cross used the clubhouse, and club members volunteered many hours to make surgical dressings for the soldiers. It remains in use today—the oldest clubhouse in Houston. Both of my grandparents also worked hard to improve the education of young people in the area. They led the movement to build the first schoolhouse in the Heights. Granddad donated the lot for the school, and Grandmother sold some of her jewelry to fund the building. The school opened in 1894 and was named the Cooley School to honor my grandparents. Granddad served for many years on the school board, and Grandmother was the first president of the mothers' club. I still have the oil portraits of my grandparents that once hung in the school. Unfortunately, the old building was recently demolished. Granddad and Grandmother also helped establish St. Andrews Episcopal Church on Heights Boulevard, and Granddad gave money to construct it. Until the church was built, the congregation met in the parlor at my grandparents' home. In the early 1920s Granddad led the effort to create a municipally chartered hospital, which was named Jefferson Davis County Hospital. I would later be on the surgical staff there.

* * *

I was named in honor of my uncles Denton and Arthur. I like to think that I am somewhat a blend of the two. Uncle Denton was tall and athletic and played football and other sports in high school. Hardworking like his father, Uncle Denton later founded the Marine Bank and Trust Company. Uncle Arthur was born with a dislocated hip that left him partially disabled. He was a particularly kind and compassionate man. He and his wife, Armine, never had children of their own, but they had many foster children who adored them, as did I.

My grandparents' youngest son, Ralph Clarkson Cooley—who would later become my father—was born in 1885. He grew into a masculine, popular, self-confident man, who could tell great stories and jokes. He was six feet tall, with blue eyes. As he got older, he developed a considerable paunch.

As a boy, my father went to Cooley School and later Heights High School along with his brothers Denton and Arthur. He was the first of many Cooleys to attend the University of Texas (UT). He had hoped to be a doctor but withdrew after ten days because an episode of hazing worsened the bronchial asthma that had troubled him since childhood. Frightened for his health, my grandmother convinced him not to return to UT. Instead, she persuaded him to enroll in the newly formed Texas Dental College, in Houston, which in those days required only a high school diploma for admission. My father graduated at age eighteen or nineteen as a full-fledged dentist—something that could never happen today. I remember his saying on many occasions that he regretted not becoming a physician. Those memories would later play a role in my decision to go to medical instead of dental school.

In about 1916 my father married my mother, Mary Augusta Fraley, who had been born to Frederick W. and Ethel Fraley on March 11, 1896, in Marshall, Texas. Ethel's father was Dr. Robert William McCutchan, who studied medicine in Alabama and later at the University of Nashville, from which he graduated in 1870. During the 1870s and 1880s, he apparently practiced medicine between Longview and Gladewater in East Texas. Perhaps I inherited a medical gene from him.

My mother had three younger siblings: Frederick, an early graduate of the Rice Institute (now Rice University), who majored in chemical engineering; Etheldra, who became an artist; and Florence, who married a New Orleans lawyer named Harry Talbot. Mother ended up in Houston because her father took a job with Houston's Sinclair Oil Company. She graduated from Central High School and was said to be the prettiest young woman in town. When she met my father, he was already a practicing dentist. After their wedding, my parents took the interurban electric train to Galveston and stayed at the Galvez Hotel, the most elegant one on the island. (I would actually purchase that hotel sixty years later.) On returning to Houston, they moved into the Rice Hotel, a posh new downtown structure that, at seventeen stories, was the city's tallest building. On April 25, 1919, my brother, Ralph Clarkson Cooley Jr., was born.

After I was born sixteen months later, my parents decided that a hotel wasn't the best place to raise two boys, so they bought a bungalow for $6,500 at 908 W. Alabama Street in the new Montrose addition southwest of downtown. It had two bedrooms and a small yard. Because this house was essentially my birthplace, my own children jokingly call it "the manger." It is still standing more than ninety years later.

By the time I came along, the Prohibition era had just begun. Ford

Model T cars were selling well, home radios were beginning to catch on, and women had just been granted the right to vote. Under Presidents Warren G. Harding and Calvin Coolidge, America was enjoying a period of economic prosperity that would last for most of the decade. A loaf of bread cost twelve cents, a gallon of milk sixty-six cents, and a gallon of gasoline thirty cents.

In many ways, Houston symbolized the pioneering spirit of Texas and embodied the state's "larger-than-life" attitude. Since 1901, when the Spindletop oil field was discovered near Beaumont, oil had made Houston's fortune. In 1914 the Houston Ship Channel was completed, and the city began to send "black gold" all over the world. Soon oil refineries sprang up along the ship channel. With the growth of the automobile industry and the demand for fuel and oil during World War I, Houston's economy exploded. The port and railroads expanded, cotton revenues reached new heights, and construction projects dotted the skyline. This was a great time to come to Houston and get rich. From 1900 to 1920, the city tripled its size to nearly 140,000 people.

My mother's small-town background made her very protective of my brother, Ralph, and me. Like Daddy, Ralph was handsome, charming, and the life of any party. Also like Daddy, he had bronchial asthma. Both of them used Green Mountain Asthma Cure, a remedy you could order via mail to relieve bronchial spasms. In those days medicine was practiced more haphazardly, and homeopathic remedies were about all we had. Green Mountain contained stramonium leaves soaked in a strong solution of saltpeter. It was misted from an atomizer. I later found out that it contained small quantities of cocaine, which may be why it made users feel so good. Ralph also had visceroptosis, or "dropped stomach," a condition thought to cause chronic gastric and intestinal symptoms and contribute to poor nutrition. These days it is regarded as an outmoded diagnosis that was something of a fad at the time. In the hope of realigning his organs, Ralph had to spend days in bed with his feet up. I hated how he suffered, and I yearned to do something to help him. His poor health, always a family focus, made me aware of how tough a chronic illness could be.

Mother devoted her life to her two sons, and we always had the deepest affection for her. I used to rejoice when anybody would say something really nice about my mother. She had brown eyes and hair and was strikingly good looking. She wasn't all that tall, but she had great style and made most of her own clothes. I thought she looked especially chic in "flapper" dresses. Mother loved talking with people and was a natural conversationalist. She even enjoyed hearing (and telling) an occasional off-color joke. She often started these jokes by saying, "Let me tell you a story the Bishop told me." Mother was very kind. She had such a great sense of humor that her grandchildren called her "Coo Coo." Though not a college graduate, she audited English courses at the Rice Institute while raising Ralph and me. Grandmother Fraley had taught piano, and my mother was also an excellent pianist. I loved hearing her play. On special occasions she would accompany my father, who sang or played his violin.

My relationship with my father was somewhat complicated. He motivated me to do my very best in whatever I undertook. He also taught me the importance of family and of loyalty to family members. He was truly considerate of the feelings of others and encouraged me to be the same way. He could not tolerate people who were "inconsiderate," and I learned that big word when I was very young. Naturally, I was quite proud of him and inspired by him.

My father was one of the finest dental surgeons of his day and constantly sought new ways to improve his profession. Being highly creative, he was able to invent several devices and materials that would improve dental practice. One was an affordable, resin-based sealant called Copalite, fondly known as "Doc's Best Cement." After a tooth is drilled, Copalite is applied between the tooth's surface and the gold or silver filling. This sealant was originally produced in our home, and my brother and I were often enlisted to help mix and package it. We enjoyed helping our father, the inventor. To encourage my interest in dentistry, he even let me cast one of my own gold inlays, which I still have in my mouth today, seventy-five years later!

At an early age, I also learned how to counsel patients. In the evenings, Daddy often didn't want to be disturbed by phone calls from patients with routine toothaches. So he instructed me to tell them his special cure: "Take an aspirin, have a shot of whiskey, and come to the office at 9:00 in the morning."

Daddy served as president of the Texas Dental Association and the American Academy of Restorative Dentistry. He took great pride in his fellowship in the International College of Dentists and wore his gold membership key, prominently displayed on a key chain, every day.

Always concerned about public respect for his profession, Daddy was annoyed at how some dentists shamelessly promoted themselves. He thought that advertising made dentists seem undignified. I remember that he would be especially irate every time we drove by the office of one particular dentist, who had a large wooden tooth hanging outside his building.

Daddy had many patients. His most prominent one was Jesse H. Jones, who was a banker, a developer, and the publisher of the *Houston Chronicle*. Jones was appointed to the Reconstruction Finance Corporation (RFC) under President Herbert C. Hoover. Later, President Franklin D. Roosevelt appointed him head of the RFC and also secretary of commerce. Those positions gave Jones enormous power. There was even some talk that he should run for president.

Of course, Daddy also took care of Ralph's teeth and mine. Like most other children, I hated the dentist's drill and dreaded having checkups. Thinking back on those days, I recall Christopher Morley's poem:

> All joys I bless, but I confess
> There is one greatest thrill:
> What the dentist does when he stops the buzz
> And puts away the drill.

In elementary school, my classmates and I regularly had to fill out a form asking about our hygiene. One of the questions was, "Do you brush your teeth twice a day and see your dentist twice a year"? I always wanted to answer, "I see my *dentist* twice a day and brush my *teeth* twice a year."

In a write-up by the Texas Dental Association, my father was portrayed as "a raconteur, bon vivant, and friend to everyone who came his way." I thought that described his public persona well. In private, though, we sometimes saw another side of him, especially if he'd had too much to drink. On those occasions, he almost became a different person. He had a hot temper and could rant and rave over fairly trivial matters but would usually apologize later. When Daddy was drinking, he sometimes abused my mother physically. I couldn't excuse him for that. Their relationship, which was happy in the early years of their marriage, unfortunately deteriorated over time. For my sake and Ralph's, however, the two of them stayed together during our formative years, keeping the family intact until we were in college.

With Ralph, left, running our first business venture: a soft-drink stand in front of our house at 908 W. Alabama. Appearing with us is a neighbor, Edgar Saper, center, who would eventually become my accountant.

CHAPTER 2

Boyhood Friends and Activities

S OME OF MY FONDEST CHILDHOOD MEMORIES are of exploring my grandfather Cooley's home in the Heights. Granddad, who died when I was thirteen, was a tall, stately gentleman with a large white moustache and a completely bald head. His house was constructed during the horse and buggy era, so the side porch had a high landing to help ladies step into and out of a horse-drawn carriage.

To a small boy, Granddad's house was filled with fascinating things. In the attic was an old saddle of my grandmother's. I loved to sit on it and "gallop across Texas." Ralph and I liked to play hide-and-seek in the attic. One of my favorite hiding places was a large, cedar-lined closet where my father had his asthma treatments as a boy. There my grandmother burned a special concoction that she made from garden leaves and herbs to relieve his bronchial spasms. The basement was another fun space. It seemed like a cave to Ralph and me. In exploring its dark, damp corners, we were constantly on the lookout for hidden treasure. The only actual "treasure" we ever found was a crop of edible mushrooms that Granddad raised down there.

The barn, or garage, was also a holdover from the horse and buggy days. Its loft held saddles, harnesses, horse collars, and various old hand tools. My grandfather owned one of the first automobiles in Houston. I still remember that car well. It was a Maxwell, the make of car later made famous by the comedian Jack Benny. Granddad's car dated from about 1908, and its license plate bore the number 3, so it was only the third car registered in Harris County. I would sit in the driver's seat and pretend to race down the road at the car's top speed of about fifty miles per hour.

In the yard were a coop for chickens and a pen for homing pigeons. During World War I, pigeons specially trained to fly home were used to carry messages from the front lines. After the war, raising such pigeons became a popular pastime, and people used their birds to communicate with friends and neighbors who shared the same hobby. Granddad let me help him train his pigeons, and I always loved to see them return home.

Granddad's house also served as the setting for many happy family gatherings, especially on major holidays. On his death in 1933, the house was taken over by Uncle Arthur, who lived there until 1965. When he died, the house was left empty, but by that time it had fallen into disrepair. My brother and I hoped to restore the house and give it to the Heritage Society, but we became worried about its safety after vandals broke in on several occasions and caused even more damage. So about six months after Uncle Arthur died, we had the house demolished. To this day, I regret that we didn't have a caretaker move in so that it would be standing today as a monument to my grandparents' life and work in the Heights. In 1979 the Houston Heights Association bought the vacant lot and turned it into a recreational area called Marmion Park, named after the last mayor of Houston Heights. One of the park's main attractions is the award-winning Kaiser Pavilion, designed to copy the unique turret on my grandparents' house. I am happy that a modernized, smaller replica of the house was later built across the street from the original site.

My maternal grandparents, the Fraleys, lived only a few blocks from our Montrose home, and Ralph and I often rode our bikes over to see them. They were avid pinochle players and always had a game underway. Ralph and I liked to peer over their shoulders and guess what card they might play next. Although Mother was good at sewing, Grandmother Fraley was even better. She was usually the one who made my special clothes, including costumes for Halloween and school plays. I remember that once in third grade when we were studying Indians, our teacher decided to put on a play. I was excited to get the part of Pooshawattaha, a Choctaw chief who sprang from an oak tree instead of being born normally. Grandmother made me a pair of fringed pants, and I appeared bare-chested onstage. I could see my mother in the audience smiling and assumed that it was because she was proud of her son the actor. When I asked her about it later, she said, "Of course I was proud of you, but I was also thinking about how much easier your birth would have been if *you'd* sprung from an oak."

Ever since then, I have jokingly called myself "Whatawamah" because I could never remember the chief's real name.

. . .

In 1926 I started the first grade at Montrose Elementary School, which was at an easy distance for walking, roller skating, or bicycling from home. No matter how unpleasant the weather, my parents never drove me to school. When warm weather arrived, many boys went to school barefoot. Mother always expected me to wear shoes to school, but I wanted to be like the other boys. So, after leaving the house, I often hid my shoes in a vacant field and didn't retrieve them until I was nearly home.

My early education was mostly traditional. I learned the three "Rs"—reading, 'riting, and 'rithmetic. My teachers emphasized writing legibly, now something of a lost art. In those days, students were taught the Palmer method of handwriting, which emphasized cursive script over printed letters. I remember making loops for what seemed like hours with sweeping, rhythmic motions of my arm. I am proud that over the years I have preserved my handwriting skill, even as a member of a profession not known for good penmanship.

Despite his health problems, my brother, Ralph, was my closest friend and playmate. I was only sixteen months younger, so we were constant companions. Like other boys, we enjoyed shooting marbles, playing shinny (a form of hockey on roller skates), and spinning tops. We also enjoyed collecting butterflies, postage stamps, and cigar bands. I was always curious, especially about the biological sciences. Our neighborhood was a bike ride away from hunting, fishing, and camping sites. At that time, nobody had private swimming pools, so we occasionally swam in Buffalo Bayou or White Oak Bayou. Ralph and I played with rubber guns, using ammunition fashioned from strips of automobile inner tubes. We soon graduated to air rifles and .22-caliber rifles. We often shot birds and squirrels, which we cleaned and took home to Mother to cook. These experiences gave me my first view of internal organs, including the heart. I was fascinated.

Within walking distance of our home was a mansion owned by oilman T. P. Lee. That place attracted Ralph and me like a magnet. Mr. Lee raised figs that we thought were the perfect afternoon snack. Ralph and I would see which of us could snatch the most figs without getting caught. "Get out of here, you naughty boys!" the housekeeper would shout, chasing but never catching us. Our fig raids may have taught us a questionable lesson: stolen fruit is sweeter than store-bought. The historic mansion is now the central office of the University of St. Thomas, a Catholic liberal-arts school.

One day, after a heavy rain, some neighbor boys joined Ralph and me in a mud-ball fight. Bored with targeting each other, we turned our attention to the cars passing in front of our house. As we happily splattered one vehicle after another with mud, one of our victims stopped his car and came after us yelling. Hearing a commotion, Daddy came outside to investigate. He quickly cut off the driver's complaints. "My boys would never do such a thing," he insisted. "Get off my property!" Unfortunately, it was only a brief reprieve. Daddy took us in the house and spanked us with the leather strap that he used to sharpen his straight razor. From then on, automobiles driving by our house enjoyed safe passage.

An earlier encounter with passing drivers was more pleasant. When I was about five, Ralph and I embarked on our first business venture, a soft-drink stand on the sidewalk in front of our house. We set up the stand on the hottest days of summer, when temperatures in Houston soared to ninety degrees or more. Drivers and other passers-by would stop for a cold Coke, which we sold for five cents. The overhead was low, and so were the profits. We may not have had a lot of customers, but we felt more like grown-up businessmen each time another nickel came our way.

Despite Prohibition, a lot of people still had access to whiskey. Late at night, bootleggers regularly came by our house with casks of corn whiskey that Daddy hid in the attic. When I was nine years old, I got an allowance of fifty cents a week. To earn this princely sum, I had a variety of household duties. One was to rock the oaken casks in the attic to keep the whiskey mixed. Another was to siphon off pitchers of whiskey for Daddy to use in entertaining his friends who would stop by. The small amount of whiskey I tasted from the siphoning tube had such a bitter flavor, I was not tempted to drink more.

One day, while prowling around the neighborhood, Ralph and I discovered some rusted golf clubs in a neighbor's storeroom. We "borrowed" the clubs and took them to our back yard, where we practiced hitting balls into a suspended canvas sheet. On tiring of that makeshift game, we decided to try our newfound sport at the nearby Hermann Park Municipal Golf Course. We biked over to the course with "our" clubs in tow. Although the green fee was only fifty cents, we were disinclined to pay it, so we left our bikes behind a tree near the twelfth hole, away from the clubhouse. After playing seven or eight stolen holes, we returned to our bikes and pedaled home. That initial unlawful exposure hooked me on the game. Years later, Mr. Spears, the golf pro at Hermann Park, told me that he knew boys like us frequently sneaked onto the course, but he simply looked the other way.

About this time, the stock market crashed. The resulting Great Depression lasted for more than a decade. Because Houston was an oil center, it did not suffer as badly as some other American cities. My family had always lived modestly and saved money, so we weren't impoverished, but we had to be really careful with our resources. My father expected Ralph and me to help out. We sold magazines, delivered newspapers, and collected glass bottles and coat hangers to sell to a junk dealer. Thankfully, we always had enough food. Sometimes, hungry men would come by our house, and my mother would give them something to eat. Despite the hard times, people still needed dental care. Even if they didn't have the cash on hand, they generally worked out some arrangement to pay. I was impressed that health care was fairly secure from the ups and downs of the economy. This was one reason why I later decided to become a doctor.

In 1931, in the midst of the Depression, I enrolled at Sidney Lanier Junior High School. I took all the usual subjects and did well in my classes. One of my favorite teachers was Miss Weinheimer, who taught seventh- and eighth-grade English. She showed us how to diagram sentences and to write properly. Even today, I hate it when people who consider themselves well educated make mistakes in grammar.

We were given a choice of electives: cooking, sewing, typing, or woodshop. When I asked my parents which one I should take, I remember my father's exact words, "If you take typing, you'll end up as a stenographer or clerk." So I chose shop, which introduced me to woodworking. Toiling over the lathe, I created a wooden stool that wasn't half bad. In fact, I gave it to my grandson Denton for his twenty-first birthday. However, I still regret not knowing how to type, especially now in the computer age. The best I can do is hunt and peck.

Because I was fairly tall, I decided to go out for the basketball team.

About that time, I had a growth spurt and soon topped six feet. I almost felt too gangly to play, but I made the team. Coach Donald Longcope became a role model for me and my teammates. Under his guidance, I had my first real experience of team sports and the thrill of athletic competition. Sports drew me out of my natural shyness. I began to understand my strengths and weaknesses, both physical and mental. And I learned to give my entire focus to the task at hand. I also learned the importance of teamwork, hand-body coordination, respect for others, and balance in life. I eventually became an accomplished player, and basketball became a lifelong passion of mine. These early lessons would be important in my surgical career.

The first time I ever received a major award was at my junior high school graduation ceremony. Every year the local American Legion chapter gave an award for service, leadership, and scholarship to one boy and girl from each junior high graduating class in Houston. That year Lanier had about four hundred graduates, and I was a straight A student. I was shy, though, and not very outgoing in school, so was surprised when the principal called out, "Denton Cooley." The award not only increased my self-confidence but also introduced me to the joys of scholastic accomplishment.

•   •   •

In 1933 Ralph and I bought our first car, a 1917 Model T Ford, popularly known as a "flivver" or "Tin Lizzie." The first automobile to be mass produced on an assembly line, the Model T was the car that "put America on wheels." At the time of our purchase, I was thirteen years old and Ralph was fourteen. We bought the vehicle for eighteen dollars at a used-car lot on Washington Avenue with cash saved from our newspaper routes. That was a lot of money to us.

Back home, when we pulled up in the car and honked the horn, our mixed-breed dog, Jack, came running, barking at the commotion. He was followed closely by our parents: "Where did that car come from? What on earth do you boys think you're doing?" Once we explained our need for "better transportation," they were skeptical but didn't make us take the car back. By their inaction, we knew they were secretly pleased by our initiative. They also probably thought that working on the car would help keep us out of trouble during our early teens. Fixing the Model T did occupy most of our free time, and our parents were amazed by our dedication to the project.

I already had some experience repairing bicycles and enjoyed working on the car even more. Ralph and I quickly learned that it needed a lot of repairs, which may be why we got it so cheaply. We immediately started exploring everything under the hood. We changed piston rings, connecting rods, distributors, carburetors, bearings, gaskets, spark plugs, and fan belts. By disassembling and reassembling those parts many times, we learned the basics of the combustion engine. Working on that old engine, the heart of the Model T, I discovered how much I enjoyed tinkering with mechanical things.

We didn't have much income for maintaining and fueling a car. When we were strapped for cash, we sometimes siphoned gasoline out of other vehicles. We began with my father's car but weren't averse to siphoning from other cars if we thought we could get away with it. About that time, many of my friends were beginning to smoke. When I was offered a cigarette, I always jokingly said, "No thanks, I am afraid the gasoline on my breath might set me on fire."

Once our Model T was running, Ralph and I were able to go where our bikes couldn't take us. We expanded our golf games to courses beyond Hermann Park—any place where green fees were nominal for kids. On these outings, Jack happily rode on the running board and barked at oncoming cars, other dogs, and people.

The car was also important during our scouting days. When I was eleven and Ralph was twelve, we joined Boy Scout Troop 15 at Palmer Memorial Episcopal Church, on South Main. The scoutmaster diligently taught us to obey the scout laws, and we quickly advanced to First Class. After Ralph and I bought the Model T, we began driving to all of our camping trips. Several other boys in our troop had old cars like ours that rattled noisily over the rough terrain, so we ended up calling our troop "the Rattlers." After a year or so, our scoutmaster quit for health reasons, and many of the boys began to be more interested in girls than in merit badges. Although satisfied with my scouting achievements, I always regretted not going on to become an Eagle Scout. I am proud that three of my grandsons—Robert Plumb, John Plumb, and Peter Kaldis—did become Eagles.

One summer, Ralph and I drove our car three hundred miles to visit our Aunt Florence and Uncle Harry Talbot in Covington, Louisiana. The Model T also took us to the 1936 Texas Centennial Exposition in Dallas. Those trips took a long time, as our top speed was only thirty-five to forty miles per hour. The car frequently broke down, and fixing it added to the time we spent on the road. "This darn car uses more oil than gas," we joked. We even carried a large tank of used crankcase oil in the car when we traveled.

Our enthusiasm for cars did not end with the Model T. Later, for thirty dollars, we bought a retired Ford racing car that had overhead Frontenac valves. We overhauled this engine, too. The racer didn't have a speedometer, and we wanted to know how fast it could go. So one day, I drove Daddy's new Lincoln Zephyr and Ralph drove the racer over to Old Spanish Trail, a fairly straight stretch of road on the southern outskirts of Houston. I drove behind Ralph as he pushed the old racer to its limit. We clocked it at eighty-five miles an hour. Afterward, we proudly announced this feat at the dinner table. Two days later, we had a mysterious offer of $150 for the racer, so we jumped at the chance to sell it for such a profit. Later, we learned that the offer had come from my godfather, Raymond Pearson, a Ford dealer, who shipped the car to a lot in San Antonio. As it turned out, Daddy paid for the entire transaction, probably saving our lives.

About this time, my interest in cars led to my first real job. At age fifteen, I worked for Daddy's friend Earl North, at his Buick dealership, during my summer vacation. My job was renovating secondhand cars and transporting new cars back and forth to other dealerships. On one occasion, I had to go as far as Oklahoma City by myself to deliver a car. On all the long hauls, I had to sleep in the car or at a tourist park. In retrospect, I'm surprised how much responsibility I was given at age fifteen. I'm also surprised that my mother let me make those trips. I guess she was beginning to see me as an adult.

Another summer, Daddy helped get me a higher-paying job working with a construction crew in an oilfield south of Houston. The oilfield workers were a rather rowdy bunch who liked to hang out at a local honkytonk called the Diddy-Wa-Diddy. One evening after work, they convinced me to go with them, which made me feel like one of the guys. Before I knew it, I'd had three or four beers and had somehow gotten into a fight outside the bar. I don't remember much about that night, but I woke up covered in mud in the back of a pick-up truck. This was not a story I ever wanted to tell my mother (or Daddy), but it taught me a valuable lesson, and I swore that I'd never overindulge again.

• • •

In 1934 I enrolled in San Jacinto High School. At first, I couldn't get excited about Latin, my language requirement, and didn't try very hard in class. Toward the middle of the semester, the teacher, Mr. Lamaster, warned me that I was likely to fail. For the first time in my school career, my work was below average and my promotion in doubt. I could only imagine what my mother would say. The thought of disappointing her made me buckle down and apply myself seriously. As a result, I finished Latin and every other high school course thereafter with an A. Looking back, I realize how important that near failure was in shaping my young life. It showed me that I should never settle for less than my best effort.

One subject that became increasingly important to me in later years was Spanish, which was taught by Señorita Esther Treviño, a lovable spinster. 'You students need to learn Spanish because Houston is so close to Mexico and has so many Spanish-speaking residents," she always told us. Some of her top students were even invited to her home, where she served us tea and cookies—insisting that we try to speak only in Spanish. Her dedicated efforts increased my awareness of Spanish culture and further stimulated my interest in grammar and composition. Señorita Treviño stayed in touch with me at college, always asking if I was practicing my Spanish. Later, because many of my patients were from Latin America, my knowledge of Spanish became a valuable asset.

Sports continued to be important during my high school career. I had played tennis in junior high but was beaten by an older, more experienced player six-love-six-love in a city tournament. I had felt so crushed that I decided to focus on basketball. I didn't become serious about tennis again until high school, when Coach Stuart MacKay showed me the potential of this sport. I would play tennis for the rest of my life, and it would even influence my medical career. At first, I didn't want to try out for the San Jacinto team, but then I found out that tennis players didn't have to take gym class. Rather than practice more tennis during that free hour, I used the time to do homework.

I've always been grateful to Coach MacKay for letting me get by with this. Years later, I was partially able to repay his kindness after he was diagnosed with a large abdominal aneurysm. When he learned that I was doing vascular surgery, he called and asked me to operate on him. Señorita Treviño also became a patient of mine when she needed a cholecystectomy. This was the highest compliment these two wonderful people could possibly have given me. Looking back, I am amazed that they would entrust their lives to someone they first knew as a teenaged boy.

Basketball continued to be my favorite sport, and during my senior year I made the varsity team. That year Coach Walter Hodges took us to San Antonio to play in the annual invitational high school tournament. We stayed on the sixth floor at the Gunter Hotel. We were typical teenagers looking for fun, and this was our first stay in a fancy place. For a while, we simply gazed out the window, marveling at how small everyone appeared six stories below. Then somebody said, "Why don't we drop some water bombs?" So we found some paper sacks and filled them with water. "Let's see how close we can get to people without hitting them." We took turns dropping the bombs. Unfortunately, one of them went awry, and the victim's scream brought the corner policeman running. Looking up, he could easily tell which room the bombs were coming from. We knew we were discovered. With nowhere to run, we were scared out of our wits.

Coach Hodges was in an adjoining room, oblivious to the situation. He had probably drunk too much and fallen asleep. We soon heard a loud knock at his door. We put our ears to the wall and listened intently, trying to learn our fate. We fully expected to be arrested, taken to jail, and withdrawn from the next day's tournament. "The manager tells me that your boys are in the room next door. They're over there throwing water bombs that are endangering people on the street below." We breathlessly awaited the coach's response: "How could you even *suggest* that my disciplined, well-mannered young men could do such a thing?" We were not sure that the policeman was convinced of our innocence, but he didn't pursue the matter any further. We were all amazed that Coach Hodges defended us so strongly, since he knew perfectly well that we were guilty. This episode only strengthened our respect and affection for him. Throughout the rest of my senior year, I continued to excel in basketball. That year, I was named to the All

City Team as first-team center by the *Houston Post*, and this honor further boosted my confidence.

At that time, high school fraternities were popular. Some were national-level Greek societies, which were frowned on by our principal and the superintendent of schools. More outgoing than I, Ralph quickly joined Theta Kappa Omega. Although my overall confidence had grown, I was still shy socially and not much interested in fraternities. With prompting from friends, I eventually did join Delta Phi Kappa. The first rush party was a "smoker," and I was only fourteen years old. When Mother saw the invitation, she was shocked. I thought she was overreacting, because in those days tobacco was considered acceptable—either to smoke or to chew. But Mother's reaction kept me from ever taking up the habit. I did try to chew tobacco once and even smoked cigars a couple of times, but I didn't enjoy those experiences.

If it hadn't been for Delta Phi Kappa, my shyness would have kept me from having even one date in high school. As it turned out, I had three dates—all with the same girl and all for the annual fraternity Christmas formal.

Unlike me, Ralph was very social and loved fraternity meetings, parties, and dances. He was an expert dancer, quite popular with girls, and a hurdler on the track team. Also unlike me, he was a lackluster student. Because our interests were increasingly different, we had a few tense moments during high school.

One day, surrounded by his older friends, Ralph jeered at me in front of my locker and jabbed his finger repeatedly into my shoulder. Hurt and barely thinking, I hit back at him. Then he really let me have it, knocking me backward against the locker. Before we knew it, we were the center of a growing throng of students. With the crowd yelling for more, we fought each other up and down the hallway. Soon my lip was bloody, and Ralph's eye was beginning to swell. About then, I felt an enormous arm reach around from behind me. "Cut it out, you guys," yelled the arm's owner, a burly football star named Buddy Gardner. He was able to separate us before we seriously hurt each other. Immediately, we realized the silliness of our quarrel. We grinned sheepishly at each other and later drove home together. We snuck into the bathroom to clean up our faces and hands, thinking we could hide our wounds. Even though we came up with some lame excuse about our bruises, I'm sure we didn't fool Mother. But after that, Ralph and I never fought each other again.

Even when we disagreed, Ralph and I didn't rat on each other. One Sunday at breakfast, Mother fired questions at us about our activities the night before: "What time did you boys get home? Did you have any girls with you? Did you race the car? Did you drink beer or smoke cigarettes?" This line of questioning went on and on, and we sat there silently. Finally, my father put down his newspaper and said, "Mary, don't ask the boys so many questions. You'll just make liars out of them."

Ralph had to withdraw from school for a few months because of appendicitis, followed by a severe asthma attack. For this reason, he ended up graduating with my class in 1937. It was no surprise that in our senior year he was voted the most popular boy. I was voted the most likely to succeed.

After we left home to enter college, Mother and Daddy divorced. Their separation had a lasting impact on me. I wish there had been some way they could have stayed together. I became painfully aware that divorce is a complex thing. In my opinion, neither of my parents ever quite regained their rightful social standing. After the divorce, Daddy's professional, social, and personal life declined. He became lonely, depressed, and more dependent on alcohol. His health steadily deteriorated, and he died in 1954 at age sixty-nine. He is still considered one of the finest dental clinicians of his era, having received almost every honor his profession could give him.

As I remember Daddy, it's hard to convey the nature of our relationship. We weren't good buddies the way fathers and sons sometimes are today. There was always a little more of a distance between us, but it was respectful. I learned many of life's important lessons from my father. Each June on Father's Day, it used to be customary to wear a flower in honor of your father—a red flower if he was alive and a white one otherwise. One Father's Day, I visited the cemetery and put flowers, red ones, on my father's grave to show that his influence was still alive in my life.

After the divorce, my mother married P. J. McGuire, a wealthy, rather selfish man. She later had a third marriage to a retired dentist named Tucker. When he died, Mother changed her name back to Cooley. In 1974 she had a severe stroke. She survived for six months with right-sided paralysis, unable to speak or to understand what was said to her. After her death in 1975, at age seventy-nine, she was buried in our family plot at Houston's Glenwood Cemetery. Each year on her birthday, I still take red roses, her favorite flower, to her grave.

I also cherish the memories of my brother, Ralph. He was the best friend I've ever had. We both enrolled at UT and even pledged the same fraternity, Kappa Sigma, but Ralph dropped out during his sophomore year. After leaving UT, he worked for a dollar a day as a cowboy in West Texas. "If I work a million days, I'll make a million dollars," he used to joke. When the war broke out, Ralph took a job in Dallas at North American Aviation. As shop foreman, he oversaw the building of P-51 Mustang fighter planes. At night, he took classes in mechanical engineering at Southern Methodist University. After the war ended, he moved around the country some but finally came back to Houston. Our uncle Fred Fraley, a chemical engineer, helped Ralph get a job working for the Harshaw Chemical Company here. By then, Ralph was married to Miriam McDorman, whom he had met in New York City. When his company tried to transfer him from Houston to Chicago, he decided not to go. Instead, he drew on his experience with the Model T and other cars and opened his own auto repair shop. He and Miriam had three children—Daniel Denton, Talbot, and Marianna. Things seemed to be going well, but, like Daddy, Ralph drank too much. He became an alcoholic and died of liver failure in 1973, at age fifty-four. I've never gotten over missing him.

Practicing basketball in Gregory Gymnasium at the University of Texas, 1939.

CHAPTER 3

"This, My Friend, is the UT"

I GRADUATED FROM HIGH SCHOOL in May 1937 at the age of sixteen, which seems early by today's standards but wasn't unusual in those days. My father was eager for Ralph and me to become dentists and eventually take over his practice. My options for college included the Rice Institute, near my home. However, I was drawn to the University of Texas in Austin, largely because of the athletic program. I was also drawn to the campus's Spanish Renaissance-style architecture, dominated by the famous Tower. Above all, I was impressed by Gregory Gymnasium, the largest university sports facility in the South.

A year earlier, a friend and I had hitchhiked from Houston to Austin, a distance of almost 150 miles, to attend the Clyde Littlefield Texas Relays, an annual track and field competition held on the UT campus. I vividly recall walking into Gregory Gymnasium, which had opened five years earlier. With 4,400 seats, it was large for its day—much bigger than any gym I had ever seen before. "What would it be like to play in a place like this?" I wondered, gazing around the gym in awe. I knew then that I wanted to go to UT, become a varsity basketball player, and wear the Longhorn uniform.

My parents, particularly my mother, thought the student body was too large. "Among 12,000 students, you'll get lost," I remember Mother saying. Despite her concerns, Ralph and I enrolled at the university together as freshmen in 1937. We both fulfilled the only admission requirement, a high school diploma with sixteen credits. Tuition came to about one hundred dollars a semester—a bargain even then. Because I'd enjoyed my high school fraternity experience, joining a UT fraternity seemed like a good idea. Although rushed by the Phi Delts, SAEs, and Phi Gams, I joined Kappa Sigma, because I knew more of its members, many of whom were from Houston. Ralph also pledged Kappa Sig. My mother gave each of us forty-five dollars a month to pay for fraternity dues, meals, and other extras.

As a freshman, I mapped out a predental course that included chemistry, biology, physics, and other sciences, along with English. At first, I felt somewhat insecure academically, but by the end of my first year, I had made A's in every class and was invited to join Phi Eta Sigma, the freshman honorary society. As a sophomore, I continued to do well and was asked to join Alpha Epsilon Delta, the premedical/predental honor society. These honors made me realize that I could successfully compete against premed students. I began to think about switching from dentistry to medicine. My father had regretted not becoming a physician, and this made a strong impression on me. Did I really want to become a dentist and spend my career looking into people's mouths? I just didn't find the mouth all that interesting.

During my sophomore year, I had an experience that helped solidify my decision. A fraternity friend, Billy Fitch, and I went dove hunting one Saturday near San Antonio, which was his hometown. That night, Billy took me to visit one of his friends, an intern in the emergency room at Santa Rosa, the city-county hospital. The place was a real madhouse—full of people, many of them drunk, who had wounds from knife fights and car wrecks. Billy's friend was covering the emergency room, and patients were strewn around everywhere. "Denton, do you want to come over here and sew up this patient's forehead?" he called. "Sure, I'll give it a try," I said, reaching for the needle and thread. I successfully sewed up the wound. On the strength of that first effort, he let me sew up a couple more cuts. By the time I left the emergency room that evening, my mind was made up: I was switching from dentistry to medicine.

The premed curriculum was demanding. Besides all the standard courses, there were requirements for a foreign language, either German or French. I decided to study German, which was taught by Professor Lee M. Hollander, chairman of the Germanic Languages Department. It turned out to be a very timely course, because the following year Germany would invade Poland, precipitating World War II. My knowledge of German would later come in handy when I was stationed in Austria with the U.S. Army. For one of my electives, a Kappa Sig brother advised me, "Don't take a hard European history course, take Roman Civilization." I asked, "Why do you say that, Mack?" "Well, it concerns ancient Rome, but the important thing is that all the cute sorority girls are in that course." That was a persuasive argument. History itself had never particularly interested me, but the professor made ancient Rome so fascinating that I have been hooked on history ever since. And my friend had been right—the class *was* full of pretty girls.

The lowest grades I made during my four years at UT were two B's, both in English composition. Yet one of my favorite professors was Dr. Hanson Tufts Parlin, dean of the School of Arts and Sciences. In an advanced literature class, he taught not only English composition but also the importance of having diverse interests. Dr. Parlin was short and overweight, had a round, cherubic face, and was always impeccably dressed. He differed from my other heroes, who were mainly sports figures. Under his tutelage, I sharpened my critical thinking skills. In his advanced creative writing class, I made feeble attempts at writing sonnets. To keep me from getting discouraged, he described my efforts as "not bad," "somewhat better," and, eventually, "almost good." My final grade of A came as a complete surprise.

In those days, many of the social activities revolved around Greek-letter fraternities and sororities. At the Kappa Sig house, I often hung out with Frank Erwin, later chairman of the UT board of regents; Homer Jester, a nephew of Texas governor Beauford Jester; Walter Woodul, the son of the Texas lieutenant governor at that time; and Kenneth Ford, who became a prominent petroleum engineer. During rush week, Walter and I spent some nights in his father's two-bedroom apartment in the State Capitol. I still recall the strangeness of the deserted corridors late at night in that otherwise bustling seat of government. This was the best "hotel" I had ever stayed in.

About a third of my pledge brothers listed themselves as premed students, although they didn't have much serious hope of attending medical school. Because of the constant commotion, it was impossible for me to study at the fraternity house. Guys were always cutting up, roughhousing, and being generally rowdy. You could always be lured into a bull session on one subject or another, especially sports and girls. There was also a loud, round-the-clock poker game. Ralph got drawn into playing bridge and partying, which is one of the reasons he dropped out of school in his sophomore year. To avoid these distractions, I usually escaped to the university library, hoping for a quiet table that faced the wall, away from the pretty girls who studied there.

For those of us who wanted to be serious students, the first semester as a lowly pledge was tough. The upperclassmen subjected us to hazing. To build our "character," they paddled us hard with one-by-four pine boards. But the torture device we hated the most was the "bee," an electric cattle prod. When we heard its awful buzz, we knew it was headed our way. Even the largest, most stalwart pledges quaked before this instrument of the devil. I am glad that hazing is no longer permitted on college campuses.

Being a pledge of Kappa Sig forced me to attend parties, dances, and other social activities that I might otherwise have skipped. On one occasion, I was assigned to take the Pi Phi president to the fraternity's annual Christmas dance. That turned out to be one assignment I really enjoyed. The guys also arranged blind dates for me with some other real beauties. For formal dances, the fraternities brought in big-name musical groups such as Henry Busse and his Shuffle Rhythm Band and Tommy Dorsey and his Orchestra. Gradually, I learned to dance and to become more comfortable with mixing and mingling. I also acquired various social graces that would stand me in good stead for the rest of my life.

I've always kept in touch with my fraternity buddies. Our pranks didn't end with our UT days. Shortly after leaving for medical school, I got a call from one of the guys, Bubba Watterworth, who wanted to go to the UT/Colorado football game in Boulder. He'd heard that the Longhorn Band wasn't going, and he had a plan to support the team but no way to get to Boulder. He knew I had a Ford V-8 that I'd bought with an allowance from my parents and some of my athletic scholarship money (see story below). Ready for an adventure, I drove to Austin and picked up Bubba and two other guys, who'd scrounged up a public address system for a makeshift "band." We set off for Boulder with a case of Four Roses Whiskey, taking turns at the wheel. During one of my turns, Watterworth said, "Bubba,[1] you're not drunk enough to drive, so why don't you get in back?" We stopped the car, and I climbed in the back seat, where there was an empty bottle of whiskey. We started off again and were soon going ninety miles an

---

[1] "Bubba" is a universal nickname in the South. Here, I am the Bubba in question.

hour. I opened the door a crack to throw out the bottle. What a mistake! With the car speeding down the highway, the force of the wind whipped the door outward, tearing it off the hinges. We pulled over, roped the door to the car body, and then motored on. When we got to the stadium the next day, the game was almost ready to begin. Each of us carried parts of the PA system into the stands. When the Buffalo Marching Band came onto the field, our quartet drowned them out with "Texas Fight!" and "The Eyes of Texas." It wasn't long until the police showed up and confiscated our equipment—but not before we had created quite a sensation. I've forgotten the final score but recall that the star of Colorado's team was Byron "Whizzer" White, who was later appointed to the U.S. Supreme Court.

• • •

The athletic program was one of the main reasons I was attracted to UT. Dana X. Bible had just been appointed the head football coach. His salary was reportedly more than that of the UT president or the governor of Texas. A remarkable, inspiring man, Coach Bible ushered in a new era in athletics. He took a lackluster program and transformed it into a national powerhouse. He emphasized success for his players not only on the field but also in the classroom. Unlike most other coaches of that day, he also believed that balance in life was important for his boys. He recruited some of the best teams in UT history.

The head basketball coach at the time was Jack Gray, who had been an all-American, all-conference, and all-everything-else athlete during his student days at UT. Ed Price, himself a Kappa Sig and a varsity athlete, coached the freshmen players. Competition to make the starting team was keen. Not having been recruited as a scholarship athlete, I decided to try out as a "walk-on" player. Most of the athletes who got scholarships had spent two years in junior college, so they were nineteen or twenty years old as freshmen, and I was just seventeen. At that age, two years made a big difference in a guy's physical development, so I felt at a disadvantage. But I did make the freshman team. As a 6-foot, 4-inch center weighing only 140 pounds, I found scrimmages against the older and larger varsity players traumatic. So between my freshman and sophomore years, I ate like a horse to gain weight, reaching a robust 185 pounds. That was also the summer I worked for the Lower Colorado River Authority, surveying for electrical lines from the Marshall Ford Dam to below the town of Bastrop. That job gave me a really good appetite.

I made the varsity team my sophomore year and immediately got a lucky break. Just before the official season opened, the varsity was playing an exhibition game with St. Edwards University, an older but smaller school in south Austin. In the third quarter, St. Edwards was actually threatening to defeat the great University of Texas. Frustrated, Coach Gray looked way down to the end of the bench at me and said, "Cooley, get in the game." I was surprised because I had only played for five or ten minutes in other games. But I ran onto the court and made thirteen points, which helped us win. The next day Coach Gray called me into his office and said, "Denton, you played so well in yesterday's game, I think it's time you had a scholarship." I was elated.

My scholarship paid forty dollars a month, which covered half of my expenses. Boys on scholarship were expected to "earn" their money. Coach Gray gave me the job of sweeping the northwest section of the stands in Gregory Gym. I did this diligently twice a week and after basketball games. After a few weeks, I noticed that no other boys were in the gym doing any sweeping. Finally, a janitor came along and said, "Son, what are you doing? You don't have to sweep. We janitors are paid to do that." So I put my broom away and never said anything to Coach Gray. Another year, Coach Gray called my teammate "Speedy" Houpt and me to his office, held up the newspaper, and opened it to the sports section. He pointed to a story and said, "Boys, you're going to help me scout for the football team. Speedy, you take these scissors. Denton, hold the newspaper so that Speedy can cut out the story. Then, you boys paste it in this book. For this year, that's your job. I'll call you if I have any more need for you." I finally realized that scholarship jobs were for appearances only. The other boys had figured this out early on.

During my sophomore year, the Longhorns played a number of tough opponents and were invited to the National Invitation Tournament in New York. We took the train all the way from Austin to New York City to play Manhattan College at Madison Square Garden. Manhattan College was considered one of the best East Coast teams. Playing at the Garden was a big thrill for me. Some 18,000 people attended the game. I was put into play as a substitute and again was lucky to score enough points to ensure the win. I still have a newspaper clipping that shows me jumping up and putting the ball in the basket. The caption under the photo reads: "Cooley was instrumental in beating Manhattan College in basketball." The night after we won at the Garden, we went to Philadelphia to play Temple University and lost by two points. We just couldn't hit the basket. Although this was disappointing, it was a good lesson in life. Success has to be earned over and over again.

My performance that year in our game against Southern Methodist University near the end of our season earned me a place on the first team for the rest of my UT basketball career. It was a thrill to have first-team status. I loved mixing it up with the older, larger boys. Every time I set foot in Gregory Gymnasium, I was reminded of my first awestruck feeling for it. My dream had come true. Listening to the screaming crowds, the band, and the UT fight song, I felt on top of the world. That season, our home games attracted 58,000 ardent fans, most wearing the burnt orange of UT. The atmosphere was different when we played against our archrivals, the Aggies, at Texas A&M in College Station. They hated us Longhorns and packed their gym with jeering students in an attempt to knock us off balance. For a guy like me, used to small high school crowds, these huge games were equally exhilarating whether our team was met with cheers or not. Despite all the jeers our opponents could muster, we beat both the Aggies and the Rice Institute Owls to win the 1939 Southwest Conference Championship.

As a result, we were invited to the first National Collegiate Athletic Association Western Regional Playoffs on Treasure Island in San Francisco. At the train station, a crowd of well-wishers sent us off by clapping and singing "The Eyes of Texas." We were wearing ten-gallon hats and cowboy boots provided by our supporters in Austin. During that train trip, I got my nickname, "Buckwheat." I was with my teammates in the train's dining car when the waiter asked for my order. "I'll have buckwheat pancakes," I replied. Coach Gray, who was sitting nearby, remarked loudly, "No buckwheat cakes for you, Buckwheat, they're not on your diet." Most of my teammates had a nickname, such as "Bounding" Bobby Moers, "Wee" Willie Tate, "Slue" Thurman Hull, and "Speedy" Walter Houpt, and now I had one too.

Until my graduation, I was known as "Buckwheat" Cooley. It was sort of a silly nickname that came out of nowhere, but I was pleased to have it. A nickname meant that I was part of the group.

Treasure Island, the site of the playoffs, had been built specifically for the Golden Gate International Exposition, which was taking place while we were there. The Longhorns had a first draw against the University of Oregon, a much taller and more experienced team. We lost the game 56-41, and Oregon went on to win the championship that year. But at least our team had a wonderful trip. My most vivid memory of San Francisco is of the Golden Gate Bridge, which had been dedicated two years earlier, in 1937. What an impressive sight for a kid from Texas!

I'd thought about going to medical school after completing my three years of premedical courses, which you could do in those days, but Coach Gray convinced me to stay on the team for my full four years of basketball eligibility. After such an exciting sophomore year, my final two seasons weren't as memorable. In 1940 the Longhorns finished second to Rice in the conference, beaten by a single, final basket. My senior year we fell to third place behind Arkansas and Rice. During a preseason game, I suffered a painful hairline fracture in my right heel bone that handicapped me throughout the season. I had to play the entire season without putting my heel down on the court. This was extremely disappointing because I'd stayed the extra year to play on the team.

· · ·

During my junior year, I was nominated for the Cowboys, a service organization that that was comprised mainly of fraternity members and campus leaders. The Cowboys chose only two new members a year from each club on campus, so being asked to join was quite an honor. At that time, the Cowboys had been on campus for about eighteen years. A standard cattle-branding iron, consisting of a T inside a U, was used in the initiation ceremony. Originally, the cattle brand was plunged into a bucket of ice water and then applied to the initiate's chest. By 1940, however, when I joined, the icy brand had been changed to a hot one.

The secret initiation took place in the hills west of Austin. Blindfolded and shirtless, we initiates lay on the ground while the Cowboys pinned our arms. The foreman took the red-hot branding iron from the fire and applied it to each exposed chest, chanting, "This, my friend, is the UT." Immediately after receiving the brand, I sat up, removed the blindfold, and looked at my chest. The letters didn't look right. "The 'T' isn't crossed," I told the foreman. "Let's give it another try." Without a blindfold, I waited for the iron to get red hot again. Once it was ready, I got my second burn. Because of that, my brand is still clear more than seventy years later. I've always been proud of it. Although the Cowboys remain an important part of UT, the branding was soon discontinued by order of Dean Arno Nowotny, who was himself a founding member of the Cowboys. In 2010 I received the first Outstanding Cowboy of the Year award at the group's annual reunion. I was deeply honored. There were a number of young Cowboys at the ceremony. I asked them, although I already knew the answer, "Did you guys get your cattle brand?" They said, "No, but we would love to have had one."

●　●　●

One of the best things about UT was that there was always something fun to do. On fall weekends, there was football, the major sport on campus. Golf, tennis, and intramural sports also provided diversions. I was lucky enough to attend most of the games. As a member of the Cowboys, I wore leather chaps, an orange scarf, and a black felt hat. In the spring, we had the UT–Roundup, which was basically a week-long, campus-wide party with a cowboy theme. There were concerts, pageants, and a parade that went along Guadalupe Street, better known to UT students as "The Drag." On nice weekend afternoons, lots of us went to Bull Creek for picnics or to Barton Springs pool—a favorite location for swimming, tanning, and showing off. At that time, I had an old, open Chevrolet, which was painted orange on white, and I used it to take my friends everywhere. During my years at UT, I had several girlfriends, but my only serious relationship was with Joy Ray, a campus sweetheart candidate and beauty, whom I met in my junior year and to whom I later gave my fraternity pin. When I left for medical school, we broke up because I was not yet ready for anything more serious, such as marriage.

In 1941 I received a B.A. degree in zoology with a minor in English. I graduated Phi Beta Kappa and with highest honors. The four years that I spent at UT gave me the knowledge and skills I would need for both medical school and life. Playing varsity basketball reinforced many lessons I had learned in junior and senior high school: the thrill of competition, the pleasure of teamwork, and the importance of sports to a well-rounded life. Basketball also taught me skills for coping with loss and disappointment. All of these lessons have been important throughout my life. I've also been able to use my experience as a university "jock" in a more humorous way: When somebody corners me with a basic scientific or philosophical question that I am unable to answer, I simply tell them, "Please don't ask me about those things. I went to college on a basketball scholarship."

All five of my daughters would eventually go to UT, and most of my grandchildren would follow them there. Because of what my alma mater gave me, I have always tried to support it in every possible way. In fact, my devotion to UT runs so deep, people say, "Denton, your blood isn't red—it's burnt orange."

Dr. Alfred Blalock, chairman of the Department of Surgery at Johns Hopkins. Eileen Saxon, who underwent the historic "blue baby" operation at Johns Hopkins, is pictured in the photograph (lower left). Dr. Blalock's portrait was taken by the famous photographer Yousuf Karsh. Courtesy of Dr. Cooley's personal collection and Johns Hopkins University.

CHAPTER 4

Becoming a Doctor

WHILE A JUNIOR AT UT, I became eligible for a Rhodes Scholarship for postgraduate study at Oxford University in England. It was an honor for me to be considered, so I decided to apply for the scholarship rather than go to medical school right away. I was scheduled for an interview in New Orleans, but shortly before that interview was to be held, the program was suspended because of the impending war in Europe. As a result, I decided to go straight to medical school. Because money was still tight from the Depression, I applied to schools close to home: Baylor in Dallas, Tulane in New Orleans, and the University of Texas Medical Branch (UTMB) in Galveston. I was accepted at all three schools but chose UTMB because I believed it was the most prestigious.

Two weeks after graduating from UT in June 1941, I moved to the city of Galveston, on Galveston Island, about fifty miles southeast of Houston. There I began my medical education. In the late 1800s, Galveston was considered the "New York City of the Gulf Coast." In 1900, however, the island was devastated by a massive hurricane that killed more than six thousand people—the worst natural disaster in the history of the United States. The city was never the same and was soon overshadowed by Houston.

By the time I arrived in Galveston, it had a reputation of being a "sin city" largely controlled by organized crime. It had become a center for illegal activities, including prostitution and gambling. Many of its citizens even considered the island to be a "free state," outside the laws of Texas. Through all of this, UTMB was a bastion of stability. The decision to locate the medical school in Galveston had actually been determined by popular vote of the citizens of Texas in 1881, when Galveston was in its heyday.

At UTMB, there were four medical fraternities, all of which held parties during rush week. I joined Alpha Kappa Kappa (AKK), largely because Dr. Bertner, who had delivered me, was himself a member and a major sponsor. The fraternity house was a mansion on Post Office Street that had once been the Swedish Consulate. Ironically, it was located only six blocks away from the most notorious brothel in Galveston. My fraternity brothers and I were amused that the brothel's street address was so similar to ours.

Right before school started, the fraternities had rush week. Around 2:00 one morning after a couple of fraternity rush parties, I was sitting alone at the bar of the Studio Lounge in downtown Galveston. An elegantly dressed, middle-aged man walked over and said, "Son, what are you doing here all by yourself?" We chatted for a few minutes, then he asked my name. I introduced myself and explained that I was a medical student. "You aren't related to Ralph Cooley, the dentist, are you?"

"As a matter of fact, he's my father."

"Well, if you seriously want to be a doctor, let me give you some advice. If you spend much time in places like this, you won't make it. You're going to have to change your way of life." The man began to walk away, then suddenly turned around. "By the way," he added, "I'm Sam Maceo, and this club belongs to me." I was so shocked, I hardly knew what to say. Of course I had heard of him and his organized crime syndicate, which "owned" most of Galveston. The next morning I felt embarrassed because I had been admonished by the notorious Sam Maceo.

That summer, American involvement in the European war seemed imminent. To provide more physicians for the war effort, the government asked medical schools to reduce the length of their programs from the traditional four years to only three years. Complying with this request, UTMB cancelled summer vacations and set up a tighter curriculum. I had to study hard, and my first year was really challenging. Every Monday morning at 8:00, we had an hour-long exam on anatomy, physiology, biochemistry, bacteriology, or another of our subjects. Although this involved only one exam per week, it just about put an end to all weekend social life. We studied hard on Saturday and Sunday, took the exam on Monday morning, then began partying on Monday afternoon.

In my spare time, I played on basketball and softball teams. The games were played in the city league, which included numerous military personnel stationed in Galveston. My basketball team was sponsored by Club Metropole, a saloon that gave the players free drinks after the games. When basketball season was over, many of the same players switched to a softball team sponsored by the Second Presbyterian Church. We found it humorous to play on two teams with such different sponsors.

Except for the occasional partying and sports activities, we medical students were a serious lot. I was determined to excel in school and so were most of my classmates—there were about eighty-five of us, as I recall. UTMB was highly competitive. Every week, numerical grades were posted by name on the dean's bulletin board. We were well aware of everyone's rank in each subject, right down to the decimal point.

UTMB had an outstanding faculty, many of whom were prominent in Texas medical education. My professors included Dr. Samuel Snodgrass, founder of the Division of Neurosurgery at UTMB; Dr. Raymond Blount, a famed anatomist; and Dr. Albert O. Singleton, chief of surgery. I was fascinated to watch him and his team operate, and I spent many a free afternoon observing in the surgical theater. It became apparent to me that the same degree of teamwork was necessary for a successful operation as for a winning basketball game. As I observed Dr. Singleton and his colleagues, I also remembered the evening when I had sewn up wounds in the San Antonio emergency room. A career in surgery began to interest me more and more.

I had just gotten settled into medical school when we were electrified by the bombing of Pearl Harbor on December 7, 1941. In response, the United States declared war on Japan, Germany, and Italy. Before long, rumors began to circulate about German U-boats in the Gulf of Mexico, and Galvestonians began to realize that they could be vulnerable to attack. Dim-out orders went into effect in June 1942, causing us to cover the hospital windows with black shades. To keep merchant vessels from being silhouetted and targeted, no lighting at all was permitted within five hundred yards of the coast. No one was allowed out on the beach at night, and the part of the beach nearest the medical school was turned into a military installation. The Galvez Hotel was even converted into the Coast Guard barracks. The bridal suite where my parents had spent their honeymoon now housed half a dozen men.

Also in 1942, the medical school began to have some internal problems that made me think maybe I should transfer elsewhere. Basically, it was a power struggle between the school's old-guard faculty and a new, autocratic dean, Dr. John Spies, who was dictating unpopular changes. As I recall, Dean Spies, being of German descent, was also suspected of being a German sympathizer. Galveston had a large German population, and officials feared that some German residents might secretly belong to a German American Bund, a pro-Nazi organization. News of the UTMB conflict reached the legislature in Austin, which created a special committee—including Texas Rangers—to go to Galveston and investigate. The committee held a kangaroo court on the stage of the school's auditorium. The Texas Rangers were quite a sight sitting on the stage in their cowboy hats, boots, and spurs, with their feet propped up on chairs. We students attended the sessions and were disheartened to hear our respected teachers air their jealousies and complaints, which seemed petty to us.

Whatever the reasons, I was afraid that the school was likely to be placed on scholastic probation. So I called my long-time mentor, Dr. Ernst Bertner, to ask his advice. "Well, Denton, you need a back-up plan. Why don't you consider applying to some other schools? I served with some doctors from Johns Hopkins during World War I and have friends on the faculty there. The school has an outstanding reputation and would be an excellent choice if you got accepted."

In fact, I already knew something about Johns Hopkins because I had recently read a popular novel about it. Written by Augusta Tucker and published in 1939, the novel was called *Miss Susie Slagle's*. It related the lives of several young men who lived in a boarding house while attending medical school at Johns Hopkins shortly before the First World War. I was impressed by the book, which was later turned into a movie starring Lillian Gish.

After talking with Dr. Bertner, I secretly began applying to other institutions to finish out my medical school requirements. Five schools interested me: Washington University, Michigan, Duke, Johns Hopkins, and Harvard. Of these five, the only school that didn't accept me was Harvard. I followed Dr. Bertner's advice and took the offer from Johns Hopkins.

Before I departed for Baltimore, Dr. Bertner gave me five letters of endorsement to division chiefs he knew personally. At that time he was probably the most influential physician in Houston. I owe him a great debt not only for helping me in this situation but also for treating me like a son. He recognized my potential and encouraged me to fulfill it.

As I had feared, soon after I left Galveston the Association of American Medical Colleges placed UTMB on probation, citing a number of deficiencies. It took a new dean and two years to bring the warring factions back together and reestablish the school's reputation. I had made the right decision in leaving when I did.

• • •

In February 1943 I arrived in Baltimore to begin my studies at Johns Hopkins Medical School. It had been established in 1893 with a gift from the Quaker merchant for whom it is named. The founders pioneered the type of rigorous, scientific programs that all accredited U.S. medical schools offer today. William S. Halsted, its first surgeon-in-chief, was the father of modern surgical residency training. When I arrived at Hopkins, it was considered one of the best medical schools in the world. I boarded at the AKK house, across the street from the hospital.

I entered Hopkins with some anxiety because of its world-class reputation. Although people think of me today as very self-confident, there was a time in my life when I fought insecurities at every new step. Whenever I faced an unfamiliar and challenging situation, I had to regain my self-confidence. At Hopkins I was uneasy because many of my classmates had received their undergraduate degrees from Princeton, Yale, Harvard, or other elite schools. They had already been at Hopkins for two years, so they knew the ropes. But after I began my classes, I realized that UTMB had prepared me extremely well, so my anxiety waned. Most of my classmates had never met a Texan before. They seemed relieved to learn that I wasn't toting a six-shooter!

Among the brightest stars on the medical school faculty was Dr. Alfred Blalock. He was a distinguished-looking forty-four-year-old man with glasses and dark, wavy hair. A native of Georgia, he had a kindly drawl and smoked cigarettes from a long holder. He had a great sense of humor and loved to hear or tell a good story. Dr. Blalock had gone to medical school at Hopkins. While there, he had made mediocre grades and was known as something of a playboy. Afterward, he completed a residency at Vanderbilt University and then stayed on, eventually becoming a professor of surgery. There he attracted much attention in the national medical community for his research on hemorrhagic and traumatic shock. His work led to the widespread use of blood plasma transfusions for severely wounded soldiers during World War II.

In 1941 Dr. Blalock returned to Hopkins as a professor of surgery and chairman of the Department of Surgery. He immediately reorganized the surgical residency program and began recruiting medical students who met his high standards. He believed that students interested in a surgical career needed more than academic skills—they needed to be well rounded in terms of character, experience, and physical ability. He admired athletes because of their agility, stamina, self-confidence, and competitiveness. To Dr. Blalock, those were essential characteristics for a surgeon. I was fortunate to have had some of the qualities he favored.

The Baltimore weather was awful that February, with rain, snow, or sleet almost every day. One morning toward the end of March, the sun finally came out. To celebrate, I invited a new friend and classmate, Lester Persky, to play tennis on the hospital's Quadrangle court. Like me, Lester was a transfer student. Our impromptu game required us to cut Dr. Blalock's surgery clinic, which was held at noon every Friday in Hurd Hall, an old-fashioned, steeply sloped amphitheater. In those days, the patients were brought to the theater, where their cases were discussed in detail. Students were seated directly to the right of the senior staff and were expected to participate in the dialogue.

As Persky and I traded tennis volleys, who should cross the courtyard but Dr. Blalock himself? With him were Dr. Mark Ravitch, Dr. Bill Longmire, and some junior residents and interns. When Dr. Blalock spotted us, he sat down with his entourage, lit a cigarette, and watched us play. I was really worried, because I assumed that cutting his class to play tennis would result in my premature and involuntary departure from Hopkins. What was I to do? There seemed to be only one option: keep my wits about me and play even harder. As Persky and I were exchanging courts after a couple of games, Dr. Blalock called out, "Mr. Cooley, come over here. I would like to talk to you." I thought to myself, "This is where you get the ax."

Instead of asking why I had cut his clinic, Dr. Blalock said, "I've been watching your tennis game. You're a pretty good player."

"Thank you, sir," was my nervous reply.

"Mr. Cooley, most tennis players can play ping-pong. What about you?"

"Well, sir, I played some ping-pong in college." Actually, I considered myself to be better at ping-pong than tennis.

"This weekend, my family and I are going to Dr. Bill Rienhoff's cabin on Gibson Island south of here on Chesapeake Bay. I need someone to come along and play ping-pong with me. Would you like to go?" Would I? *Would I?* Of course I said "yes."

I couldn't believe my good fortune at being selected from a class of about eighty students to spend a weekend with Dr. Blalock and his family. And I was selected in such an unlikely way. He hadn't found me working diligently in the library or laboratory. Perhaps he thought that I showed good sense to be outdoors on such a beautiful day. Maybe he, too, would have liked to skip surgery clinic. Once I got over my initial thrill, nervousness about the pending trip began to set in. I managed to survive the car ride without showing how anxious I was.

After we got settled at the cabin, Dr. Blalock asked me to mix us a couple of bourbons before we had our first ping-pong match. I was uneasy about mixing a drink for the professor and didn't have any idea how much bourbon to pour into his glass. In the kitchen, I turned to his wife, Mary: "I don't know what to do. If his drink is mixed too weak, he may think I'm a sissy. If it's too strong, he may think I'm a toper." She replied, "Don't worry. You can't mix a drink too strong for my husband." So I mixed the drinks, a strong one for Dr. Blalock and a weaker one for me. He was waiting by the ping-pong table, eager to start our first game.

Dr. Blalock played with great energy, but I won the first game easily. Maybe beating him by such a margin wasn't all that wise, especially for a new student. After the second game, he said, "You're pretty good at this, Denton. I'm impressed." Then he smiled and said, "If you'll let *me* fix the next drinks, we can resume playing." This time, my drink was so strong, my eyes watered every time I took a sip. The final game was a much harder victory for me.

The rest of the weekend, I felt more at ease. Dr. Blalock and I swam with his wife and two children and played some more ping-pong. We discussed a wide variety of topics, including athletics, medical school, my childhood, and my experiences at UT. By the end of my stay, I knew for certain that transferring to Hopkins had been the right choice. I also knew for certain that I wanted to be a surgeon. Throughout my years at Hopkins, my relationship with Dr. Blalock remained warm and personal. He made me want to excel at Hopkins as much as I had at UT. His close personal interest greatly affected my surgical career and those of his other trainees. His relationship with us was almost like that of a father with his sons, and his influence was profound. Later, many of us would head academic surgical departments around the country.

Although medical school kept me extremely busy, I really missed playing basketball. Some of the other interns and I decided to organize a team of students and house staff, each of whom had previously played on varsity teams at major universities. We were called the "Student Book Store" team, because the store's owner, Ed Foster, supplied our uniforms. Every Sunday night, we played in the Baltimore City League, mainly at the Fourteen Holy Martyrs Church gymnasium. Each Monday morning, Dr. Blalock read the sports page to see how our team had done and often asked me for reports of the weekend's game.

One Saturday night, the fraternities had a big party, and I overserved myself at the bar. The next day, I woke up with a terrible hangover. About 3:00 that afternoon, Dr. Blalock called me: "Denton, I read in the newspaper that your team has a game tonight. I've finally gotten some faculty friends together to come and watch y'all play: Walter Dandy [a nationally known neurosurgeon]; Philip Bard [the head of physiology]; and Alan Woods [a professor of ophthalmology]." At the time, I had a splitting headache and couldn't keep any food down. "Dr. Blalock, I don't think it's going to be much of a game. Maybe you and your group should come next Sunday, when we'll be playing a better team." This didn't convince him. "No, we're looking forward to tonight's game. With our schedules, it's not easy to get us all together. We'll see you this evening."

In desperation, I called my good friend Jim Davis, who was also on the house staff and currently working in the gynecology service. I said, "Jim, I've got a serious problem. I haven't been able to hold anything down all day, and Dr. Blalock is coming to our basketball game tonight. Would you give me a jolt of glucose and saline? I need an energy boost." He said, "Sure, anything you want." I went on over to his clinic, where he put a big needle into one of the veins in my arm and quickly infused about a liter of a glucose and salt solution.

Afterward, I felt a little better, so I went to the gym. My stomach was cramping badly, but I took some paregoric I'd also gotten from Jim. That helped some. Our team was playing against one sponsored by the Knights of Columbus. Somehow I pulled myself together enough to score thirty-two points. After the game, I was exhausted, had terrible stomach cramps, and couldn't wait to go home. But Dr. Blalock stopped me. "Denton, you certainly amaze me. You work so hard and keep such long hours all week, yet you're in such splendid physical shape." I thought to myself, "Dr. Blalock, you may be one of the most famous doctors in the world, but you don't know a dying man when you see one."

I was also affected by the war while at Hopkins. To ensure that enough doctors would be available for the war effort, the United States conscripted medical students into the Army Specialized Training Program, or ASTP. We liked to call it "All Safe 'Til Peace." I was conscripted as a private first class before my second semester. As soldiers, we participated in Saturday morning inspections and infantry drills—with shoes shined and uniforms pressed. Our olive drab uniforms weren't nearly as fancy as the U.S. Navy uniforms. However, we did have shoulder patches that depicted a lamp of knowledge on a field of gold. When we were out in the bars, "real soldiers" often asked us, "What outfit are you guys in?" We proudly replied, "the Flamethrowers."

My annual tuition at Hopkins was 650 dollars per year, which was quite a contrast to the 45 dollars a year I had paid at UTMB. To pay the tuition my first semester, I had to ask my father for 500 dollars. Once I was conscripted, I got a small monthly salary, and my tuition was reimbursed, so I repaid the 500 dollars to my dad. From then on and throughout medical school, the U.S. Army funded everything. In this way, I got a nearly free medical education.

The next step after medical school graduation would be an internship, and I had to decide where to apply. Somehow I thought that I needed to diversify my training, so I started to look outside of Hopkins. After some thought, I applied to the University of Michigan, as I had heard good things about its surgical program.

When Dr. Blalock learned that I had not applied to Hopkins, he called me into his office and asked for an explanation. "Why aren't you on the list of applicants for a surgical internship here? I think you have a special aptitude for surgery, and I would like you in my program if you want to stay." I realized that it made sense to accept his offer. To this day, I am amazed at how fortunate my decision was, as staying at Hopkins proved to be pivotal for my career. I became exposed to heart surgery early in my internship—much sooner than might otherwise have been the case.

In August 1944 I received my M.D. degree, sharing first place in my graduating class with another student, Richard Kiefer. I was accepted into Alpha Omega Alpha, the honorary medical scholastic fraternity. Although commissioned as a second lieutenant, I received a deferment from active duty for eighteen months, so that I could continue my surgical training. The army required me to begin an accelerated postgraduate program called the mini-mini program, in which I would spend nine months as an intern and nine months as an assistant resident.

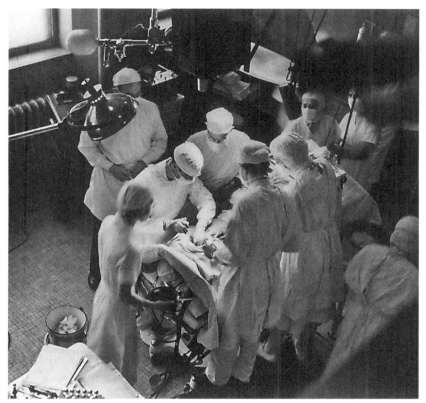

Blue baby operation at Johns Hopkins Hospital in 1945. I am at the right side of the operating table, facing Dr. Blalock. Courtesy of Dr. Cooley's personal collection.

CHAPTER 5

The Dawn of Heart Surgery

A S A SURGICAL TRAINEE, I was privileged not only to witness the dawn of heart surgery but also to participate in the evolution of the field. Until the late 1930s, few surgeons had even considered operating on the heart. Occasionally, operations were undertaken to sew up cardiac wounds, but more complex heart procedures had to await improved anesthetic techniques, the development of blood banking, and the discovery of antibiotics. World War II provided a major stimulus for cardiac research and treatment. However, a planned, or elective, operation on the heart itself was still almost unthinkable.

In 1943 I was a third-year medical student at Johns Hopkins. That year, I had a chance to work in the school's Hunterian Laboratory, where I was exposed to surgical research for the first time. The facility was named in honor of John Hunter, an eighteenth-century Scottish surgeon who was an early advocate of the scientific method. The lab was located a city block away from the main hospital building. Although devoted mostly to neurologic studies, it was also used for other types of research. By the time I arrived there, the building was old, dilapidated, and dreary.

The lab was overseen by Vivien Thomas, an African American surgical technician. An extremely intelligent and pleasant man, Vivien was about thirty-three years old when I first met him. After high school, he had dreamed of going to college and medical school, but his parents didn't have the money to send him. He worked as a carpenter to save for college, but the stock market crash wiped out his hard-earned savings. So he was forced to put his college plans on hold and look for other work. At that time, Dr. Blalock was still at Vanderbilt University in Nashville, where Vivien lived. A friend told Vivien that Dr. Blalock had a position open for a surgical technician in his laboratory. Vivien applied for the job and got it. However, because he wasn't white, the Vanderbilt administration classified him as a janitor and paid him a janitor's wage.

In those days, because of segregation, blacks and whites led separate lives. Despite these racial and social differences, Dr. Blalock and Vivien Thomas worked well together in the laboratory. Dr. Blalock immediately realized that Vivien had amazing hand-eye coordination and began teaching him to perform operations on the lab animals. Vivien was such a precise, talented, and effective surgical technician that he was soon made responsible for most of Dr. Blalock's experimental procedures.

In 1941 Dr. Blalock left Vanderbilt to head the surgery department at Johns Hopkins. He asked Vivien to go with him. Although Vivien got a slight raise in pay, he often moonlighted as a bartender to make ends meet. Occasionally, he worked at parties given by Dr. Blalock or by the surgical house staff. So Vivien sometimes ended up serving drinks to those of us he taught during the day. I never felt quite right about that.[1]

During my internship, which began in 1944, I got to know Vivien well. His work in the Hunterian lab included teaching the interns and medical students to perform surgery on dogs. He became a role model for many of us. He taught us how to anesthetize the animals, make incisions, tie knots, and perform a variety of operations. Like other aspiring young surgeons, I took some string to my room at night and practiced tying knots with one or both hands. There is a rumor that I practiced tying sutures inside a matchbox, but that's an exaggeration. I also got a scalpel and practiced cutting a piece of meat. That helped me learn how to hold my fingers and to operate gracefully. As part of my work in the laboratory, I assisted Vivien in creating heart defects and then repairing them in dogs. Dogs were chosen for these studies

---

[1] Eventually, Vivien did receive a more reasonable salary. Also, in the late 1970s, Johns Hopkins University gave him an honorary Doctorate of Laws, and he was appointed to the faculty in Surgery.

because their heart and great vessels are similar to those of humans and about the same size.

One of my teachers was Dr. Helen Taussig, a pediatric cardiologist who had graduated from Hopkins, the first U.S. medical school to admit women. By the time I arrived there, she was director of the Children's Heart Clinic. Because of a complication of whooping cough, Dr. Taussig had been nearly deaf since childhood and had to use a special stethoscope that amplified her hearing. Congenital cardiac anomalies were her specialty. She was particularly interested in tetralogy of Fallot, a complicated birth defect that usually resulted in death. Named for the French physician who first described it, this condition consists of four structural defects that limit blood flow to the lungs. As a result, not enough oxygen is available to meet the baby's needs, and the skin, lips, and nails develop a bluish tint, called cyanosis. In tetralogy, the main problem causing the cyanosis is a severe narrowing of the pulmonary artery and valve, which channel blood to the lungs.

Dr. Taussig had noted that babies with tetralogy of Fallot are not always intensely cyanotic at birth. She theorized that some oxygenated blood was being circulated through what's called a patent ductus arteriosus, a vessel that routes blood around the lungs before birth. Normally the ductus closes at birth, when the lungs begin to work. In some cases, though, it remains open, or patent. Ironically, the patent ductus actually helps in cases of tetralogy. When the ductus is open, some blood returning from the body can reach the lungs through the ductus. When the ductus closes after birth, the only way for blood to go is through the obstructed pulmonary artery, so the baby doesn't get enough oxygen and turns blue.

Dr. Taussig reasoned that the principle of the patent ductus might be useful in correcting the cyanosis of tetralogy. She proposed this operation to Dr. Robert Gross, the surgeon who, in 1938, had first successfully closed a patent ductus—the first repair of a congenital heart condition. He didn't think her idea would work. She then discussed her idea with Dr. Blalock. Why couldn't a surgeon create an artificial ductus by joining the patient's subclavian and pulmonary arteries? Dr. Blalock had been experimenting with a similar idea for creating a canine model of pulmonary hypertension. He told Dr. Taussig that he thought he could create an artificial ductus in a patient. They decided to modify his technique for use in tetralogy. Vivien began performing additional dog experiments for that purpose. Once the technique was perfected, Dr. Blalock practiced the operation with Vivien on dogs in the lab.

In April 1944 an eight-month-old baby named Eileen Saxon was diagnosed with tetralogy of Fallot by Dr. Taussig. Because nothing could be done for Eileen, she was sent home. She was readmitted to Johns Hopkins Hospital in November 1944 in serious condition. Eileen was extremely frail and weighed only nine pounds. Drs. Taussig and Blalock believed that their procedure was her only chance for survival, so they scheduled the operation. Dr. Blalock asked Vivien to be present in the operating room. As news of the daring plan spread throughout the hospital, many wondered whether Eileen would even be able to survive general anesthesia. Could the surgical procedure be accomplished at all?

The surgery took place on November 29, 1944, in an operating room on the top floor of the Halsted Clinic. The room was lit by two large windows and was heated by cast-iron radiators. Along one side of the room, about three feet from the operating table, there was a balcony-like observation stand for a few visitors. Vivien Thomas stood on a stool behind Dr. Blalock's right shoulder. Dr. William Longmire, the chief resident, was first assistant. As a surgical intern, I was automatically scheduled to be a member of the team, albeit the lowest person on the totem pole. I was twenty-four years old at the time. My main task was to administer intravenous fluids and blood transfusions. I inserted a needle in a small vein in Eileen's ankle for this purpose.

On opening her chest, Dr. Blalock could see that Eileen's vessels were less than half the size of those in the dogs he had practiced on. As he began to free the subclavian and pulmonary arteries, he encountered more bleeding than expected, which made it difficult to prepare these two vessels for attachment. He seemed to have an almost impossible task. As he resolutely proceeded with the operation, he often asked Vivien questions. "Is this an appropriate length for the subclavian artery? Will it reach the pulmonary artery? Is this suture close enough to the one I just placed?" Vivien gave his opinion. Dr. Longmire watched to ensure that each suture was precisely placed. By today's standards, the instruments used were crude and the sutures cumbersome. But the connection was finally accomplished, although the arteries were under some tension.

The operation went on for ninety minutes. At its end, Dr. Blalock unclamped the artery that would allow blood to flow into the lung. Dr. Taussig exclaimed, "Al, the baby is turning a glorious pink!" Many in the operating room shed tears of joy and relief. After a rocky two-month postoperative course, Eileen was discharged from the hospital. Unfortunately, she soon became cyanotic again, so we did a similar procedure on the other side of her heart. She died within a few days.

Although this original operation was only moderately successful, it did pave the way for later, more successful ones. I have always been proud of being part of the team that performed that historic first Blalock-Taussig procedure. Few other events in my career have influenced me as much. Over the next several months, I participated in more blue baby cases.

One day, Dr. Blalock called me into his office and shut the door behind us. "Denton, you seem to have a reputation around the hospital for getting along well with the women."

"Do I, sir?"

"Yes, that's the rumor." After a brief pause, Dr. Blalock continued, "Dr. Longmire is becoming chief resident for the surgical service, so I need a new cardiac resident. I want you for that position. It may seem a little premature for you, but I believe you're up to the task. And I want you to do one thing for me. I want you to get all those damn women out of my hair."

"What do you mean?" I asked.

"Dr. Taussig, Ruth Whittemore, Peggy Hanlon, and Mary Allen Engle."[2] It seems that Dr. Taussig's female staff members were hovering over the pediatric patients postoperatively and calling Dr. Blalock at all hours with requests and suggestions.

"That's your assignment. Do you think you can handle it?"

I could only reply, "I'll try, Dr. Blalock." From then on, I interceded with Dr. Taussig and her staff in managing the postoperative care of her patients. Although Drs. Blalock and Taussig continued to have

---

[2] All of these protégés of Dr. Taussig later became prominent pediatric cardiologists.

their differences, he was a very humble man and always acknowledged her contributions. He always said openly that it was Dr. Taussig who first proposed the concept of the blue baby operation.

My unusual promotion to cardiac resident came as a complete surprise. I had been out of medical school for less than a year. Today, caring for hospital patients is generally the responsibility of staff surgeons. Back then, however, the surgical training program at Hopkins was set up so that senior-level trainees had the authority of staff surgeons. As chief cardiac resident, I had my own set of patients and was responsible for their entire hospital stay. Although Dr. Blalock and the staff surgeons were available, I was not expected to seek their help unless a problem came up that I couldn't solve.

I was now also Dr. Blalock's first assistant in the operating room, so I was performing procedures that were well ahead of my actual experience as a surgeon. I had done an appendectomy and a couple of inguinal hernia repairs but had never done even a basic gallbladder operation.

As more people found out about the Blalock-Taussig procedure, patients began coming to Hopkins from near and far, and visiting surgeons crowded the operating rooms.[3] Soon I was able to perform the operation myself, as the principal surgeon. I even suggested modifications that added to its success. Later, at a meeting of the Society of Vascular Surgeons in Atlantic City, I listened from the back of the room as Dr. Blalock described some technical aspects of the operation. Then he said, "My resident Dr. Cooley made some modifications that have improved the results." Those words meant more to me than I can say. Dr. Blalock was always quick to acknowledge the contributions of his trainees. In turn, we felt a special comradeship and pride to be members of what we called the "Blalock school of surgery."

In my opinion, the Blalock-Taussig procedure marked the dawn of heart surgery. Before that operation, doctors were afraid to perform any invasive procedures in children with tetralogy of Fallot. Dentists

---

[3] Eventually, we found that the Blalock-Taussig procedure worked best in children aged three years or older, whose arteries were more fully developed. By 1964, when Dr. Blalock retired, more than fifteen thousand patients worldwide had undergone the Blalock-Taussig procedure, and at least two thousand of those operations had been performed at Johns Hopkins.

would not pull their teeth, and surgeons would not operate on them. Any child with tetralogy and acute appendicitis or tonsillitis would have been in dire trouble. The Blalock-Taussig procedure proved that these children could tolerate anesthesia easily and gave other surgeons the courage to operate on very sick children. As these pediatric procedures became more successful, surgeons began to think about operating on adults with acquired heart diseases.

In my army uniform after induction into the Army Specialized Training Program as a private first class.

CHAPTER 6

Army Doctor

IN AUGUST 1945 JAPAN SURRENDERED, bringing an end to World War II. Even though the war was over, I was required to fulfill my military service as originally planned, because new medical personnel were needed to relieve those who had been on duty during the war. This meant that I would have to interrupt my surgical training and leave Johns Hopkins for two years. In late 1945 the army notified me that I would be called to active duty as a first lieutenant within a few months. I hoped that I might be lucky enough to be assigned to Walter Reed Army Hospital in Washington, D.C., where my surgical training would be broadened.

When I shared my concern with Dr. Blalock, he said that he would write a letter to the surgeon general, Dr. Norman T. Kirk, requesting that I be sent to Walter Reed. The key was for me to deliver the letter personally to General Kirk so that it wouldn't get lost in the army bureaucracy. Letter in hand, I made the short trip from Baltimore to Washington. When I got to the building and reached General Kirk's floor, I was directed to his adjutant, who was bent over a desk piled with papers and books. I had to stand there for a few minutes before he glanced up. I immediately recognized him as Dr. Michael E. DeBakey, a surgeon from the Ochsner Clinic in New Orleans. Dr. Blalock had introduced me to him a few months earlier, when we were attending a meeting of the Southern Surgical Association in Hot Springs, Virginia. Dr. DeBakey had a black mustache, a prominent nose, heavy eyebrows, and a receding hairline. He looked up at me without saying anything. His large, dark-rimmed glasses emphasized his intense gaze.

"I'm Denton Cooley, and this letter is from Dr. Alfred Blalock at Johns Hopkins. He asked me to deliver it personally to General Kirk." I handed Dr. DeBakey the envelope. He opened it and quickly glanced at the letter. "I'll keep you in mind if anything comes up," he said curtly. He returned to his work, and I was obviously dismissed. I never knew whether the letter made it to General Kirk, but I doubt that it did. At the time, I little guessed that Michael DeBakey would soon play an even more decisive role in my career.

Two weeks after delivering the letter, I was disappointed to learn that I had been assigned to the European Theater of Operations. I was given orders to report in January 1946 to Fort Sam Houston, in San Antonio, Texas, the largest army post in the United States. I don't remember the exact date when I was expected to arrive. My friend Jim Davis had received the same orders. We drove my car to Texas and decided to stop for a farewell to civilian life at my father's vacation home (*El Rancho Dontia*, or "The Tooth Ranch") on Lake Travis, near Austin. When we finally got to Fort Sam three days late, we were reprimanded but not penalized. Thankfully, the sergeant was reluctant to question and offend commissioned officers. At Fort Sam, I was indoctrinated into military life along with some seventy-five other young physicians. I was taught the basic protocols of being an officer, including how to interact with enlisted men and to work with my superior officers.

A month later, the army sent Jim and me to Camp Kilmer in New Jersey. The camp had been built specifically as a staging area for troops awaiting departure for Europe. After a few days of boredom, I got a pass to go to New York City, which was about twenty miles north of us by train. I spent the weekend enjoying Manhattan nightlife with a friend. Early Monday morning I returned to the base a few hours late, only to find that our orders had been delivered and everyone was heading out. I scrambled to gather my belongings, including a tennis racket. When we reached New York harbor, we boarded the USS *Wheaton Victory*—one of the Victory ships built during the war and equipped for transporting large contingents of soldiers. Our destination was the port of Bremerhaven, Germany.

My accommodations onboard the ship were low in the hold, close to the screw. The bunks were stacked four deep, with about eighteen inches between each one. As soon as the boat reached open water, I became so seasick I couldn't get out of my bunk. I lay there for five days, vomiting into my helmet liner. By the sixth day, my kidneys had stopped functioning. A bunkmate got me to the infirmary, where I was given an infusion of glucose. The infirmary doctor had graduated from the University of Maryland, Hopkins' archrival. He seemed amused by my plight. Thankfully, it would be only a few more days before we arrived in Bremerhaven. I was never so glad to set foot on terra firma. Motion sickness has continued to plague me all my life. Even today when I get offers to go deep-sea fishing, I always decline. I tell my fishing buddies that I'm not going out on the ocean until they pave the damn place!

In Bremerhaven, I learned that I'd been assigned to the 124th Station Hospital in Linz, Austria. Feeling a need for some R&R after my grueling voyage, I convinced Jim, who had also come on the *Wheaton*, to hitchhike the thirty miles to Bremen, where we had a little holiday—partying and playing golf at the officers' club and resort. When we returned to Bremerhaven, we were surprised to learn that our units had already left by train. Although we had arrived late, the corporal decided to look the other way. As officers, we were issued tickets on a comfortable passenger train. This was a stroke of luck because the others in our group had gone via boxcar. When we arrived, we couldn't locate our units. As it turned out, the heavily loaded troop train had somehow bypassed Stuttgart and gotten lost somewhere to the south. It didn't get back for two more days. So Jim and I took it easy at the officers' club in the Hotel Graf Zeppelin before meeting up with our units to leave for our assigned hospitals.

I finally arrived in Linz—three days late. Located in the north-central region of the country, Linz is one of Austria's largest and most beautiful cities. Adolf Hitler was born nearby and always considered Linz his hometown. The 124th Station Hospital was originally a *Frauenklinik*, or women's hospital. When the city was liberated by the U.S. Army, the hospital was occupied by the medical corps. According to regulations for station hospitals, only emergency treatments or minor surgical procedures could be done there. All nonemergency major surgical cases had to be referred to hospitals in Munich or back to Walter Reed.

As a first lieutenant, I was outranked by other surgeons on the staff. I felt as if I'd been demoted, having just left Hopkins as a promising junior resident. But, after only a few months, the army sent the higher-level officers home, and I was appointed chief of surgery. My responsibilities included orthopedics, obstetrics, urology, and gynecology. After a year I was promoted to the rank of captain. With this appointment, I had more authority to do what I thought necessary to improve the hospital's services.

As soon as possible, I acquired a nurse anesthetist to give anesthesia and monitor patients during surgery. Before then, anesthesia had been managed by the surgeon. Most of my patients were GIs who had been injured in road accidents after partying too hard or otherwise misbehaving. Because I had to treat a variety of injuries, the surgery was interesting and often challenging. One soldier arrived at the hospital with a complex skull fracture that required me to perform my first brain operation. I learned how to do many types of operations while on the job—literally. If I wasn't thoroughly familiar with a procedure, I read about it in the library beforehand, then kept the book close at hand in the operating room in case I needed to refresh my memory.

As chief of obstetrics, I delivered forty babies. Some of the women assigned to my care were local war brides, or "*Fräuleins,*" but others were wives of American servicemen stationed there. At Hopkins, I'd seen a delivery in which an infant was accidentally injured by a resident using forceps. Because of that experience, I was determined not to use forceps. For complicated deliveries, I performed a cesarian section instead—never even having seen one done before! Fortunately, all of the babies in my care were delivered successfully. I've even gotten thank-you letters from some of them years later.

At first, I was living in a spartan billet adjacent to the hospital. After a year there, I was offered a much better accommodation in an elegant private estate, the Villa Guglhof, located on a hill on the west side of Linz. I believe the house had belonged to a wealthy family who were Nazi sympathizers. The move made an amazing difference in my standard of living. Several other young officers were assigned to the villa, and we all received royal treatment. At lunch and dinner, we were entertained by a string quartet as we ate gourmet meals prepared by the villa's chef, who had managed the kitchens on the luxury liner *Normandie*.[1] He was a master at cooking all sorts of wild game and edible plants from the countryside around Linz. Some of his best dishes contained ingredients I had never heard of before.

---

[1] In 1942 the *Normandie* (then renamed the USS *Lafayette*) caught fire, capsized, and sank in New York harbor as she was being converted into a troopship.

The army discouraged officers from fraternizing with Austrian or German civilians. Even so, I became friends with an Austrian count who had a large estate along the Danube, including a private game park for hunting. His wife, the countess, reminded me of the lovely Austrian-born actress Hedy Lamarr. I also got to know a *Jägermeister*, or gamekeeper, who had access to other hunting properties. I bought a prewar double-barrel shotgun and often hunted pheasants with one of the *Jägers*, or professional hunters.

On one occasion, I was invited to a major hunt organized by the count on his estate. This was a part of aristocratic life that I'd read about but never expected to see firsthand, and it was worlds away from the type of hunting my brother and I had done as boys. The hunt conformed to traditions and formalities that dated from the Middle Ages. Guests of the host brought their own shotguns. There were beaters, *Jägers*, and hunters, and each group had its own place on the hunting field. A *Jägermeister* was in charge of the event and signaled each phase of the hunt by blowing a horn. At the first sounding of the horn, the beaters walked into the field with their sticks to drive the game into one area. The horn sounded again, and out went the *Jägers*, who assisted the beaters in flushing out the birds. Along with the pheasants, numerous *Hasen*, or hares, tried to escape. The hares were as big as Texas jackrabbits, but fatter. Finally, at the third sounding of the horn, we hunters began to shoot as game appeared. We ended up with 150 cock pheasants (hens were not targeted) and more than 200 hares. The invited hunters, or "guns," were invited to the local village for food and wine. The spoils of the hunt were displayed at the village. It was an amazing sight. All the participants in the hunt could choose either a hare or two pheasants. All of the locals chose a hare, because it had more meat than two pheasants. The rest of the game was taken to a "cool house," where the villagers could later buy it for a modest fee. Blocks of ice chopped from the local lakes in winter were used for refrigeration.

In this immediate postwar period, almost all of Europe had a bleak economy. Many cities had been heavily damaged, and food and other basic necessities were in short supply. Although Linz had escaped serious physical damage, its economy was poor. The currency had almost no value, so bartering of goods became the standard means of exchange. My net pay was 215 dollars a month. Of that amount, I designated 212 dollars to be transferred to my bank account in Houston and kept only three dollars for personal needs. How could I get by on so little? In addition to my salary, I got a weekly allotment at the post exchange that included toiletries, chocolates, twelve packs of cigarettes, and other items. The cigarettes became currency for any personal items not already supplied by the army.

At the PX, I also bought a surplus jeep with a canvas top for 125 dollars, an opportunity available only to officers. I paid two cartons of cigarettes to an Austrian craftsman to customize my jeep with comfortable seats from a used, prewar Mercedes and with a hard top for winter. Although the vehicle was mechanically sound, it had been reclaimed from a battlefield. I named it "Pamela" in honor of a cute girl I had met at Piccadilly Circus in London while on leave. My jeep, Pamela, took me to many unforgettable places, including Mondsee, Gemünden, and St. Wolfgangsee in the Salzkammergut region of Austria. At all the resorts, lodgings were cheap for American officers. As "conquerors," we were given luxurious rooms and wonderful meals. I remember that at Mondsee, a town on a large lake, the fanciest hotel had been designated an American Army Officers' Club. About eleven or twelve o'clock one night at the bar, somebody yelled out, "Let's have a jeep race around the lake!" Despite—or perhaps because of—their advanced state of inebriation, many of the officers jumped into their jeeps and took off. I'm surprised they weren't all killed.

I'll never forget the overwhelming beauty of the region—the white-capped mountains, shimmering lakes, and fragrant forests— or the hospitality of the villagers, some of whom had never met an American before. Often I'd take my army buddies with me on my trips in Pamela. We were young, the war was over, and we were ready to party whenever we could. On one such occasion, we visited Kitzbühel, a popular prewar ski resort. I'd never snow skied before, but with minimum instruction, I gave it a try. I strapped on the skis with some trepidation. They were eight feet long, made of heavy mahogany, and difficult to manage. After I made it down a gentle slope, my buddies convinced me that I was ready for something more challenging. I struggled hard to get down a steeper run in one piece. What a relief to finally get back to the inn, with its roaring fire and hot buttered rum! That brief flirtation with snow skiing reaffirmed my commitment to tennis.

One of my best friends in Linz was Mildred Dunshee, a Red Cross worker at the local USO. One day, she told me that the canteen was about to discard a large box of stale, water-stained cigarettes. I knew that I could make good use of those cigarettes. Jim Davis and I had been planning a trip to Italy, so we decided to take the cigarettes to Rome to "pay" for our trip. We hid them under Pamela's hood. We were worried that customs guards would confiscate the cigarettes when we crossed into Italy, but Pamela was so "fancy" that the border guards just waved us on without a search. At that time, Lucky Strikes were a top-selling brand because their tobacco was toasted rather than sun-dried. We could honestly claim, tongue in cheek, that although our cigarettes weren't Lucky Strikes, they too were toasted—by the heat from Pamela's engine. We sold them on the black market in a rather sleazy alley in Rome. With the resulting bundle of Italian lira, we lived in comfort on our vacation, which included visits to Naples, Capri, Florence, and Venice.

In Linz the officers were expected to organize intramural activities for the enlisted personnel at the hospital. We had tennis, softball, and basketball teams that competed against other military teams in the area. My basketball team traveled to Vienna to play in a tournament, which we won. Also, in a tennis tournament for military groups in Austria, I joined a young lieutenant who had played varsity tennis at West Point, and we won the doubles event. After that win, I was scheduled to go to Bremen to represent Austria in a tennis tournament for the European theater.

Unfortunately, my love of tennis caused me to miss a great opportunity in my young professional career. Early in 1947 Dr. Blalock wrote and told me that he'd been invited to demonstrate the Blalock-Taussig operation on a European tour. He asked me to join him. Because I wanted to play in the Bremen tournament, I declined the invitation with a fake excuse that the army would not grant me leave for the tour. It was one of my dumbest-ever decisions, which I regret to this day. I not only missed the tour with Dr. Blalock but was also eliminated in the first round of the tournament. Because I had declined his invitation, Dr. Blalock instead brought my friend Dr. Henry "Hank" Bahnson, at that time his assistant resident. They operated at Guy's Hospital in London and at Broussai's Hospital in Paris and were received with much acclaim in both cities. They were given a spectacular reception at the Royal College of Surgeons in London. The tour had a profound impact on the development of cardiac surgery in Europe and brought great prestige to Dr. Blalock and Hank. If I'd made a better choice, I could have shared that experience.

While in the service, I did take advantage of other professional opportunities. I went to Vienna for a six-week course in surgical pathology led by the famous professor Hermann Chiari, director of the Pathological-Anatomical Institute at the University of Vienna. At that time, an autopsy was automatically performed on everyone in Vienna who died. So each morning, thirty to forty cadavers were waiting in the morgue for autopsy by the staff of pathologists. On one occasion, Professor Chiari himself performed the autopsy before our class. He sliced away half of a cadaver's lung, scraped off a portion with his long knife, and held it under my nose. "*Was ist das?*" he asked. "*Kanker milch, Herr Professor,*" I responded. Thankfully, I knew that the milky, cheesy appearance of the liquid indicated squamous-cell carcinoma. My experience with the professor really broadened my knowledge of anatomy and medicine. At the end of the course, I received a certificate in surgical pathology from the University of Vienna.

At the university, I was also exposed to other illustrious faculty members, including Professor Hans Finsterer, a world-famous gastrointestinal surgeon. I marveled at his precise suturing techniques and his ability to simplify complex operations. He preferred straight needles without a holder rather than the customary curved needles used in American hospitals. As a result, he had an almost tailor-like technique. Anesthesia was primitive and inadequate. I remember one poor man who was having part of his stomach removed for ulcers. The procedure was being performed under local anesthesia, so the patient was awake. In the middle of the operation, he moaned, "*Herr Professor, Schmertz, Schmertz—bitte,*" which means, "Pain, pain—please." The professor then injected additional amounts of novacaine. Further surgical manipulations increased the patient's pain. In a soft and kindly voice, the professor whispered to the nurse, "*Schwester, Ether bitte.*" A small amount of ether put an end to the patient's complaints, and the operation was completed.

My stay in Vienna was filled with excellent courses and interesting learning experiences. The surgeons there were having to deal with shortages resulting from the war. Critically needed anesthetics and other medicines—as well as surgical instruments, sutures, and other essential equipment—were always difficult, and sometimes impossible, to obtain. Even if medicines were available, they were often used for only the severest of cases. Because of the rubber shortage, most surgeons had to wear previously used and patched surgical gloves. On occasion, some even operated with their bare hands.

On another note, I also enjoyed the city itself, with its historical and cultural offerings. Vienna had an active nightlife centered around musical performances of all kinds—operas, symphonies, chamber music, and waltzes. I took them all in. I even rode horseback in the Vienna Woods.

All in all, I enjoyed my stay in Europe, on both a personal and a professional level. Back in the States I had been deeply immersed in the rigors of college and medical training. Although I was originally disappointed to be assigned to Europe, my tour of duty there provided me with a much-needed change of pace and a new perspective on surgery. At the end of two years, though, I was eager to return to Baltimore to resume my surgical training. In treating battlefield injuries during the war, surgeons had found that the heart was more amenable to the scalpel than they had earlier realized. Dr. Dwight Harken, a young surgeon in a military hospital, had successfully removed shrapnel in and around the hearts of soldiers. About the same time, Drs. Harken, Charles Bailey, and Russell Brock pioneered techniques for manipulating the impaired mitral valve within the human heart. Clearly, the day was fast approaching when complex operations would be performed inside the heart. I wanted to participate in this progress. I was ready to go home.

Just before leaving Linz, I broke my ankle playing basketball, so I disembarked from the ship in New York City wearing a plaster of Paris cast. Some of those on hand to greet the ship probably thought I was a "battle casualty."

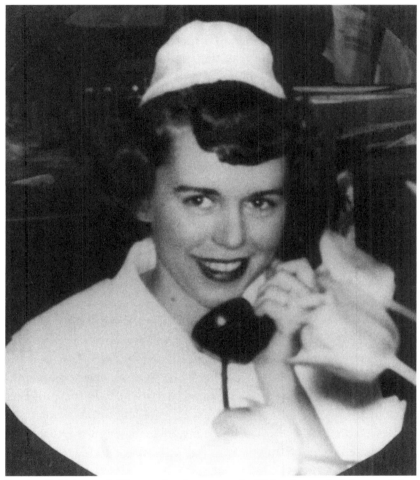

Louise Goldsborough Thomas, head nurse on the Halsted 5 surgical floor at Johns Hopkins Hospital.

CHAPTER 7

Residency at Hopkins

FTER LEAVING THE MILITARY in the spring of 1948, I returned to Baltimore to complete my residency training at Johns Hopkins. In the army, I'd successfully dealt with a wide range of medical problems and surgical procedures, so I came home a more confident doctor and surgeon.

At Hopkins, I resumed my job as chief resident on the cardiac service—the most active unit in the hospital. While I'd been away, Hank Bahnson had become its brightest young star after taking my place on Dr. Blalock's European tour. One of his interests was tissue transplantation for patients whose parathyroid glands had been removed during a thyroidectomy. One day, Hank asked me to implant a pair of fetal human parathyroid glands into his abdominal wall to see if his body would reject the tissue. The operation would be simple, so I agreed. All that was required was local anesthesia. As we expected, the glands did not survive. Dr. Blalock was out of town at the time, but when he returned, he called Hank and me to his office to confirm a "crazy rumor" about our experiment. When we confessed that it wasn't a rumor, Dr. Blalock shook his head and called us "a couple of damn fools." Hank Bahnson was an outstanding surgeon who eventually went on to the University of Pittsburgh School of Medicine, where he created one of the leading departments of cardiac surgery in the country. He was especially close to Dr. Blalock and even named his son Alfred Blalock Bahnson. Hank and I remained good friends until his death in 2003.

• • •

Over the years, I'd had a number of women friends but had not been seriously involved with any of them. Then, in the fall of 1948, I met a pretty twenty-four-year-old nurse with blonde hair and big blue eyes. Louise Goldsborough Thomas was the head nurse on Halsted 5, the main surgical floor of Johns Hopkins Hospital, where many of my patients recovered after their operations. Louise had majored in psychology at the College of William and Mary. After graduating from there, she earned her certification as a registered nurse at the Johns Hopkins School of Nursing. Her father, Edward P. Thomas, was a prominent general practitioner and surgeon in Frederick, Maryland, and a friend of Dr. Blalock's. Because of our schedules, Louise and I had mostly informal dates—near the hospital and after 9 p.m., when I could get away. We'd go to a local hangout, the bar of the new Broadway Hotel, where we enjoyed listening to the jukebox. Occasionally, we'd take in a movie downtown.

I soon decided that Louise was the one for me. A month after we met, we drove to her parents' home in Frederick. I had planned to ask her father for her hand and, if he agreed, to ask Louise to marry me. For my twenty-first birthday in 1941, my father had given me a bluish-white, one-carat diamond ring. I seldom wore the ring, so I had the stone removed and put into an engagement ring, which was designed by Kirk Jewelry in Baltimore. I took it with me to Frederick and showed it to Louise after proposing in her living room. But I was so nervous that I dropped the ring. Her boxer dog, Clipper, picked it up in his mouth. I had to grab the dog in a stranglehold to keep him from swallowing the ring. I managed to retrieve it from his mouth and give it to Louise. This was not a very romantic beginning to our engagement. However, back at Hopkins, everyone admired the ring and enjoyed hearing the story.

On January 15, 1949, we were married in a huge wedding at the Evangelical Reformed Church in Frederick, Maryland, which was followed by a reception at the Francis Scott Key Hotel. Besides the hundreds of guests who attended from the Frederick, Baltimore, and Washington, D.C., areas, numerous friends and relatives of mine had flown up from Texas. I was really pleased to have both my mother and father there, along with my brother, Ralph, who served as best man.

Louise and I spent our honeymoon in Sea Island, Georgia, where we stayed at the Cloister Hotel. We drove there in the green Chevy that I'd recently bought with money saved while I was in the army. We spent our first night at the Shoreham in Washington, D.C. We also stopped at the historic Williamsburg Inn in Virginia. Louise told me that the inn had been an officers' club during the war. On Sea Island, she and I played tennis, swam, and walked on the beach. I also managed to sneak in a few rounds of golf.

During the weeks before our wedding, we had found an apartment on Wolfe Street, adjacent to the hospital. It was on the second floor of a typical Baltimore row house. We spent evenings cleaning, painting, and even wallpapering to make it look livable. When we returned from our wedding trip, we stocked the pantry closet. During the first night, we were awakened by a scuffling, crackling noise in the kitchen but decided it was probably just the house creaking. The next morning, we found a large hole in the door of the pantry, which had been made by ravenous rats trying to get to our breakfast cereals. When our baby Mary arrived a year later, we purchased a Kiddy Koop, a heavily screened crib on wheels, to protect her in case the rats came back.

• • •

That same year, Dr. Jack Handelsman and I both became chief residents at Hopkins. The cardiac service had become so large that two chief residents were needed instead of the usual one. Unfortunately, the budget allowed for only one chief resident. Dr. Blalock took this problem to the hospital board. The board members had an easy solution: The budget was one hundred dollars a month for the chief resident's position, so each of us would get fifty dollars. Hopkins was a tight-fisted outfit in those days. Despite the low pay, there was no question about my accepting the post. Chief resident on Dr. Blalock's service at Hopkins was one of the most prestigious postgraduate positions in the country.

Louise and I were able to get by on her salary of 187 dollars a month as head nurse, my savings from active military service, and my stipend from the federal GI Bill. In addition, I made fifty dollars for donating blood, which I did at least once a month. All in all, we were able to live well. On February 1, 1950, our first child, Mary Fraley Cooley, was born. Louise had continued to work as a nurse almost until the day of our daughter's birth. Mary was the first girl to be born to the Cooley family in generations. Louise and I were exceedingly proud of our beautiful baby. Jubilantly, I called my father to announce the news. After a pause, he responded, "You had a *girl*, son?? What were you doing—chewing gum or looking out the window?" Later, when my four other daughters arrived, I hesitated to call him with the news.

· · ·

Outside the operating room, Dr. Blalock had a warm, congenial personality and was completely modest. When he walked into a room, everyone seemed eager to greet him, not merely because he was famous but because he was such a genuinely friendly person. I never heard anyone say a derogatory word against him. He had the gift of making everyone who knew him feel special, or at least equal to himself.

In the operating room, however, Dr. Blalock could be somewhat difficult. I never felt that he was entirely comfortable there. He could be nervous, impatient, and quarrelsome while operating. I remember once when he encountered a problem during a procedure, he whined plaintively, "Will someone help me? *Please* help me!" On another occasion, Dr. Blalock was dissecting to free the right pulmonary artery. He had made a small incision in the chest wall, and the structures inside were difficult to see from my side of the table. He complained, "Denton, why don't you get on the ball?" I was embarrassed by his comment, especially because some visitors were observing the case. I finally said quietly, "Dr. Blalock, I can't even *see* the damn ball." After that, the patient's position was changed, and Dr. Blalock's complaints ceased. Later, he apologized to me for his conduct. Such episodes were typical of him and made me realize the importance of emotional control for a surgeon.

Dr. Blalock was not exactly what I would call scholarly, but he was always a solid thinker. He had a genuine curiosity and a practical approach to solving problems. He also had a determination to persevere, even when things seemed to be going badly. I remember a disastrous day when one of our small patients died in the operating room and another one died on the surgical ward. Extremely depressed, I went to Dr. Blalock and said, "Today's events must have been hard on you. I think we should cancel tomorrow's surgical schedule so that you can have a day's rest."

Frowning, he replied, "No, that's not the way to face adversity. We have to keep on working. We didn't do anything wrong—the situations were simply beyond our control. You schedule a full day of surgery for me tomorrow. This afternoon, I am going to play nine holes of golf with Dr. Rienhoff. After that, I will have cleared my mind."

I have never forgotten that incident. Dr. Blalock liked to work and was trained like an athlete to cope with both winning and losing. I recognized the wisdom of his approach and have tried to follow his example in my own career. After a disappointing day, I may leave the hospital to play a round of golf or tennis and regain my perspective. The next day, I can return to the hospital in a better frame of mind.

Another episode at Hopkins strongly influenced my development as a cardiovascular surgeon. In 1949 an emergency arose involving a patient of Dr. Grant Ward, who was best known for operating on tumors of the head and neck. The patient previously had undergone an operation for cancer in his sternum, or breastbone. Part of his sternum had been removed and replaced with a metal prosthesis devised by Dr. Ward. After several weeks, the prosthesis had eroded into the ascending aorta, causing an aneurysm—a ballooning of the vessel wall—that had begun to leak. The patient was in severe pain, and he soon went into shock. He was urgently taken to the operating room. It was a Saturday afternoon, and only Dr. Ward and I were available for an emergency. Once the patient was anesthetized and the chest exposed, Dr. Ward quickly removed the metal prosthesis. Behind it, the aorta had ruptured, and there was a pool of blood that spurted so high, it hit the operating room light. Dr. Ward immediately thrust his left hand into the patient's chest and blocked the opening with his left index finger. However, he himself had formerly undergone an operation for a spinal cord tumor, which impaired the function of muscles in his right shoulder. He was required to wear a special shoulder splint that partially disabled his right arm. With his left hand in the patient and his right arm immobilized by the splint, he turned to me and said, "It's your operation now. See what you can do to get my finger out of the hole." I set about repairing the aneurysm by removing a section of muscle from the patient's chest wall and using it as a graft to patch the hole. I placed the muscle patch over Dr. Ward's finger without tying the final knot. He then quickly removed his finger while I tied the suture. "What shall we do now?" he asked. I replied, "We could put a clamp on the side of the aorta to stop the blood flow temporarily. Then the hole could be sewn over without a need for the muscle patch." Dr. Ward told me to proceed. This operation saved the patient's life.

The procedure was of great interest to the staff surgeons, who were impressed by the result.

Previously, treatment of aneurysms had been limited to "indirect" techniques, such as introducing wire into the aneurysm to promote blood clotting or applying cellophane to the exterior of the lesion to induce scarring and reinforce the wall. These techniques might keep the aneurysm from rupturing, but they were only minimally successful. Our direct aneurysm repair was an entirely new approach to this usually fatal condition. It attracted a lot of attention in the medical community. Because of that operation, I became convinced that it should be possible to cut out aneurysms and reconnect the remaining, healthy segments of the vessel.

I would soon test this theory when Dr. Blalock left me in charge of his practice while he went to Honolulu for two weeks as a visiting professor. After he left town, one of his patients, a thirty-two-year-old man, was admitted in severe pain with a mass in the right upper part of his chest. The mass was diagnosed as a large aneurysm of the right subclavian artery, which supplies blood to the right upper extremity. The aneurysm was in danger of rupturing. Two months earlier, Dr. Blalock had repaired an aortic narrowing, or coarctation, in this same patient. Although the subclavian aneurysm was present at that time, Dr. Blalock decided to delay treatment. Now that the aneurysm had enlarged, it needed to be treated. We took the patient to the operating room and removed the aneurysm by applying a clamp across its base from the aorta. In 1950, vascular grafts for repairing aneurysms did not exist, so surgeons had fewer options for treating aneurysms than they have today. In this case, collateral circulation was present to support the region originally supplied by the subclavian artery.[1] The patient did well and was back at work soon after the operation.

When Dr. Blalock returned from Hawaii, he was astounded that I had repaired the aneurysm. At his clinical conference, he said to the faculty, "This proves that if any of you staff surgeons have a problem that you are reluctant to deal with, just leave town. When you come back home, maybe a resident will have taken care of it for you—that

---

[1] You can read surgical details of this operation in the *Annals of Surgery*, vol. 135 (1952), pp. 660–680.

is, if your resident happens to be Denton Cooley." That was his way of complimenting me, and it made me immensely proud.

During my residency, I learned many other new techniques and made some contributions of my own. In 1949 we operated on a lovely little redheaded girl who had a patent ductus arteriosus. During the operation, anesthesia was induced with cyclopropane, which is now known to cause irregular heartbeats. The little girl developed a very rapid heartbeat called tachycardia. This led to ventricular fibrillation, a condition in which the heart muscle contracts in an uncoordinated manner. We tried all of the medical treatments known at the time, but to no avail. She died in the operating room.

Because of her death, I read everything I could find about ventricular fibrillation. I wanted to create a defibrillator—an electrical device to shock the heart back into a normal rhythm. I decided to modify the techniques used by Donald Hooker and Claude Beck, both of whom had previously worked in the Hunterian lab. In 1947 Beck had performed the first successful defibrillation of a human heart by using electrical countershock. Dr. Blalock showed little interest in my project, so I developed the device alone. When I couldn't find the components I needed, I made them with the aid of the machine and carpentry shops at Hopkins. The total cost of the device was ninety-two dollars, which I paid out of my salary of fifty dollars a month. The defibrillator functioned on alternating current from a normal wall outlet. I tested the device in the animal laboratory with Vivien Thomas. The final version was used in the Hopkins operating room for almost ten years before commercial devices became available. In 1950 I published a paper in the prestigious *Annals of Surgery* about the use of this defibrillator for cardiac resuscitation.[2] Although Dr. Blalock gave me comments about the paper, he said that I should be the only author because it was my work. During this time, I also pioneered some other procedures, including a partial gastrectomy (removal of the stomach) for treating acute perforation of peptic ulcers.

As a result of his successful congenital heart surgery program, Dr. Blalock became the most influential surgeon in the United States. An impressive number of his house staff at Hopkins eventually ended up in fulltime academic positions for which they received widespread rec-

---

[2] This report can be read in the *Annals of Surgery*, vol. 132 (1950), pp. 930–936.

ognition. William Longmire, who was Dr. Blalock's closest associate when I was at Hopkins, later became the chairman of the Department of Surgery at the University of California at Los Angeles. Several other Blalock trainees eventually became chairmen of major departments of surgery, including Hank Bahnson at the University of Pittsburgh, David Sabiston at Duke University, William Harry Mueller at the University of Virginia in Charlottesville, and Mark Ravitch at Mount Sinai Hospital in New York City. Dr. Blalock imparted something special to each of us, and we felt obligated to repay our debt for having the privilege of working with him.

One day, close to the end of my tenure, Dr. Blalock called me into his office and said, "You know, Denton, we've invested a lot of time in you. I don't know what you're going to do with your life, but I hope you'll have an interest in academia and write some clinical reports. However, I predict that you'll probably go back down to Houston and become a society doctor." His words unsettled me. I was planning to return to Houston but was determined that I would not be just a "society doctor."

Mr. Russell Brock, Britain's foremost cardiac surgeon and my mentor in London. Courtesy of Dr. Cooley's personal collection.

CHAPTER 8

A Year at the Brompton

INSTEAD OF BECOMING A SOCIETY DOCTOR as Dr. Blalock feared, I decided to enter the world of academic medicine, which meant finding a teaching and research position at a medical school. Luckily for me, in 1943, Baylor University College of Medicine, the only private medical school in Texas, had moved from Dallas to Houston. By 1950 Baylor had settled into the recently constructed Cullen building at the Texas Medical Center. Dr. Michael DeBakey, the army colonel whom I suspected of "deep-sixing" my request for assignment to Walter Reed Hospital, had joined Baylor's faculty as head of the Department of Surgery. Dr. DeBakey was determined to make Baylor a first-rate medical school. During a visit to Houston, I contacted him to see if I could have a job on his staff after I completed my residency. This time, our encounter was more successful. He offered me a faculty position in surgery, and I quickly accepted.

In 1949, near the end of my residency, Mr. Russell Brock,[1] Britain's foremost cardiac surgeon, spent a month at Hopkins as a visiting professor working with Dr. Blalock. Although deliberate and precise, Brock was intrepid at performing new surgical procedures. He was a pioneer of intracardiac surgery for stenosis of the pulmonary and mitral valves, which he repaired with "closed" techniques, guided by feel instead of sight. Intracardiac surgery was a new approach, and I was eager to learn it. I had assisted him in several of these very aggressive procedures while he was visiting at Hopkins. I was also interested in learning more about Brock's technique for a blue baby operation. I

---

[1] In the British system, surgeons are known as "Mister," and other medical doctors are known as "Doctor."

wondered how his results compared to those of the Blalock-Taussig procedure.

Before Brock returned to London, I asked if I could spend some time with him on his service at the Brompton Hospital for Chest Diseases. He said I could come for a year and serve as his senior surgical registrar, or first assistant. I called Dr. DeBakey to tell him about Brock's offer and to ask if he'd hold my position at Baylor for a year while I broadened my training in London. He agreed that a year of training abroad with such a distinguished surgeon would benefit not only me but also Baylor. He promised that a job at Baylor would be waiting for me when I returned.

In June 1950, having completed my training in general and thoracic surgery at Hopkins, I sailed for England on the *Queen Elizabeth* with Louise and our baby, Mary. Because of my tendency for seasickness, I was dreading the week-long trip. The *QE* was the largest ship of its day, so it was extremely stable—much more so than the Victory ship that had transported me to Germany. Although I wasn't violently ill during this cruise, I never felt entirely well on board.

Great Britain was still struggling to overcome the economic devastation resulting from the war. Consumer goods, including food, clothing, and fuel, continued to be rationed even five years after the war's end. Living conditions were less than optimal. Among the decisions that Louise and I had to make was whether we wanted a cold- or hot-water flat. Cold-water flats didn't have warm, running water, so bathing would require heating the water. Louise and I looked at several apartments—mostly stark, dreary, places—a few of which were nearly 150 years old. We finally rented an apartment at Latimer Court, which was considered a "modern block" because it was only about ten years old and had hot water and regular bathrooms. The rent was a thousand pounds a year, and my annual salary from the Brompton was only twelve hundred pounds. Even so, we got along very well. I again drew on the stash of money I had saved from my military years. Since I was still in training, I also continued to receive some money from the GI Bill. We were doing well enough that we were able to buy a Hillman Minx, a small four-door sedan. We drove that little car all over the United Kingdom and the continent. We could even afford a cleaning lady, or charwoman, as they are called in England. Her name was Mrs. Moore, and she babysat for Mary.

Cooley family portrait, ca. 1912. Seated: Daniel Denton Cooley (grandfather), Helen Winfield Cooley (grandmother); standing: Ralph Clarkson Cooley (father), Denton Winfield Cooley (uncle), and Arthur Waugh Cooley (uncle).

The Daniel Denton Cooley house at 1802 Heights Blvd., built in 1893.

Prize Winning Roadster, Floral Parade, Deep Water Jubilee, Houston, 1914.

My father with his prize-winning Kissel roadster in front of my grandfather's house. Daddy, who was about twenty-nine years old, had decorated his car for a local parade.

Ralph Clarkson Cooley (father).

Mary Fraley Cooley (mother).

My maternal grandparents, Ethel and Frederick W. Fraley.

Mother, holding my brother, Ralph, and me (left).

Me, nine months old.

Mother at her stylish best.

Mother sitting at the piano in our home. My framed portrait is hanging on the wall.

With Daddy and Ralph (right) on Armistice Day in 1922. Toward the close of World War I, Daddy had a brief stint in France as a captain in the U.S. Dental Corps.

With Daddy and Ralph (left) in front of our boyhood home at 908 W. Alabama (the "manger").

Daddy holding the Cooley Clinic Cup, which was given yearly until 2003 to the winner of the "table clinic" at the Texas Dental Association Meeting. The awarding of a trophy was originally Daddy's idea, so the trophy was named for him. The table clinics allowed private practice dentists to showcase and promote new and innovative ideas and techniques through visual media, written reports, and oral explanations.

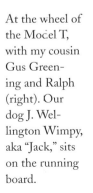

At the wheel of the Model T, with my cousin Gus Greening and Ralph (right). Our dog J. Wellington Wimpy, aka "Jack," sits on the running board.

Ralph Cooley Θ.Κ.Ν.

MOST POPULAR BOY

High school photo of my brother, Ralph, who was voted the most popular boy in the 1937 graduating class at San Jacinto High School.

With Pi Beta Phi sorority beauty queen Betty Munson at a Kappa Sigma dance, UT.

The UT Longhorn basketball team, 1939 Southwest Conference Champions. Bottom row: Nelms, Granville, Hull, Captain Tate, Moers, Spears, Finley; top row: Houpt, Wiggins, Coach Gray, Moore, King, me.

1939 UT Longhorn basketball team on the steps of Gregory Gymnasium before leaving for the National Invitation Tournament at Madison Square Garden. I am standing third from the right with Chester Granville's arm on my shoulder.

Making some points at the 1939 UT basketball game against Manhattan College at Madison Square Garden.

The 1941 headline said, "Cooley Leads UT with 14 Points." We beat Baylor 45–44 in Gregory Gymnasium. I am driving for the basket, and Baylor's no. 7 player is working hard to block me.

With Ralph (right) and Mother at Littlefield Fountain on the UT campus.

With Joy Ray, my college girlfriend.

"Bubbas" Watterworth and Cooley with our two other "band members" behind the Ford V8 that we drove to Boulder, Colorado, for the UT/Colorado football game in 1941.

AN AKK TRADITION WINTER 1942

Alpha Kappa Kappa poker party during my medical school days in Galveston. I'm in front of the rightmost plaid curtain.

Dr. Ernst W. Bermer, who presided over my birth and remained my lifelong mentor.

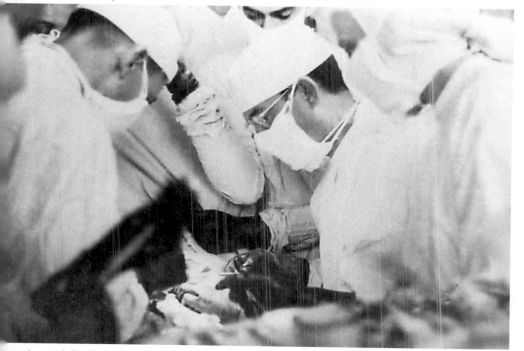

...erating with Dr. Blalock at Johns Hopkins. I'm on the left.

With my jeep, Pamela, in front of my billet at the 124th Station Hospital in Linz, Austria.

The Villa Guglhof in Linz, Austria, where I lived during my second year of service—nice quarters for a young army officer.

With Mildred Dunshee, a Red Cross worker and good friend, and Jim Davis at the Eiffel Tower on a getaway weekend.

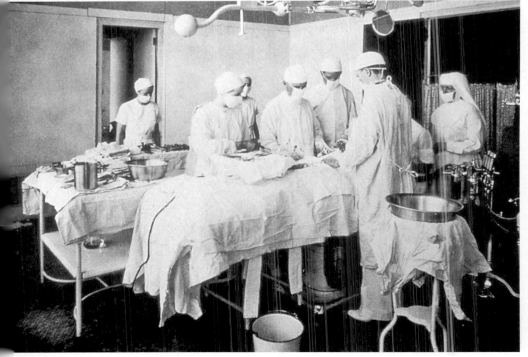

. Finsterer's operating room in Vienna. I am on the left at the head of the table.

With Louise at our wedding reception, January 15, 1949, at the Francis Scott Key Hotel in Frederick, Maryland.

The Johns Hopkins Hospital surgical house staff (interns and residents) and Dr. Blalock, 1949. I am denoted by the arrow, and Dr. Blalock is in the gray suit. To his right is Jack Handelsman, with whom I shared the position of chief resident. In the second row, between Dr. Blalock and me, is Albert Starr, an intern who later became famous for his innovations in valve surgery.

Dissecting lungs on our dining room table in London. Louise's comment on the back of this photo was 'Ugh.'

Trafalgar Square, London, with Louise and baby Mary.

The Texas Medical Center in its infancy (1951), looking northeast. The only recognizable buildings in this photo (left to right) are the Hermann Professional Building, the two buildings comprising Hermann Hospital, Methodist Hospital (center of photo), Baylor University College of Medicine, and M. D. Anderson Hospital. The intersection is Holcombe and Main.

The Jefferson Davis Hospital house staff (residents and interns) and medical staff. I am standing next to Mike DeBakey (end of second row, right). E. Stanley Crawford, another pioneer in the repair of aortic aneurysms, is seated second from left.

Those were enjoyable times for me. Each morning I took the London Underground (the Tube) northeast from Hammersmith Station to the Brompton on Fulham Road. Founded in the 1840s to treat tuberculosis patients, the hospital was a venerable institution whose early patrons included Charles Dickens, Jenny Lind, Prince Albert, and Queen Victoria. Because of Brock's work, it had earned a reputation for innovative techniques in heart as well as lung surgery.

Mr. Brock contrasted sharply with Dr. Blalock in personality. Brock was serious and formal. He was a stern but considerate chief. Although many of his associates thought he lacked a sense of humor, I didn't agree. His humor was subtle, understated, and sometimes downright odd. For example, once when I told him that a certain surgical procedure he disfavored had been done many times with success, he answered, "Cooley, people commit adultery frequently, but that doesn't make it right."

Soon after starting on Brock's service, I learned his technique for opening the mitral valve in patients with isolated stenosis or for opening the pulmonary valve in patients with tetralogy of Fallot. In both cases, he opened the obstructed valves directly with his finger or an instrument to increase blood flow. Although this technique seemed to work well for mitral stenosis, his results were not as good as Dr. Blalock's for tetralogy.

One of the other procedures that I wanted to learn at the Brompton was endoscopy—both bronchial and esophageal. In these procedures, a long tube known as an endoscope is inserted through the mouth and advanced into the trachea or esophagus. For bronchoscopies, the tube is advanced into the lung. At Johns Hopkins the otolaryngologists performed these procedures exclusively, so surgeons weren't given an opportunity to learn them. Nevertheless, being able to perform endoscopies seemed essential to me for planning operations on the lung or esophagus.

On my very first day in the surgical suite at the Brompton, there were three "bronchs" to be done. That morning, Brock asked me, "Cooley, you know how to do a bronchoscopy, don't you?" I untruthfully replied, "Yes, sir." So I nervously entered the endoscopy room, where there was an orderly named Colles, who had been working at the Brompton for more than fifteen years. Although only an orderly, he knew how to do a bronchoscopy. When the first patient was brought in, I picked up the rigid bronchoscope and said, "Mr. Colles, I'm going to be honest with you. I've never done one of these procedures. I know what I'm supposed to do, but maybe you will help me." He said, "Mr. Cooley, all you've got to do is hold that bronchoscope real steady, and I'll thread the patient up on it for you." On the basis of that initial experience, I soon became proficient at the procedure.

Compared to Brock, Mr. Oswald ("Os") Tubbs, who shared the surgical "firm" with Brock, had a more relaxed attitude. About two months after my arrival, he was diagnosed with tuberculosis in the right lung. At that time, an antibiotic that would cure "tubercle" (as the English called it) was not yet widely available for human use, so TB was still rampant in England.[2] One of the few available options was to remove part of Os's affected lung. Brock was to perform this procedure, and Os requested that I be Brock's first assistant. Two hours before the operation, Os called me to his bedside to explain how he wanted the surgery to be done. He asked me to persuade Brock to perform a phrenic nerve crush on the side of the affected lung. This would temporarily keep that side of the diaphragm from moving, thereby resting the lung and helping the bronchus heal more quickly. The nerve would recover in a few months. Brock had said he didn't think the procedure was necessary. Rather than bother him about it, I simply went ahead and crushed Os's right phrenic nerve before I closed the incision, as he had requested.[3]

Os asked me to take over his National Health Service (NHS) practice, which had a waiting list of two hundred patients, while he was convalescing. I was happy to do it because I wanted to increase my surgical experience while I was in London. I could consult with Os, if necessary, for problem cases. Faced with that overwhelming waiting list, I decided to double the daily number of surgical cases, knowing that I could do twice as many as were currently being done. By convincing the operating room personnel to work overtime, I was able to achieve this goal, greatly reducing the number of patients awaiting

[2] An interesting finding from my work with tuberculosis at the Brompton was later described in one of my first medical papers, "The Clinical Significance of Cavernolithiasis," which can be found in *The Journal of Thoracic Surgery*, vol. 25 (1953), pp. 246–255.

[3] In 1978 I saw Os at a meeting of the Denton A. Cooley Cardiovascular Surgical Society, which was being held in London. He had retired by then but was still doing well.

surgery. I also had the patients get out of bed quickly after their operations, so they recovered faster.

At the Brompton, I gained not only extensive surgical experience
but also firsthand exposure to Britain's NHS. The service had been in
effect for only about two years, and some practical details were still
being worked out. Under this system, everyone who could get to England was eligible for health care. People would come over from the
continent to have routine procedures done. They would cross the English Channel merely to pick up a free walking cane, a wig, or whatever else they needed. Because so many people claimed these routine
services, there weren't enough resources to provide major services to
everyone who needed them. For instance, Brock would not do a thoracotomy on NHS patients older than sixty-five. I asked, "Why do you
draw the line there, Mr. Brock? That elderly man I examined on the
ward this morning has cancer, and you might be able to cure him."
Brock responded "Well, we're spending society's money, so we want
to use it to do the most good. To operate on a man of that age merely
to extend his life for a few months would not be useful to society."
Although I understood his point, I didn't agree. I felt that the man
should have been given a chance to be cured.

During my year in London, I was able to work and socialize with
many pioneers of cardiac surgery, and my friendships with those eminent surgeons have lasted throughout my career. One such person was
Clement Price Thomas, a staff member at the Brompton. In one of his
famous cases, he removed King George VI's cancerous left lung in an
operation performed in Buckingham Palace. In 1951 Thomas became
Sir Clement Price Thomas.

Another eminent friend was Norman ("Pasty") Barrett, a thoracic
surgeon for whom Barrett's esophagus was named. In this disorder,
the lining of the lower esophagus is damaged by the frequent regur-
gitation of gastric acid. Barrett had a keen, self-deprecating sense of
humor. One day, I walked into the operating room when he was doing
a mitral valvotomy. Barrett probably had no business doing that procedure because he wasn't that good a technical surgeon. I immediately noticed more free blood than would be expected. I asked, "What
are you doing Mr. Barrett?" He replied, "Cooley, what I'm doing here
should be awfully simple, but I seem to be making it simply awful." He
had torn part of the left atrium, causing the patient's chest to fill with

blood, and had placed his index finger in the heart to stem the flow. He asked if I could assist him, so I put on some gloves and placed a clamp on the torn atrium, allowing us to complete the repair and save the patient.

One day, I was invited to give a lecture on tetralogy of Fallot before a cardiac surgical society at the National Heart Hospital. I was nervous about this talk, because a number of prominent surgeons were to be present. Afterward, when I asked Os Tubbs how the audience had received my lecture, he commented, "They weren't so much interested in *what* you said as in *how* you said it." They had never heard the King's English twisted into a Texas drawl before.

The year I spent at the Brompton was an invaluable and unforgettable experience. I consider Lord Brock[4] to be one of the people who had the greatest influence on my surgical career.[5] Brock impressed me by his perseverance and dedication to advancing surgical techniques. Of course, the other major influence on me at this time was Dr. Blalock.

Before our year in London was over, Louise and I took a couple of driving trips. One that I especially remember was to Edinburgh. I had always wanted to play golf at the Royal and Ancient Golf Club at St. Andrews, which was located there. We arranged the trip for Easter, a time of year that would have offered great golf weather back in Houston. But when I arrived at St. Andrews, the temperature was about forty-five degrees, and there was a stiff wind coming off the North Sea. Luckily, I met up with a couple of other golfers who invited me to fill a threesome. They were both wearing kilts. As we were going along, I noticed that, at every tee, they were pulling bottles out of their golf bags. After a couple of tees, they asked me, "Mr. Cooley, would you care for a wee nip?" *"Would I?"* So we nipped around the course together. They were memorable guys and avid golfers.

---

[4] Brock became Sir Russell (Lord) Brock after receiving his knighthood in 1954 and was later admitted to the peerage, becoming Baron Brock of Wimbledon.

[5] At that time, one of my ambitions was to become a fellow of the Royal College of Surgeons of England. To reach that goal would have required me to study, attend classes, and sit for exams. Mr. Brock advised me not to pursue this arduous route but, rather, to concentrate on receiving an honorary fellowship. In 1988 I was named a fellow of the Royal College of Surgeons of England. I have also been named an honorary fellow of four other royal colleges of surgeons.

Right before my year with Brock was over, Louise and I took our mothers on a driving tour of the continent. We visited Paris, Munich, and other cities, then headed over the Brenner Pass into Italy. We went all the way to Naples and the island of Capri. I did the driving and juggled the fourteen pieces of luggage. Strapped to the roof of our little car, they made it so top-heavy, we were surprised it didn't turn over.

After that trip, Louise, Mary, and I returned to Houston, where Dr. Michael DeBakey had a job waiting for me at Baylor University College of Medicine.

Dr. Michael E. DeBakey, chairman of the Department of Surgery at Baylor University College of Medicine. Courtesy of Dr. O. H. Frazier's personal collection and Baylor University College of Medicine.

CHAPTER 9

Pioneering Cardiovascular Surgery

LOUISE, MARY, AND I returned to the United States in the early summer of 1951. Louise was two months pregnant with our second daughter, Susan, who would be born at the beginning of 1952. After a visit in Baltimore with my mentor, Dr. Blalock, I began the long drive to Houston with Louise and little Mary. The trip was uneventful until we reached Louisiana. A few miles outside of Opelousas, on a two-lane highway and in a torrential rainstorm, we encountered a stalled truck in our lane and an oncoming vehicle in the left lane. Our car skidded and struck the truck's bed, smashing the right side of our windshield and its supporting post. Louise instinctively threw herself across Mary, who was in a baby seat between us, to protect her from the impact and the flying glass. Unfortunately, Louise's back wasn't spared from the glass shards. I wrapped my fingers in a clean handkerchief and removed the larger pieces. Then I had her press back tightly against the car seat to slow the bleeding. I covered the broken part of the windshield with my raincoat and spread a blanket across my wife and baby. We drove to a local roadhouse, where we dried our clothes and bandaged Louise's wounds. A traveler there named Dudley LeBlanc was most kind and helpful, offering to take us to a hospital.[1] Although Louise was in pain, her injuries were bearable. Mary and I were unscathed, but it had been a close call. I admired Louise for her instinctive reaction to protect Mary. We drove on to Houston and arrived safely at my mother's home, where we spent a

---

[1] We later found out that LeBlanc was a Louisiana state senator and the well-known promoter of a controversial patent medicine known as Hadacol, which was popular in the early 1950s. Marketed as a dietary supplement, Hadacol had almost an ounce of ethyl alcohol in each bottle.

couple of weeks. I didn't have much time to reflect on the accident, because my new responsibilities in Houston soon occupied all of my attention.

On Monday, June 11, 1951, I assumed my position at Baylor as an instructor of surgery for a salary of $4,500 a year. Louise and I rented an apartment on South Boulevard, not far from Rice University and the Texas Medical Center. Chartered in 1945 the Texas Medical Center is now the largest healthcare complex in the world, with nearly fifty buildings. It covers an area larger than downtown Dallas and is soon expected to surpass the area of downtown Houston. But when I arrived in the summer of 1951, the Medical Center had only two completed buildings: Hermann Hospital and Baylor University College of Medicine. Methodist Hospital opened later that year. St. Luke's Episcopal Hospital and Texas Children's Hospital were under construction and would not open until 1954. Baylor's associated hospitals were Jefferson Davis (the city-county hospital), located a few miles away on Allen Parkway; the Veterans Administration Hospital, near the Medical Center; and Hermann Hospital.

My earliest mentor, Dr. Bertner, served as the first president of the Texas Medical Center. Unfortunately, he died the year before I returned to Houston. I credit him with founding the Medical Center because he was the major medical advisor to the M. D. Anderson Foundation trustees. Monroe Dunaway Anderson was a wealthy Houston businessman who established a charitable foundation, partly to avoid a large estate tax that could have crippled his company should he die. The M. D. Anderson Foundation's charter did not specify how its money should be used. The foundation trustees decided that Anderson's money should be used to establish a major Houston medical center that would have many different hospitals, academic institutions, and support services. Thus, the Texas Medical Center was born. Through Dr. Bertner's persuasiveness, the foundation matched a gift from the Texas Legislature for building a cancer hospital in Houston. That hospital became the University of Texas M. D. Anderson Cancer Center, as it is known today.

My arrival at Baylor University College of Medicine launched my professional relationship with Dr. Michael DeBakey, who was chairman of the Department of Surgery there. Mike was in his early forties at the time. He was a native of Lake Charles, Louisiana, where his father, a Lebanese immigrant, owned and operated a drugstore. Mike graduated from Tulane University Medical School. He was a protégé of the famed surgeon Alton Ochsner, another of my own role models. After completing his residency at Tulane, Mike continued his training in Europe, first at the University of Strasbourg and then at the University of Heidelberg. As I mentioned earlier, Mike had possibly influenced my military assignment to Europe when he was serving on the staff of Surgeon General Kirk. After leaving the army, Mike returned to Tulane, where he worked for two years until he was invited to chair Baylor's Department of Surgery. Baylor recruited Mike not only because of his talent as an investigative surgeon but also because of his connections with federal agencies that were granting large sums of money for medical research. He did not fail Baylor in either capacity.

Mike DeBakey was an extremely hard worker and a powerful organizer, promoter, and achiever. He slept little and basically spent his life in the hospital or at the medical school. I soon learned that he was much feared by his junior staff of residents. Mike's temper tantrums in the operating room were far in excess of anything I'd ever witnessed with Dr. Blalock. When a surgical assistant did not meet Mike's standards, he would denounce that assistant loudly and would send him from the operating room like a schoolboy to the principal's office. Mike was unforgiving. It was not unusual for residents dismissed in that manner never to return to any of his operating rooms—essentially, their careers at Baylor were over.

When I started at Baylor, Mike assigned me to lecture medical students and to work with interns and residents at Jefferson Davis, the city-county hospital. I did most of my surgery at Jeff Davis and at Hermann Hospital. Like other southern cities at that time, Houston was still segregated, and there were limited beds for black patients. For this reason, separate hospitals, including St. Elizabeth's and Riverside, were designated specifically for black patients, and I also saw patients there.

To augment my salary, I was permitted to retain surgical fees from paying patients at the private hospitals. Then, as my practice grew, I developed a plan with Mike that we felt would be advantageous both to Baylor and to us. All of our collections went into a fee pool. Once our salaries and overhead were covered, we could retain a percentage of the remainder. The rest went to support the Department of Surgery and the school, which had only a meager income. This plan was a stimulus for increased surgical productivity and was an important source of revenue for Baylor. Other medical schools soon copied this approach.

My first day on the job, I accompanied Mike and the house staff at Jeff Davis Hospital on their morning rounds. One of our patients was a forty-six-year-old man who had a large aneurysm of the innominate artery and aortic arch. The aneurysm threatened to rupture through the overlying skin. As we gathered around the patient's bed, Mike reviewed the chart and said, "We have a new staff man here today. Maybe he has an idea. Dr. Cooley, what do you consider ought to be done?" When I responded that I thought the aneurysm should be surgically removed, Mike frowned and asked what I meant. I replied that I had some experience with clamping sacciform, or sac-like, aneurysms and repairing the aorta. I would put a clamp across the neck of the aneurysm, remove it, and sew the aorta back together. I was certain that this was the patient's only chance for survival. Mike asked me to explain what I meant by "experience." I told him that I had twice done the procedure successfully during my residency at Hopkins. Surprised, he said, "Well, why don't you give it a try tomorrow?"

To reach the aneurysm, I would have to make an incision in the patient's chest and cut through the sternum. This approach, known as a sternotomy, was not standard back then, and Jeff Davis lacked the proper instruments for performing it. So the evening before the surgery, I drove to the Veterans Administration Hospital to borrow a special mallet and chisel. The next morning, I used these tools to open the patient's breastbone. I then excised the aneurysm by clamping its neck and tying off the innominate artery and its branches.[2]

About 9:30 that morning, Mike DeBakey arrived in the operating room, assuming that he would be seeing a surgical disaster in progress. He was scrubbed to operate, expecting to have to bail me out.

"How are things going, Denton?"

"Well, the aneurysm is over there in the bucket if you want to look at it. I am now repairing the aorta."

That procedure, known as an aneurysmectomy, ushered in a new era involving the repair of aortic aneurysms. In its own way, it was as important a milestone as the blue baby operation had been in 1944.

[2] You can read the details of this operation in the *Annals of Surgery*, vol. 135 (1952), pp.. 660–680.

It was possibly the first aneurysm repair of its kind to be performed anywhere in the world. Mike was so impressed by the result that he became convinced that we could treat other aneurysms in an aggressive manner. At first, I worked with him while he learned to do the procedure. Within a few weeks, we'd performed four more aneurysmectomies. Later in 1952, Mike presented those four cases and my first two Hopkins cases at a meeting of the Southern Surgical Association. His presentation was met with great acclaim. Because five of our six patients had syphilitic aneurysms, however, the renowned Dr. Evarts Graham of Barnes Hospital commented that, although our technique was remarkable, it probably wouldn't be used very often because the advent of penicillin would soon make aortic syphilitic aneurysms rare. That turned out to be true but failed to account for the increasing numbers of atherosclerotic and traumatic aneurysms, which would be equally amenable to the removal technique.

To repair larger, spindle-shaped, fusiform aneurysms, surgeons required some type of graft for bridging the gap where the aneurysm was to be cut out, thereby restoring normal blood flow. The first type of graft that surgeons used for this purpose was called a homograft because it came from human cadavers. Young accident victims were the ideal source because their aortic tissue was unlikely to be diseased. When kept in a special preserving solution that also contained penicillin, the refrigerated grafts were usable for up to two weeks. In the early 1950s a few surgeons, including Jacques Oudot and Charles DuBost of France, had used homografts to repair abdominal aortic aneurysms. In 1952 Mike and I became the first surgeons to use a homograft in repairing a large aneurysm of the thoracoabdominal aorta—the long, straight part of the aorta that stretches from the abdomen to the aortic arch. To remove the aneurysm, we had to clamp the patient's aorta on both sides so that blood could no longer flow through it. However, the clamp time (the time during which aortic flow was disrupted) had to be short so that the blood supply to the spinal cord wouldn't be interrupted for too long. Otherwise the patient might have become paralyzed. Fortunately, though, he did well and went back to work as a county sheriff a month after the operation.[3]

---

[3] You can read more about this procedure in *The Journal of the American Medical Association*, vol. 152 (1953), pp. 673–676. The aorta was occluded for forty-five minutes, but there were no residual ischemic changes in the spinal cord, kidneys, or other organs.

Within a year, a method for freeze-drying homografts was developed. When the freeze-dried grafts were soaked in saline, they became soft and pliable again. Because fresh homografts were scarce, Mike and I began using mostly freeze-dried ones. By early 1954 we had reported a series of forty-seven cases in which we repaired aortic aneurysms or other types of aortic disease with homografts, including twenty-six cases of abdominal aneurysms.[4] One of the patients happened to be the first man I operated on at Jeff Davis. He had developed another aneurysm in the abdominal portion of his aorta. At the Southern Surgical Association meeting that year, Mike reported our experience. In the discussion portion of the meeting, he responded to the congratulatory comments by saying, " . . . my own colleague, Dr. Cooley, deserves more credit than I do in this work." I was pleased by that recognition.

About the same time, I had an even greater challenge in trying to repair a ruptured abdominal aneurysm—the first time this had ever been attempted.[5] Although the patient survived the operation, he died of kidney failure five days later. I soon repaired four more ruptured aneurysms. These operations were all done under emergency conditions. I had only a small window of time to make the repairs, so my ability to operate rapidly was an important advantage. The last two patients survived and had no complications.

Mike and I soon learned that neither fresh nor freeze-dried homografts were very durable for our aneurysm cases. A strong synthetic graft was needed. Like other surgical investigators, we began experimenting by making tube grafts with a variety of fabrics—nylon, Vinyon-N, Teflon, Orlon, Ivalon, and polyester. But with all of these different fabrics, durability remained a serious problem. Some of the fibers, including nylon, deteriorated rapidly in the body, and Teflon failed to form a strong bond with surrounding tissues. One day, Mike went to buy some more nylon from a local department store. When

[4] These cases and an overview of treatment at that time are described in an article in the *Annals of Surgery,* vol. 139 (1954), pp. 763–777.

[5] This case is included in a report of the first five repairs of ruptured abdominal aortic aneurysms, which was published in *Postgraduate Medicine,* vol. 16 (1954), pp. 334–342.

[6] Ironically, when Mike was ninety-seven years old, his life would be saved by an improved version of this type of graft. The graft was implanted to repair a dissecting aneurysm of the aorta.

he got there, the store was out of nylon, but it had just received a shipment of a new polyester fabric called Dacron. Mike, who had learned to sew from his mother, occasionally used his wife's sewing machine to fabricate prototype grafts. He decided to fashion some grafts from the new Dacron fabric. About this time, he operated on a man who owned a textile company in Pennsylvania. Mike asked him if he would start producing a graft that could be used for vascular procedures. The man agreed.[6]

The fabric grafts were either woven or knitted. In a woven graft, the threads are interlaced in an over-and-under pattern. In contrast, knitted fabrics are made with looped threads that form a continuous, interconnecting chain. The early woven grafts were too stiff to be used for anything but large vessels, but these grafts would not leak blood. The knitted grafts could be used for vessels of any size but were so porous that serious intraoperative bleeding often occurred. Different substances were tried for coating the fibers to make the knitted grafts more impervious to bleeding. One of our Baylor researchers, Dr. Oscar Creech, developed a crimped, semiporous Dacron graft that could be easily tailored. The graft required only preclotting with the patient's blood to seal the surface before being used in the surgical procedure. The fabric provided a lattice on which human tissue could grow, thus incorporating the graft into the aorta. Mike and I continued to work on developing grafts of knitted or woven Dacron to suit our special needs. DeBakey grafts and Cooley grafts are still being used today.

By the summer of 1955, Mike and I had performed 245 aneurysm procedures, and our work was attracting much attention from the international medical community. Some of these procedures involved our first use of synthetic materials for grafts. That same summer, with our wives Diana and Louise, we toured northern Europe to demonstrate our techniques in Oslo, Stockholm, and Copenhagen for the surgeons there. After returning home, I received a letter from Russell Brock saying how impressed he was that I was "making a name" for myself in this field. Because of Mike's tireless promotion of our results with aortic aneurysms, these early operations established Baylor as a leading center for vascular surgery. By late 1960 we had repaired 3,324 aortic and major arterial aneurysms.[7]

[7] These cases are summarized in *Postgraduate Medicine*, vol. 29 (1961), pp. 151–162.

During this period, I also did numerous procedures on peripheral arteries in the legs.[8] I first tackled an artery leading to the brain in March 1956, when I performed the first successful endarterectomy for carotid stenosis.[9] In an endarterectomy procedure, a small incision is made in the diseased artery, and the blockage causing the stenosis is removed. This particular procedure was done at the Methodist Hospital in Houston. The patient was an otherwise healthy seventy-one-year-old man from a small town in East Texas. He had gone to his family doctor because of dizziness and a swishing noise in his left ear.

I had some misgivings about operating, because the patient's symptoms were relatively mild and neurologic damage might result from the temporary lack of oxygen to the brain caused by clamping of the carotid artery. I knew that during the operation, there had to be some plan for protecting the brain. I'd already done some research on paraplegia after thoracic aortic aneurysm resection. And in dog experiments, my colleagues and I had tried cooling or draining the spinal fluid to induce hypothermia of the spinal cord.[10] I even had some experience with spinal fluid and cord cooling in human patients. In this case, I decided that we would attempt to cool the patient's brain by putting his head in a bucket of cracked ice for about thirty minutes. I also devised a bypass shunt using a small plastic tube with large-bore needles at each end to divert blood flow around the blockage during the procedure. I clamped the artery and made an incision over the blockage. I then peeled out the calcified plaque and sutured the incision closed. Although the circulation to the brain was interrupted for only eight minutes, the patient's right leg and arm were weak after the operation, and he had trouble speaking. To my relief, these symptoms disappeared within twelve hours. He was especially grateful that the operation had ended the swishing noise, which was a result of the blockage in the artery.

Within two years Mike and I had improved the procedure enough to have operated on seventy-five patients.[11] Throughout his career,

[8] The first ninety such cases are documented in the *Texas State Journal of Medicine*, vol. 51 (1955), pp. 700–703.

[9] I reported this case in the *Journal of Neurosurgery*, vol. 13 (1956), pp. 500–506.

[10] The results of this early experimental work can be found in *Surgical Forum*, vol. 11 (1960), pp. 153–154.

[11] These seventy-five cases are described in the *Annals of Surgery*, vol. 149 (1959), pp. 690–710.

Mike would always claim to have done the first successful carotid endarterectomy. I actually helped him with the case he claimed as the first, which occurred a few months earlier than the one I've just described. However, he merely opened the carotid artery and closed it again because the blockage was chronic and too adherent to remove.

Mike was mainly interested in aneurysm and vascular surgery and had little experience with congenital anomalies or valve procedures. While remaining active in aneurysm surgery, I also continued to perform the Blalock-Taussig and other congenital procedures and to expand my experience with valve operations. I did aortic coarctation repairs, patent ductus closures, and valvotomies. During my first year in Houston, I performed twenty-one mitral valvotomies and had only one death. In the series was a twenty-eight-year-old woman in her fourth month of pregnancy. This was one of the first mitral valve operations ever successfully performed in a pregnant woman. She delivered a healthy baby five months later. Not long afterward, I did a similar operation in a twenty-three-year-old woman in her last month of pregnancy, and her baby was born a few days later. Because of these successes, I soon began doing the same procedure on the aortic valve. In 1954 I reported a series of 115 mitral and aortic valvotomies at the American Medical Association meeting in St. Louis.[12] That was quite a large number for back then.

By today's standards, heart surgery at that time was rather primitive, and the outcomes were unpredictable. The operations were all "closed" procedures, performed without opening up the heart to see inside, so only a few conditions could be treated. To repair valve stenosis, we inserted a finger, or a tiny knife attached to our finger, into the valve to open the leaflets. Later on, we used an expanding dilator that I designed—a blunt instrument that separated the scarred and fused leaflets. We had to feel for the defect and correct it while the heart continued to beat. We could also "blindly" repair an atrial septal defect, or hole in the wall separating the upper chambers of the heart.[13] We had to make a finger-sized incision in the heart and introduce an index finger to search for the defect. We then manipulated the tissues so that

[12] A report of these 115 cases can be found in *The Journal of the American Medical Association*, vol. 155 (1954), pp. 234–239.

[13] My early surgical operations to repair atrial septal defects are described in *Surgery, Gynecology and Obstetrics*, vol. 100 (1955), pp. 268–276.

we could sew the sides of the defect together and close it as completely as possible. We also had the option of using hypothermia, a technique that had been introduced in 1952 by Dr. C. Walton (Walt) Lillehei and Dr. F. John Lewis in Minneapolis to close a septal defect under direct vision. The idea was to reduce the body's metabolism enough that blood flow could be clamped off for about five minutes without harming the brain. Because of the time limitations, these operations had to be extremely hurried, and we couldn't open much of the heart to see what we were doing. So most of the procedures were "incomplete." We simply couldn't do as thorough a repair as we would have liked. Thinking back to those days, it's hard to imagine that we could do any of these procedures, but our success rate was mostly good. Over the years, I have been gratified to receive letters and visits from patients who were saved by these early operations.

A major breakthrough that would help make open heart operations possible was cardiac catheterization and angiography, which came into use in the 1950s to confirm preoperative physical findings. In these techniques, a flexible tube, or catheter, is inserted into an artery or a vein in the patient's arm or leg and is advanced into the heart or the diseased artery to examine its structures. Before catheterization and angiography became available, we had to rely mainly on the patient's symptoms and our physical examination to make a diagnosis. The only other diagnostic tools we had were the electrocardiogram and standard X-rays. None of these methods could clarify the extent—or sometimes even the location—of the defect. In contrast, cardiac catheterization and angiography provided detailed structural information about the inside of the heart and the arteries, thereby revolutionizing the diagnosis of heart disease. What we needed now, however, was a revolution in *treatment*. This would require a way to keep blood flowing through the body, so that the heart could be stopped and opened. Not until a usable "heart-lung" machine came along would open heart surgery be possible.

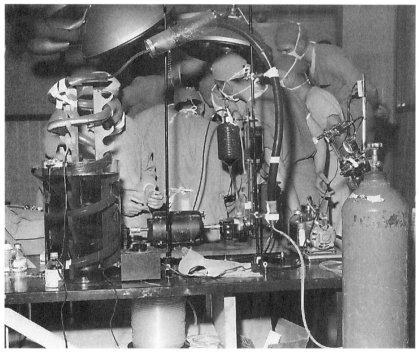

The DeWall-Lillehei heart-lung machine that we built and used in the first open heart operation in Houston.

CHAPTER 10

Opening Up the Heart

A FEW SURGEONS HAD ALREADY BEEN WORKING to create a mechanical heart-lung machine. By 1953 Dr. John Gibbon, at Jefferson Medical College in Philadelphia, had devoted about twenty years to developing and testing such a machine but had used it only in animals. In 1946 he'd met with Thomas J. Watson, then chairman of the board of the International Business Machines (IBM) Corporation, to seek engineering help in designing a device that would be efficient enough to be used in human patients. Over the next seven years, they came up with a workable device at IBM's expense. With this device, oxygen-poor blood from the veins was drained through a catheter into a reservoir and pumped over a series of vertical metallic screens (the oxygenator), where it was exposed to oxygen. The blood was then pumped back into the arterial circulation. In other words, blood was rerouted through the machine in order to be oxygenated, bypassing the heart and lungs. Without blood flowing through the heart, that organ could be opened, and repairs could be performed under direct vision. This heart-lung machine, or cardiopulmonary bypass pump, was cumbersome to use and damaged blood elements. But it promised to give surgeons more time—up to an hour—in which to make repairs inside the open heart.

In 1953 Gibbon and his team first used the pump successfully to repair an atrial septal defect in an eighteen-year-old girl. They also tried the technique in five other patients, all of whom died. Two of these cases were never reported. Because of these deaths, Gibbon abandoned the device, but he never discouraged others from further developing it. Meanwhile, in 1952, John Lewis had successfully done the first open heart operation by cooling the patient and clamping off blood flow to the heart, but this method succeeded only for simple defects. A better heart-lung machine was still needed, but most surgeons were pessimistic about its development.

In February 1955 I attended a meeting of the Society of University Surgeons in Houston, where Walt Lillehei, of the University of Minnesota, presented his results with cross-circulation. Lillehei, who was a friend of mine, had introduced this technique for heart-lung bypass during open heart surgery. At the Houston meeting, he showed a movie of an intracardiac operation on a child, which made a great impression on me. In this technique, one of the parents was anesthetized and connected to the patient via long, plastic tubes, thereby serving as a living oxygenator. Blood flow was routed from the child to the parent, where it was oxygenated by the parent's lungs, then pumped back into the child. The circuit was similar to that of the umbilical cord and placenta during pregnancy, when the placenta provides oxygenated blood to the fetus. Although Lillehei's technique worked, he was criticized for potentially subjecting a healthy person, the parent, to risk. Some critics said half jokingly that this was the only heart operation that could possibly have a 200 percent mortality. From March 1954 to July 1955, Lillehei performed forty-five cross-circulation procedures. Twenty-eight patients survived the operation, and only one parent had a complication, which resolved without any permanent damage. The success of both Gibbon's device and Lillehei's cross-circulation technique proved that temporary heart-lung bypass could make open heart surgery feasible. I decided that I wanted to go to Minnesota to see Lillehei's procedures myself.

Also in 1955, Dr. John Kirklin, of the Mayo Clinic, in Rochester, Minnesota, reported eight cases in which he used an improved version of Gibbon's pump and oxygenator—four of the patients survived. His report attracted great interest at that year's meeting of the American Surgical Association. Mike and I were both there. In the presence of Jack Gibbon, I told Mike that we should do as Kirklin had done and make a modified copy of Gibbon's machine. Buying a Mayo-Gibbon machine would have been expensive, and I thought we could make one more cheaply. I believed that we should be part of this pioneering work. However, Mike had other ideas. He stated that he and two other Baylor faculty members, Dr. Stanley Olson and Dr. Hebbel Hoff, were planning to build a pump of their own. If they needed my assistance or advice, Mike said, they would call on me. I was obviously being excluded. That gave me even more incentive to develop my own pump.

So, in June 1955, I visited the only two hospitals in the world that were performing open heart surgery—the University of Minnesota Medical Center, where Lillehei worked, and the Mayo Clinic, where Kirklin operated. The two institutions were only ninety miles apart. I wanted to learn as much as possible about their procedures and techniques and to develop my own system. I invited my Baylor colleague Dr. Dan McNamara to travel with me. He was the first pediatric cardiologist in Houston and a trainee of Helen Taussig.

At the University of Minnesota, Dan and I visited with Walt Lillehei. He took us to a recovery area and showed us a few children he had operated on for a variety of cardiac anomalies. Some of them were recuperating in oxygen tents, and they didn't seem to be doing that well. A few had obvious heart failure, and others had complete heart block, a rhythm disturbance that causes a slow heartbeat. Dan was rather critical of their condition, but their long-term results turned out to be amazingly good.[1] Walt invited us to return the next morning to observe his cross-circulation technique in a child.

Being very hospitable, Walt then said, "Let's go out and have a steak dinner." He took us to a little roadhouse on the edge of town. The bartender recognized him immediately. "Howdy, Doc. Gonna have the usual tonight?"

"Yeah, I'll take a double, and bring my friends each a double, too." The bartender brought us each a double martini. Barely ten minutes later, Walt said, "Hey, Sam, let's have another round." Another double martini appeared before each of us. When it came time for the third round, I said, "I think I'll pass this time." It wasn't too long before Walt called for a fourth round. Over the entire evening, Dan and I had two or three martinis, while Walt had perhaps five or six. We enjoyed a steak dinner and around 11:00 found ourselves, like Walt, dancing with the waitresses and having a good old time. We got back to the hotel around 1:00 in the morning. Because hotel rooms were scarce, Dan and I were sharing a room that had only one double bed. The next

---

[1] According to the thirty-year follow-up report, twenty-eight of forty-five children survived the operation and were discharged. Of those, only six died in the next thirty years. All of the others were doing well. *The Annals of Thoracic Surgery*, vol. 41 (1986), pp. 4–21.

morning, I woke up about 8:30 or 9:00, feeling awful and wondering why there was a man in my bed. I soon gathered my wits and realized that we were scheduled to watch Walt perform surgery within the hour. I said, "Dan, come on, we have to get over to the hospital, or we'll miss the operation."

We jumped out of bed and rushed to the hospital without even shaving. We arrived in the operating room about 9:30. Walt Lillehei and his small team, mostly residents, were planning to correct a ventricular septal defect. The patient, a child, was on one table, and the father was on an adjacent table, already hooked up for cross-circulation. But Walt was nowhere in sight. At about 10:00, he finally arrived—looking clammy, sweaty, and in need of medical attention himself. Although I was concerned about both the patient and the father, Walt and his team performed the operation superbly and successfully.

That afternoon, Dan and I drove the short distance to Rochester to visit with Dr. John Kirklin. He greeted us in his usual reserved but friendly way and introduced us to each member of his impressive team of about fifty skilled people. All of them were devoted to maintaining the complex Mayo-Gibbon heart-lung machine. The team included physiologists, biochemists, pathologists, cardiologists, engineers, and other specialists. He showed us the device and explained how it worked. Afterward, he invited us to his home to spend the night with him and his family. We got there about 6:30. Before dinner we were served a thimbleful of sherry—in sharp contrast to the libations of the previous evening. An hour later we sat down to dinner with Dr. Kirklin and his wife, and everything was most genteel. He explained that in the morning we would observe him using the machine to repair a ventricular septal defect. At about 8:45 he said, "Well, everybody to bed! We have to operate tomorrow morning." Sure enough, the next morning he started the operation on schedule at 9:00 sharp and performed it with the utmost precision and care. The patient did well. Through our entire visit, Kirklin's demeanor sharply contrasted with Lillehei's.

While in Minneapolis, Dan and I had also visited Dr. Richard DeWall, an associate of Walt Lillehei's, who had been working on a different concept for a heart-lung machine. His device was much simpler and more practical than earlier ones. It was sterilizable with heat, fairly easy to assemble, and had no moving parts—a complete contrast to the Mayo-Gibbon machine. In the DeWall-Lillehei device, the blood was channeled through Tygon tubing, where it was exposed to bubbles of oxygen. The blood was then defoamed in a helix-shaped coil before being returned to the patient. Lillehei had used the device for the first time a month before we got there, but the patient died the next day.

Being most impressed with Dr. Kirklin but not with Dr. Lillehei, Dan McNamara said to me during our return to Houston, "Denton, you are not going to operate on any of my patients until you can duplicate what Dr. Kirklin and his team can do." I was greatly disappointed because I would never be able to afford the expensive, complicated Mayo-Gibbon device without institutional funding. Mike DeBakey had made it clear that he would not support any of my efforts to develop a heart-lung machine. If I was going to perform open heart surgery, I knew that it would have to be with the less expensive DeWall-Lillehei device.

I kept up with Walt and eagerly followed his progress with the new heart-lung machine.[2] By August he had used it in seven patients and had stopped using cross-circulation altogether. I was impressed by his results and knew that I could make a system like this work for me. I enlisted the help of two medical students, Robert Bloodwell and Albert Shirkey, who helped me make a DeWall-Lillehei device.

We were still testing our system in dogs in the Baylor lab with rather poor results when I got a phone call from Dr. Sidney Schnur, a local cardiologist. He had just admitted a forty-nine-year-old man to St. Joseph Hospital. The patient had suffered a serious heart attack that caused a rupture of the septum between his ventricles. An open heart operation was his only chance for survival, and Schnur knew about our efforts to develop a heart-lung machine. He asked if it was ready for human use. Because our lab results had not been all that successful, I needed to know more about the patient before giving an answer. Dr. Schnur responded, "Without surgery, the patient will die within a day." "In that case," I replied, "we're ready."

---

[2] Years later, I would remark at a national surgical meeting, "Walt Lillehei brought the 'can opener' to the cardiac surgery picnic." The can opener was, of course, the DeWall-Lillehei bubble oxygenator. I've always admired Dr. Lillehei for his contributions to open heart surgery and his perseverance in the face of criticism regarding his early work.

On April 5, 1956, I operated on the patient with the aid of the DeWall-Lillehei device, which we assembled at Methodist Hospital. I was able to repair the extensive septal rupture by patching the hole with a polyvinyl Ivalon sponge. I managed to do the entire procedure in only twenty-five minutes of cardiopulmonary bypass time,[3] which was quite a feat in such a complicated case. This was the first time a heart-lung machine had been used anywhere south of Minnesota. It was also the first time anyone had ever attempted to repair a ruptured interventricular septum. After the operation, the patient steadily improved, but he developed a new heart murmur after four weeks. Unfortunately, he died two weeks later of heart failure.[4] Nevertheless, the operation itself was a success, ushering in the open heart era in Houston. During the six weeks before the patient died, I used our DeWall-Lillehei system for six more operations, all of which were less complicated. These patients survived. So many referrals began to pour in that my team and I soon had as many patients as we could handle. Within eight months we had used the heart-lung machine in ninety-four more patients.

Although the DeWall-Lillehei device worked effectively, the Tygon plastic tubing was scarce, expensive, and not reusable. For this reason, I decided to design my own version of the machine. Rather than seek federal or institutional support, I approached C. J. (Tibby) Thibodeaux, a Houston oil broker, who was a close friend and a former patient. I explained that I wanted to build a heart-lung machine and could use his help. He asked, "How much money would it take?" I replied, "Three or four thousand dollars should do it." He sent five thousand by messenger that afternoon, with a note assuring me that there was more if I needed it. That was a promise Tibby would keep. Until his death in 1962, he would be one of my most generous benefactors.

With Thibodeaux's money in hand and a couple of small grants from local chapters of the American Heart Association, I formed a

---

[3] Surgeons call this support period the "pump time."

[4] An autopsy showed that one of the sutures had torn out of the sponge, causing a small opening between the left and right ventricles. The left lung was also collapsed. The sponge was still attached to the septal defect and had begun to endothelialize. Details of this case can be found in a scientific article in *Surgery*, vol. 41 (1957), pp. 930–937.

research team to design a reusable oxygenator based on the DeWall-Lillehei device. The team included my colleagues Joe Latson and Bob Leachman. I talked with them about designing a more compact, metal device that could be sterilized easily. We decided to use stainless steel. Luckily, Latson was friends with Bruce and Irene Weaver, who owned the Commercial Kitchens in Houston. Their company had welders who could fabricate the oxygenator.

We finished our prototype in early 1957. Because it looked and acted like a percolator and was made with kitchen supplies, it was dubbed "Cooley's coffeepot." The oxygenator had three main components. There was a gas exchanger column through which oxygen was bubbled and carbon dioxide was eliminated. There was also a defoaming spiral, or helix. In addition, there was a reservoir, or pot, to hold the blood. To further improve the defoaming system, a stainless steel scrubbing pad was sprayed with silicone antifoam and placed at the top of the defoaming spiral in the upper chamber. A Sigmamotor pump moved the blood through the oxygenator and then back into the patient through a main artery.[5] Within four months of its completion, we'd used the "coffeepot" in thirty-nine cases. By that time, our total of 134 open heart cases was more than had been done anywhere else.[6]

One afternoon, I learned that Mike DeBakey had scheduled a ventricular septal defect closure using my "coffeepot" device and "pump" team. Stanley Crawford, a young surgeon on the Baylor staff, was to help him. I immediately went to Mike's house and confronted him. I told him that it wasn't right for him to use my machine without consulting me. He said, "It's not your machine. It belongs to the Baylor Department of Surgery." I disagreed, as my machine had been privately funded, and I'd created it without Mike. Now he was planning to use my system without asking. Mike finally relented, saying that I could do the scheduled procedure with Stanley. Apparently, Stanley had not wanted to participate in the operation anyway and declined to be further involved. So I ended up doing the procedure at Texas Children's Hospital. This episode, in which Mike claimed ownership of

[5] The Sigmamotor pump had metal "fingers" that progressively squeezed blood through the tubing.

[6] All 134 cases are described in an article in *Postgraduate Medicine*, vol. 22 (1957), pp. 479–484. The 95 cases done with the first device are described in the *Texas State Journal of Medicine*, vol. 53 (1957), pp. 397–400.

anything developed at Baylor, foreshadowed later, more far-reaching incidents. I think it also marked the beginning of what would become a longstanding rivalry between him and me.

The ability to do open heart surgery on a "production-line" basis greatly simplified the process. Because of our volume of patients, my team and I had several more of our oxygenators produced commercially.[7] In all of these cases, we kept the operations as simple as possible and the time patients were supported by the heart-lung machine brief. Back then, we even measured the pump time in seconds, not in minutes as we do today. Part of what made me so successful was that I could operate fast enough to keep my pump times extremely short compared to those of other surgeons. For example, in 1957 I typically repaired an atrial septal defect in about seven minutes of pump time.

At the beginning, our procedures were restricted mainly to small children and infants, some of whom were only a few weeks old. We soon learned that children older than two years had better survival rates, so whenever possible we postponed surgery until the child reached that age.[8] Because of the success of these procedures in children, we expanded our program and began operating on adults. By the beginning of 1959, we had performed six hundred successful operations using our pump oxygenator, with some additional modifications. Pump oxygenators were making open heart surgery almost routine, at least for me.

We used a version of our device for two hundred and fifty operations. However, as more patients were referred for treatment, it became apparent that we needed an even simpler oxygenator that didn't require cleaning or resterilization after each procedure. Luckily, we didn't have to wait long. Dr. Vincent Gott, one of Walt Lillehei's trainees, greatly simplified and improved the DeWall-Lillehei oxygenator by developing a disposable model that was basically a large plastic bag, dubbed the "pillowcase," with channels that carried the oxygenated blood from top to bottom in a zig-zag pattern. The zig-zag pattern was used to remove any air bubbles that weren't caught in the debubbling chamber

---

[7] The devices were produced by the Mark Company in Randolph, Massachusetts.

[8] Once the equipment for open heart surgery improved, younger children were able to undergo these procedures successfully. Today, a membrane oxygenator is used, which has improved results even further.

at the top.[9] Baxter Travenol, a medical equipment company in Illinois, manufactured the devices. We modified the disposable pillowcase by putting a stainless steel sponge in the defoamer to improve its function. We used it with a roller pump to circulate the blood, which was massaged through tubing by the roller.

With steady improvements in pumps and oxygenators, we were able to make dramatic breakthroughs in the treatment of all sorts of heart conditions. By January 1958 I had used cardiopulmonary bypass successfully to treat calcified aortic valves in seven patients. I wrote Lord Brock of these procedures. He was especially pleased to hear of our success, having pioneered the treatment of this condition in closed operations. By 1962 I had done an additional sixty aortic valve procedures, and my total number of open heart surgery cases reached 1,430. Nobody else had done nearly that many cases or had come close to my success rate.

For the earliest open heart operations using an elaborate system with a Gibbon console, blood infused with heparin was used to "prime" the system, as with any other pump. On the morning of surgery, blood had to be collected from ten or twelve donors of the same blood type. This greatly complicated the procedures. Often, even though we started to collect the blood before dawn, we didn't get enough matching units to start a procedure until the afternoon or evening. Although the red cells were cross-matched, the other blood components couldn't be tested. Once the individual units were mixed together, minor incompatibilities sometimes produced adverse reactions. This problem was originally described by Dr. Howard Gadboys and Dr. Robert Litwak, who believed that it could be solved by using a non-blood prime. They had used this method successfully in dogs.

In 1961 my associate Dr. Arthur Beall and I began to perform dog experiments with a prime consisting of 5 percent dextrose in distilled water, and we were impressed with the results. We began to use this solution instead of blood to prime the pump for open heart operations in our patients.[10] Before long, my team and I were doing eight or ten operations a day, whereas institutions that still used a blood

<hr>

[9] You can read more about how this device was made in *Diseases of the Chest*, vol. 32 (1957), pp. 615–625. My early use of it in 175 cases is described in *Medicine of Japan*, vol. 14 (1959), pp. 511–521.

[10] Our early work in patients is described in *Surgery*, vol. 52 (1962), pp. 713–719.

prime did only one or two operations a week. I think we convinced the surgical world that a non-blood prime was a practical solution to the demand that open heart surgery was putting on blood-banking facilities. By August 1962 we had operated on one hundred patients using this technique,[11] which not only greatly facilitated open heart surgery but also eliminated blood-borne illnesses. Our simplified methods were a major advance. Within a year we'd done 241 cases using a non-blood prime. I believe that my popularizing this technique silenced the remaining critics of open heart surgery and led to the rapid acceleration in its growth. For this reason, I think it is one of my most important contributions. Although others, including Dr. Nazih Zuhdi and Dr. Allen Greer, had used a similar technique in a few cases, no one else had pushed to make it an accepted method.

The use of a bloodless prime also allowed me to pioneer open heart surgery on patients of the Jehovah's Witness faith. Jehovah's Witnesses refuse to receive blood transfusions or any other blood products because of their interpretation of several verses in the Bible. Refusal of blood places them at high risk for any surgical procedure in which serious blood loss could be an issue. Unless the operation is done quickly and precisely, the patient could bleed to death. Shortly after beginning to use a non-blood priming solution, I did the world's first open heart operation on a Jehovah's Witness. That was in May 1962, and within a year I had done six more cases.[12] In no instance was blood given before, during, or after these operations. The fact that I could operate very quickly meant that less blood was lost, so my cases were more likely to be successful. For many years I was the only surgeon willing to operate on Jehovah's Witnesses.[13]

Between 1956 and 1963 I used cardiopulmonary bypass to perform many other groundbreaking operations, some of which were considered "firsts."[14] I developed operations to repair other types of congenital heart defects, such as total anomalous pulmonary venous drainage,

---

[11] The first report of this work can be found in *Surgery*, vol. 52 (1962), pp. 713–719.

[12] My first seven Jehovah's Witness cases are described in detail in *The American Journal of Cardiology*, vol. 13 (1964), pp. 779–781.

[13] My team and I would eventually operate on more than 1,500 Jehovah's Witnesses.

[14] See Appendix B for a list of my procedures considered to be "firsts" in the field of cardiovascular surgery.

a very complicated defect involving blood flow to the lungs.[15] The first two patients I operated on for anomalous venous drainage are still doing well. They found each other via the Internet and decided to come personally to thank me—fifty years after their operations. In 1958 I was the first to use cardiopulmonary bypass during excision of a large left ventricular aneurysm—a complication of a heart attack. By November 1959 I had repaired thirteen more such aneurysms. Before the advent of open heart surgery, patients with left ventricular aneurysms had little chance for survival.

Pulmonary embolism was also usually fatal at that time. In this condition, clots form in the lower extremities and travel upward to lodge in the lungs, blocking blood flow. A few surgeons had tried treating pulmonary embolism, but no one had figured out a way to disrupt flow to the lung for long enough to remove the blockage and keep patients from dying. Interestingly, Gibbon had initially conceived the idea for his heart-lung machine after one of his patients died of a massive pulmonary embolus. However, neither he nor anyone else had tried to use a heart-lung machine to remove an embolus. The emergency nature of the procedure simply precluded surgeons from obtaining enough units of blood to prime the pump.

On April 16, 1961, Arthur Beall called me about a thirty-seven-year-old woman who had collapsed at home and been taken to the emergency room at Jeff Davis Hospital. Twelve days earlier, she had undergone pelvic surgery for a ruptured tubal pregnancy, and later she was discharged from the hospital. Now she was being readmitted with acute, massive pulmonary emboli and was barely alive. I told Arthur, "The only hope is for us to use the heart-lung machine, which could give us enough time to remove the clots. But since Jeff Davis doesn't have a machine, we'll need to move our pump oxygenator over there from St. Luke's. Can you get all of the necessary equipment to the loading dock? I'll meet you with my station wagon." I backed my car up to the dock, but the long, narrow machine didn't quite fit in the car. Arthur had to climb in the back and hold on to it tightly to keep it from sliding off the tailgate. We made the two-mile drive to Jeff Davis

---

[15] You can read about my first repair of total anomalous pulmonary venous drainage in *Surgery*, vol. 42 (1957), pp. 1014–1021. This paper describes three cases, the first of which was done in 1956.

safely, unloaded the equipment, and got it to the operating room. The pump was primed with glucose solution. I removed many large clots from the patient's lungs, and she survived. The operation, which was the first of its kind, took only fifteen minutes of pump time. This widely acclaimed case[16] dramatically demonstrated that by priming the pump with a non-blood solution, surgeons could use heart-lung bypass to operate on patients with acute cardiovascular emergencies.

In the early 1960s, we also began to replace aortic and mitral valves when repair wasn't feasible. Various surgeons had been working in the late 1950s and early 1960s to develop an artificial heart valve. A number of improvised devices were tried, most with limited success. The first artificial valve to become commercially available was developed by Dr. Albert Starr and his engineering colleague, Lowell Edwards. It was called a "caged ball" valve because it was designed with a solid Silastic ball inside a molded Lucite cage. With each heartbeat, the ball was raised or lowered, mimicking the opening and closing of the native valve. I started implanting the Starr-Edwards valve in 1962 and within a year had a series of 111 cases.[17] The overall mortality rate in that series was 13 percent, which included deaths up to three months postoperatively. In the last eighty-nine patients, the mortality had dropped to 9 percent.

After using several valves developed by other surgeons, I decided to design one of my own. The new valve, called the Cooley-Cutter, was produced commercially by Cutter Laboratories and had a much lower profile than previous valves. It had a biconical disc, which was held inside the circular rim by simple struts instead of a tall cage. The disc was made with a new substance called pyrolyte carbon, which was durable and resisted blood clots. Introduced in 1971,[18] the Cooley-Cutter was eventually used in more than 3,300 patients, mostly at the Texas Heart Institute. I used this valve until better ones designed by other surgeons became available. Overall, I was pleased with the results and am gratified that some patients still have their Cooley-Cutter valves today.

---

[16] This case was reported in *The Journal of the American Medical Association*, vol. 177 (1961), pp. 283–286.

[17] The results of the 111 cases are described in an article in *The American Journal of Cardiology*, vol. 14 (1964), pp. 148–153.

[18] By early 1974 we had used the Cooley-Cutter valve in 438 patients.

• • •

These advances in heart surgery attracted the attention of Princess Lilian, wife of Leopold III, the king of Belgium. Their first child, Prince Alexander, had been born with coarctation of the aorta, which was corrected by Robert Gross, of Boston, in 1957. This experience caused Princess Lilian to establish a foundation to educate the scientific community about congenital heart disease and to fund operations for needy children with congenital anomalies. Because she became disillusioned with Dr. Gross and knew of our successful results, she began referring patients to Texas Children's Hospital. She assumed that Dr. DeBakey was performing the surgeries.

Princess Lilian visited Houston in 1961, expecting to watch Mike perform an operation on one of her young subjects. Soon after arriving, she met with Dr. George Primo, a young Belgian trainee on my service. Primo told her that Mike had never operated at Texas Children's Hospital and that I had performed all of the operations. Lilian felt deceived and betrayed. She also was embarrassed because she had planned a celebration to honor Mike during her visit. When I met with her, she was upset about the deception and suggested that he be exposed in the media. I convinced her not to do this because Mike was a highly valuable asset to the Baylor program and the entire Texas Medical Center. I also knew that any adverse publicity could upset the rather sensitive balance between Mike and me.

We scheduled the operation as planned. I assured the princess that I would be present and would assist in the procedure. In the operating room, I connected the child to the heart-lung machine and made a standard incision in the chest. Mike came in, already scrubbed and gowned. George Primo also participated in the procedure. Princess Lilian arrived in the operating room wearing a surgical gown, cap, and mask with a rather unusual set of accessories: an elaborate diamond necklace and large, dangling diamond earrings. She watched intently. Because Mike was unfamiliar with congenital heart anomalies, I began guiding him through the operation. He then asked me to take over the repair. From that point on, he simply assisted me. Fortunately, the operation was successful, and the crisis was calmed. The princess was determined, however, to do something special for me.

On returning to Belgium, she organized a cardiac symposium in

Brussels so that I could demonstrate my use of non-blood prime and stimulate interest in open heart surgery there. My nurse perfusionist, Mary Martin, accompanied me and brought a suitcase containing several sterile, disposable bubble oxygenators. In Brussels, I performed a televised repair of tetralogy of Fallot in a child, which was successful. I then performed additional operations on other patients in Brussels and in Ghent. As a result, the Belgian Cardiological Society made me an honorary member, and the University of Ghent awarded me its Grande Medaille. I deeply appreciated both honors.

While in Belgium, I was a special houseguest of Princess Lilian and King Leopold at their elegant home, Château d'Argenteuil, near Waterloo. Princess Lilian was a charming hostess and spoke four languages. At a large, formal banquet held in my honor on the grounds of the chateau, I sat between her and Leopold. The dinner guests included numerous prominent cardiologists and surgeons, mostly from Western Europe. They also included Mary Lasker and Florence Mahoney from the United States, both of whom were influential at the National Institutes of Health. These women were actively lobbying the U.S. Congress for an increase in health care funding.

One morning during my visit, Princess Lilian invited me to accompany her to a golf club to hit practice balls. She drove us to the club in a Lamborghini convertible at racecar speed. I was surprised to see that she could hit a ball better than most men could. The next day I was Leopold's partner in a planned golf tournament held in my honor. The tournament was on a golf course located on the battlefield of Waterloo, about eight miles from Brussels, where Napoleon had his final defeat. King Leopold was warm, congenial, and an accomplished golfer. As we proceeded along the eighteen holes, he explained details of the battle. He identified the chateau on the hillside adjacent to the battlefield, where commissioned officers of the English coalition army had been billeted and had even fraternized with the Prussian officers. According to Leopold, the evening before the battle, the officers enjoyed a splendid dinner, card games, and fine brandy. Afterward, an attendant rang a bell and informed them that the battle would commence at 10:00 the following morning, June 18, 1815. That starting time would allow the valets and servants time to groom and saddle the officers' horses, polish the officers' boots, and prepare the uniforms. At the appointed time, the officers mounted their horses and watched the battle from the hillside. I thought to myself, "How civilized!" What a contrast to the war then being fought in Vietnam.

The mid-1950s to early 1960s were exciting times, both for my practice and for my family. During this period, Louise and I were graced with three more daughters: little Louise; Florence, who was named for my aunt; and Helen, who was named for my paternal grandmother. I felt very blessed.

Granite monument, *A Symbol of Excellence*, in front of the Texas Heart Institute.

CHAPTER II

Ar Institute for the Heart

A S OPEN HEART SURGERY EVOLVED, the Texas Medical Center continued to grow. During the 1950s a variety of new institutions had opened in rapid succession. Some of these were devoted to specific diseases or patient populations. However, the Medical Center didn't have an institution devoted specifically to the heart. We did have a cardiovascular program at Methodist Hospital, but it was dominated by Mike DeBakey. Although I was attracting an increasing number of patients of my own, his cases always took priority. There didn't seem to be room for me at Methodist anymore. Besides, I preferred a working style different from Mike's. I strongly disapproved of his abusive treatment of the residents and junior staff. He tested them to the limits of their emotional and physical endurance.

The situation was partially relieved when, in 1954, two new adjoined hospitals—Texas Children's and St. Luke's Episcopal Hospitals—opened within a few hundred yards of Methodist. Texas Children's opened first, and I performed the initial heart operation there a few weeks later. I continued to operate temporarily at both Methodist and Texas Children's, but running back and forth between the two hospitals was not the most efficient use of my time. St. Luke's, an all-adult hospital, opened later that year. My increasingly difficult relationship with Mike led me to move my office and my practice to Texas Children's and St. Luke's, although I remained a full-time faculty member at Baylor. For a while this solution worked well. Because the two hospitals shared operating rooms and other facilities, I was able to operate on children and adults in the same surgical suite. Dr. Arthur Keats, another colleague from Baylor, was my anesthesiologist. Dan McNamara was our pediatric cardiologist, and Dr. Edward B. Singleton was our radiologist. Ed and I had met at the University of Texas, where we were both Kappa Sigs and good friends.

By the end of the 1950s, I was operating on so many patients that they filled the wards of Texas Children's and St. Luke's Hospitals to overflowing, and the need for more space was again becoming urgent. We needed a major expansion of our facilities.

St. Luke's and Texas Children's were originally chartered as general hospitals, but they now had the most active cardiac surgical program in the world—because of my practice. Baylor and its clinical partner Methodist didn't have nearly such a successful heart program. At St. Luke's and Texas Children's, we were doing three or four times as much heart surgery as they were doing. But Mike was a good lobbyist, so he got a lot of grant money and much attention in the press. Even though his program was much smaller than mine, he was better known to the public.

I began to think about creating an institute for the heart that would give my program a unique presence in the Medical Center. I thought back to my days at Johns Hopkins Hospital, which had several specialty institutes for research and education devoted to different diseases. The institutes' personnel could focus on research because they did not have to run a hospital, while the hospital benefited from a steady stream of patients funneled through the institutes. I felt that this concept would be a good model on which to build. I wanted my institute to be supportive of St. Luke's and Texas Children's. Like the Hopkins' institutes, its focus would be research and education, and it would be partly funded by my professional fees and by donations from local supporters and patients. At that time, only a few so-called heart institutes existed—one each in London, Miami, and Mexico City. They were flourishing because of the demand for their specialized services. I believed that one would flourish here.

My plans didn't begin to solidify until early 1962, when I learned that Methodist was on the verge of launching a major fundraising campaign to create a new cardiovascular unit. Clearly, I was not going to play much of a role in this new program. I now had all the motivation that I needed to move forward with my own plans. My experience at Baylor had shown that government funding came with a lot of bureaucratic red tape. Raising money privately would be the only way to build my institute quickly.

I called my friend, attorney Bill Taylor, of the law firm Butler & Binion, explained what I wanted, and asked him to prepare a charter to incorporate a nonprofit organization called the Texas Heart Institute. Because the heart and circulation are so closely allied and because the public would most likely identify more readily with the word "heart" than the term "cardiovascular," I thought that the name Texas Heart Institute would be simple, descriptive, and easy to remember.[1]

Within a few days, Bill took the paperwork to Austin and registered it at the secretary of state's office. Using seed money from the fledgling Denton A. Cooley Foundation, I had the architectural firm of Starr, Rather, and Howes design a plan for a building that would be attached to St. Luke's and Texas Children's. The building would house the institute's research and educational facilities and have space for a clinic, patient beds, and staff offices.

On July 13, 1962, at a joint meeting of the two hospital boards, I presented my proposal, explained the need for the institute, and showed the model. I said that the estimated cost would be $4.5 million. St. Luke's and Texas Children's were already trying to raise money to expand their facilities, mainly in response to the increased numbers of my patients, who were filling their beds. I assured the board members that I could raise money for my building from private sources. I reminded them that, like cancer and pediatric diseases, heart disease could touch anyone's life. I didn't think it would be hard to raise money for an institute devoted to eradicating this condition. The joint hospital boards tentatively approved my plan, and on August 3, 1962, the State of Texas granted our charter. As I had promised the joint boards, the nonprofit charter precluded the institute's generating revenue from patient care. For me, that charter was a dream come true. I now had the formal legal approval to move forward. The Houston newspapers quickly picked up the story, and Mike DeBakey read about it. I learned indirectly that he was quite disturbed about the announcement.

I had hoped that I could count on a sizable donation from Benjamin Clayton, of the Anderson Clayton cotton firm. I had operated successfully on his beloved chauffeur, and Clayton had given money over the years for the care of my indigent heart patients. As it turned

---

[1] Later, we would register the words "Texas Heart" to prevent other institutions from using a name similar to ours, which might confuse the public.

out, "Mr. Ben" had no interest in brick and mortar projects or in having his name associated with them. This was a major setback. I made a few other calls to individuals but found little enthusiasm. My busy schedule left hardly any time for me to seek support from foundations, corporate contributors, and philanthropic individuals in the city. Gradually, I realized that I would not be able to raise enough money to construct the size and type of building that I had envisioned initially. The only option was to combine my fundraising efforts for the institute with the ongoing campaign of St. Luke's and Texas Children's to raise money to expand their programs.

Eventually, the joint boards and I agreed to incorporate the Texas Heart Institute within their own expansion programs. This arrangement combined all our efforts to raise money for building, and it satisfied those who were concerned that the Texas Heart Institute could become an independent hospital. I was somewhat disappointed because I thought we might lose our identity in a huge hospital complex, but the new plan seemed the only way. The final price tag for everything would be $50 million. My part would be $10 million. Many of the board members felt that this was too extravagant. However, Mr. Leopold Meyer, president of Texas Children's Hospital and a local retailer, had the vision and the courage to be outspoken on behalf of the full project. The boards finally agreed.

The final plans allowed for twenty-eight stories, seven of which would be a shell construction to be finished when the space was needed. We would have three joint institutions: St. Luke's Episcopal Hospital, Texas Children's Hospital, and the Texas Heart Institute. Although each institution would have its own separate board, they would meet together.[2] Patient beds would remain part of the St. Luke's and Texas Children's facilities. Areas within the hospitals would be designated as the research and educational facilities of the Texas Heart Institute. By the end of 1962 we had a solid plan in place, but it would take us five years to raise enough money for the ground to be broken.

In 1966 a chance encounter at a neighborhood party brought me

[2] Texas Children's eventually developed its own separate administration. The Texas Heart Institute also developed a separate administration, but it remained closely affiliated with St. Luke's. Today, we are officially called the Texas Heart Institute at St. Luke's Episcopal Hospital.

the funds I needed. At the party, I visited with my neighbor and friend Robert "Bob" Herring, an executive with the Houston Natural Gas Corporation. During a casual conversation with him, I learned that he had recently been appointed head of the Ray C. Fish Foundation, a multimillion dollar trust left by a successful engineer who had died of heart disease. The foundation was seeking a project worthy of a hefty donation. Herring asked me if I could suggest such a project. Of course, I didn't have to think twice. We met the next morning to discuss it. Bob said that the Fish Foundation could possibly fund the entire $10 million which was the amount I had to raise for the project. I believed it would be better for long-term fundraising if other donors and foundations in Houston also contributed to the effort. Bob saw the wisdom in that approach, so the Fish Foundation donated a total of $5 million, which was paid in $500,000 installments over ten years. News of this generous gift soon inspired other philanthropic groups and former patients to provide most of the remaining $5 million. I approached Ben Clayton again, and this time he agreed to make a substantial donation to pay for operating rooms and a cardiology research lab. Other donors included Gus Wortham, a civic leader who was a former patient of mine; the Houston Endowment, established by Jesse H. Jones; and the Brown and Abercrombie Foundations.

About this time, I received one of the most memorable contributions. On a Saturday afternoon, I got an urgent call from a physician in Chicago who wanted to refer a patient with a rupturing abdominal aneurysm for emergency surgery. The patient turned out to be Harry S. Blum, chairman of the Jim Beam Whiskey Distillery. He was flown by private jet from Chicago to Houston and nearly bled to death en route. I managed to repair the aneurysm, and Mr. Blum did well. Ten days later, he invited me to stop by his suite at the Shamrock Hilton Hotel, where he was recuperating. After I examined him and confirmed that his recovery was complete, he put his shirt back on and said, "That's the good news. Now for the bad news—what is your fee?"

Hoping that he might donate to the building fund, I replied, "There is no fee. I can't put a price on your life."

Of his own volition, Mr. Blum remarked, "In the hospital lobby, I saw the model for the new expansion. How much would it cost to endow the whole thing?"

"I don't need for you to endow it all, but I could use a million dollars."

"You've got it!"[3]

I picked up a pen and paper from the desk in his room, and we drew up a simple handwritten contract on the spot. From there I went straight to the Texas Children's Hospital auditorium, where I knew that a fundraising event was in progress. Waving Mr. Blum's agreement, I told Ralph McCullough, the leader of the fundraising program, "I don't know how much you'll raise today, but I just got a million dollars from a single donor." This had the effect I intended. Seeing how close we were to achieving our goal, several of those in attendance stepped forward and added to Mr. Blum's gift.

On June 26, 1967, we held the groundbreaking ceremony for the hospitals' expansion and my heart institute. Much of the tower was a reality by 1972, and the new operating suites were full of patients.[4] Although I would still have preferred my own building, I finally had a surgical home. Every time I saw the name Texas Heart Institute on the front of the building, on stationery, on programs—anywhere in the hospital—I felt a great sense of pride.

I'll always be grateful to sculptor Theodore "Ted" McKinney, who gave me the idea for the symbol that would ultimately represent the Texas Heart Institute. In 1954 I operated on Ted's young daughter to correct a congenital heart defect. Eighteen years later, I performed a triple coronary artery bypass on Ted himself. Some time afterward, he showed me a drawing of a large, heart-shaped figure that he'd conceived during his hospital stay. I was impressed with the abstract, open heart design and thought that it could make a striking monument to honor all those, including patients, who helped further the goals of

[3] Years later, another donation came my way in a similar manner from Houston's famed trial lawyer, Joe Jamail, the "King of Torts." I performed bypass surgery on him, and he later kidded me about how much it was going to cost. I told him, "Joe, I'm not sending you a bill. You couldn't afford it anyway." I knew that was a challenge Joe wouldn't be able to resist. Sure enough, he donated $10 million for research and for help with indigent patients. The donation came with a note: "Denton: This is what you get for not sending me a damn bill!"

[4] In 1983 a "skybreaking" ceremony officially began construction of a four-story expansion of the southernmost wing of the hospitals, which would give additional space to THI. In 1986 the first floor of the seven-story shell at the top of the tower was completed. The others followed soon thereafter, completing the entire twenty-eight-story tower.

the institute. We settled on a seven-foot, red granite heart, which was erected in 1977 and still stands in front of the Texas Heart Institute. It was called *A Symbol of Excellence,* and the design eventually became the institute's official logo. The statue remains a lasting tribute to the institute's excellence in research, education, and patient care. The *Symbol* so impressed me that I had a replica in gray granite created by a local sculptor and placed on our family plot at Glenwood Cemetery in Houston.

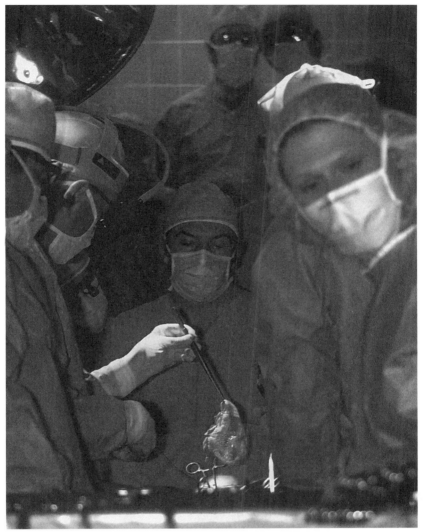

Holding a removed, diseased heart during a transplant operation. Dr. George Reul, my longtime associate chief of surgery, is at the head of the operating table. Courtesy of Ken Hoge, photographer.

CHAPTER 12

Transplanting Hearts

THE 1960S WERE AN EXCITING TIME not only for me but also for Americans in general. Overall, the period was one of prosperity and optimism. The decade started with the inauguration of John F. Kennedy, a young, idealistic president who was extremely charismatic. Under his leadership, Americans began to think that even the moon might be within their grasp. In September 1962 President Kennedy visited Rice University in Houston and spoke about the exploration of space—calling it the greatest adventure on which man had ever embarked. Earlier that year, two U.S. astronauts had actually orbited the earth for the first time. We in Houston were especially interested in space exploration because the newly established Manned Spacecraft Center[1] was located just south of town.

The day after Kennedy's speech, I read some excerpts in the newspaper. One struck me as being particularly applicable to my own field: "We meet in an hour of change and challenge, in a decade of hope and fear, in an age of both knowledge and ignorance." Despite the many advances heart surgeons had made until then, the treatment of severe cardiac disease remained a difficult and challenging problem. Those of us working in this field were acutely aware of what remained to be done. For instance, we had no way to save a patient whose heart was so badly damaged that surgical repair was impossible. Nothing short of total heart replacement—with either another human heart or an artificial heart—seemed to be the answer for these patients.

---

[1] The Manned Spacecraft Center in Clear Lake, Texas, was part of the National Aeronautics and Space Administration (NASA) In 1973 it was renamed the Lyndon B. Johnson Space Center in honor of the late president.

The concept of total heart replacement was not new. The actual surgery wouldn't be that difficult, and several techniques had already been developed in dogs, with a survival time of up to three weeks. Before transplantation could be tried in a human being, though, we had to solve two major challenges—one medical and the other legal. The medical challenge was how to keep the patient's immune system from rejecting the new heart. Dr. Norman Shumway, at Stanford, and Dr. Richard Lower, at the Medical College of Virginia, had been working to solve that problem by using several antirejection drugs. These researchers had come up with a regimen they thought would work, although they had tried it only in animals. The legal challenge, which was a huge barrier at the time, involved determining the time of death of a potential donor. According to the traditional view, death occurs when the heart stops beating. However, by then the heart tissue may have deteriorated too much to be usable for a transplant. In contrast, if the heart keeps beating but the brain activity stops, the line between life and death is not as clear. So, in the 1960s, the key was to get brain death legally accepted as an alternative definition of death. It was well known that Shumway and Lower were both prepared to perform a transplant once their institutions agreed to the concept of brain death. Other surgeons, including myself, were eager to start transplant programs, but most of us assumed that Shumway would be the first.

On December 3, 1967, however, the shocking news came from Cape Town, South Africa, that Dr. Christiaan Barnard, a trainee of Walt Lillehei's, had performed the first human-to-human heart transplant. Chris had been testing the procedure in dogs, but no one believed that he would be the first to do a human transplant. His patient, fifty-five-year-old Louis Washkansky, received the heart of a twenty-five-year-old woman who had been struck by a speeding car. Her heart was still beating when she arrived at the hospital, but she had severe brain damage and flat brainwaves. Chris applied the concept of brain death to declare her dead and proceeded with the transplant.

Barnard's feat captured the imagination of both the medical profession and the world at large. Probably no operation in history has ever generated so much publicity. Like most other surgeons, I was surprised by the news. In an interview the day after the story broke, I predicted that the transplanted heart would fail within forty-eight hours. Frankly, I was envious of Chris Barnard's success. I regretted

very much that I had not been the first. The day after the news broke
about Chris's feat, I sent him a telegram "Congratulations on your
first transplant, Chris. I will be reporting my first hundred soon." The
next surgeon to report a transplant, however, was Dr. Adrian Kantrowitz, in Brooklyn. Three days after Barnard's procedure, Kantrowitz performed a transplant in an eighteen-day-old baby who died a
few hours later.

Mr. Washkansky, Barnard's first transplant patient, died after eighteen days, but Chris was not discouraged, nor were those of us waiting to begin our programs. Chris soon performed another transplant,
this time in a fifty-eight-year-old Cape Town dentist named Philip
Blaiberg, who lived for nearly twenty months before dying of tissue
rejection. On January 6, 1968, Shumway finally performed his own
transplant, but the patient survived for only fifteen days and was never
discharged from the hospital.

Mike DeBakey soon appointed a committee at Baylor to explore
the possibility of establishing a heart transplant program. He did not
include me. Maybe it's immodest of me, but I thought that since I
was the most experienced heart surgeon in the world, I was the one
best qualified to perform transplants in Houston. Under these circumstances, I didn't feel that I had to get Mike's approval to proceed
independently. I asked my surgical associates, Dr. Grady Hallman and
Dr. Robert Bloodwell, who had joined me at St. Luke's and Texas
Children's, to be part of my team. I let them know that I was planning to do a transplant at the first opportunity. It would be almost five
months, however, before that opportunity arrived.

I understood the technique intuitively even before performing it.
The operation would be technically easier than many other heart procedures I'd been doing. It simply required removing the diseased heart
and leaving the remnants of the heart's upper chambers (the atria) in
place. I would then attach the donor heart to the atrial remnants, the
pulmonary artery, and the aorta. Ideally, once blood was allowed into
the coronary arteries of the new heart, it would begin to beat and soon
regain its normal function.

On May 2, 1968, I was in Shreveport, Louisiana, giving a talk to the
medical society there. Just before my presentation, reporters had asked
whether I was planning to do a heart transplant. I answered, truthfully,
that I had no "immediate plans." A couple of hours later, I got a call

from Bob Bloodwell in Houston. He told me, "Boss, I think we've got a donor—a fifteen-year-old girl who shot herself in the head with a .22 pistol after arguing with her nineteen-year-old husband. Her brain waves have been flat for several hours, and I have permission to take her heart." I immediately chartered a plane and returned to Houston.

When I learned that a potential donor was at St. Luke's, I thought of Everett Thomas, a forty-seven-year-old accountant whose heart had been severely damaged by rheumatic fever. He'd had two heart attacks and two strokes. Three of his heart valves were now heavily calcified and needed to be replaced. Mr. Thomas came to Houston from Phoenix after hearing of my successful record with valve replacement. He had been bedridden for six weeks, and his prognosis was bleak. We had already planned to do a triple valve replacement, but the odds were greatly against his surviving the procedure. Nonetheless, he and his wife had decided that he should go ahead with the surgery, so we had scheduled it for the morning of May 3. After the donor heart became available and I returned to Houston on May 2, I met with the Thomases. If during his valve replacement operation, it became clear that Mr. Thomas could not survive, would they consent to my placing our donor's heart in his body? They agreed.

Five different neurologists independently examined the donor, and each concluded that her brain could not possibly recover its activity. It was a peculiar coincidence that she was our first heart donor, as I had operated on her for a coarctation of the aorta when she was nine years old. That condition had left her with a permanently enlarged heart, which would be better able to handle the circulation of a large man.

Shortly before midnight, members of my team transferred the donor from the municipal Ben Taub Hospital emergency room to an operating room at St. Luke's. Everett Thomas was in an adjacent operating room. Once I saw the inside of his heart, I knew that it could not be repaired. The valves were more heavily calcified than I'd expected, and the septum was also involved. A transplant was the only option. I notified Grady Hallman in the other operating room and asked him to remove the donor's heart and bring it to me. I then removed Thomas's heart. I was assisted by Hallman and Bloodwell. Dr. Robert Leachman managed the pump oxygenator, and Dr. Arthur Keats was in charge of anesthesia. It took me only thirty-five minutes of pump time to do the transplant. As I sutured the donor heart into Mr. Thomas's chest,

I wasn't certain that it would regain function. When we removed the vascular clamps, the heart went into ventricular fibrillation. I asked for the defibrillator paddles and held them against the heart. After a single electrical jolt, the heart began a regular beat. Mr. Thomas's blood pressure soon increased to a normal level.

The five or ten minutes during which my team and I waited for the heart to begin beating strongly and regularly were some of the most anxious moments of my career. When the heart did begin to work properly, we felt as if we had witnessed a miracle. Mr. Thomas was then moved to another operating room that had been converted into a sterile intensive care unit.

At 6:30 that morning, a public relations team from St. Luke's notified the news media about the transplant. The announcement unleashed a storm of press coverage, and the wire services spread the story around the world. Mike received the news of the transplant when he arrived at Methodist that morning. He was so upset that he cancelled his scheduled surgery and spent the morning sequestered in his office. Not surprisingly, our rift widened even more.

Because of the media blitz, St. Luke's was immediately beset by people seeking a heart transplant. Within a few days of Thomas's procedure, two men with irreparably damaged hearts were admitted to the hospital. One was forty-eight years old, and the other was sixty-two. Luckily, the media blitz also briefly increased the number of donors, and one heart became available within the next few days. Ironically, the donor was the teenaged son of close friends of mine. He had been mortally injured in a motor scooter accident. I met with the parents and asked them to donate their son's heart. After gaining approval from their priest, the parents agreed.

I now had to make a difficult decision: I had one donor heart and two dying patients who needed it. Because they both had the same blood type, I decided to base my decision on age, which I felt was the most objective criterion. I gave the heart to the younger patient. Thankfully, the older man didn't have to wait long for his new heart, although the donation was complicated by legal tangles that no one could have anticipated. The donor was a thirty-two-year-old welder who had suffered a head injury during an eight-man brawl outside the Peek-a-Boo Lounge, near the Houston Ship Channel. Five days later, he slipped into a coma and was hospitalized. His brainwaves were flat.

Because homicide charges would be filed if the patient were to die, Dr. Joseph Jachimczyk, the county medical examiner, asked me not to do the transplant, as it might compromise the autopsy evidence. I told him that the situation was desperate: "The recipient is prepared for surgery and will die without the transplant. Hearts are so scarce, we can't waste this one. We would like to save at least one life out of this tragedy." Jachimczyk asked me to wait until he could get the district attorney to prepare a set of legal guidelines to govern such situations. I told him that I felt compelled to go ahead with the transplant because my main consideration was for the living, not the dead. I did the transplant that same day. The coroner did not press charges against me. However, the larger issue of using the hearts of murder victims remained unresolved legally for many years.[2] In such cases, there was even debate about whether the transplant surgeon who removed the heart could be considered the actual murderer. If so, the accused killer might either be set free or convicted of a lesser charge.

· · ·

My second and third transplant patients both had serious problems with lung congestion and pneumonia and died within eight days—a major disappointment. Meanwhile, Mr. Thomas, my first transplant patient, was on his feet and doing extremely well. Within a couple of months, he was discharged from the hospital, but he had to report back twice a week for tests and medication, which kept him from returning home to Phoenix. Fortunately, the manager of a bank just across the street from St. Luke's gave Mr. Thomas a job in the trust department.

My fourth transplant patient, a used car salesman, also took a job in Houston after being discharged from the hospital. He was an outgoing, friendly guy who enjoyed a good joke. I remember telling him that he was "the only used car salesman in the world who ever had a change of heart." He lived another four and a half months, one of the eight transplant patients in my series who survived for more than four months.

By mid August of 1968 I had done nine transplants. This was a stimulating and exciting time, but it was also very intense and emo-

---

[2] Although the use of homicide victims as donors was not prohibited, the Texas Legislature did not pass a law regarding such use until 1989.

tional. Some of the recipients appeared at news conferences, and people who saw them were impressed with how well they looked. In those early days, transplant surgeons were glorified like movie stars or other celebrities. In my own case, the adulation was sometimes uncomfortable but also highly gratifying, so I rather enjoyed it.

About this time, I gave in to my wife's insistence that we take a family vacation to Acapulco. We had been invited to stay at the Las Brisas resort—famous for its little pink jeeps—in a beautiful villa belonging to a former Mexican president. I was somewhat reluctant to go because one of my patients, a five-year-old girl, was seriously ill with a congenital condition that had weakened her heart. A transplant was her only hope for survival, but we did not have a donor. She was not in immediate danger, and I didn't want to disappoint my family, so we left on the trip to Mexico. A few hours after we arrived in Acapulco, however, I got a call saying that a donor had been found for the little girl. I returned to Houston immediately, promising my family that I would soon rejoin them.

Back at St. Luke's, I performed the transplant on the child—my first pediatric transplant. No more than twenty-four hours later, she was sitting up in bed with her coloring book. I did a transplant on another patient the next day and then flew back to Acapulco. Four days later, my youngest daughter, Helen, who was almost eight, fell off the high diving board at the resort. She hit her head on the cement below and was knocked unconscious. The fall tore her scalp. I stanched the flow of blood with strands of her hair. In my wet bathing suit, I put her in our pink jeep and drove her to the local municipal hospital. Carrying her into the emergency room, I said, "I'd like to get some sutures and a dressing so I can take care of this laceration." The hospital personnel asked me for identification. "I'm a surgeon from Houston, Texas." On the desk was a recent issue of *Life* magazine with a cover photo showing me doing a heart transplant. I pointed to the magazine, "*That's* who I am." They immediately got me the surgical materials I needed. As I sat anxiously waiting for the X-rays to see if Helen had a skull injury, I thought how ironic it would be if my own little girl ended up as a heart donor. I was greatly relieved when she regained full consciousness and we learned that her skull injury was minor. Sadly, my little girl patient in Houston died the day after Helen's accident.

· · ·

Within a few months of Barnard's first transplant, most scientists and intellectuals accepted the concept of brain death, but there was no law in place. By August 1968 a Harvard committee had published an ad hoc report that defined irreversible brain death,[3] lending further credibility to the concept. With such a definition, usable organs could be removed from the body for transplantation after proper permission was obtained from the next of kin.

Many in the lay community were not convinced, however. For them, the heart was widely regarded as the seat not only of life but also of the soul. Some people even worried that St. Peter might get mixed up if John Doe showed up at the heavenly gates with Jane Smith's heart. Others thought the recipient might take on the donor's personality. These views didn't make sense to me because I'd always felt that the heart was just a pump, a servant of the brain. I believed that when the brain died, the heart became unemployed. To me, the real moral failing was to refuse to reemploy the heart when someone desperately needed it.

At the end of August 1968, Mike DeBakey's team at Methodist Hospital, led by Dr. Ted Diethrich, finally performed its first transplant. Ted orchestrated a multiple transplant from a single teenaged suicide victim. The donor heart, a single lung, and both kidneys were harvested and transplanted into four separate recipients by different surgical teams. When Mike got to the operating suite, he was reluctant to participate in this spectacular series of operations. I later heard that Ted had taken Mike aside and told him that Denton Cooley wouldn't hesitate to do it. Only then did Mike agree to proceed. The newspaper headlines read, "DeBakey Team of Sixty Performs Multiple Transplant." Mike received all the credit, and Ted Diethrich was not mentioned.

On September 6, 1968, I attempted a heart-lung transplant on a baby girl, two-and-a-half months old and desperately ill with a com-

[3] "A Definition of Irreversible Coma. Report of the Ad Hoc Committee of the Harvard Medical School to Examine the Definition of Brain Death," *The Journal of the American Medical Association,* vol. 205 (1968), pp. 337–340.

plex heart defect and pulmonary hypertension. The transplant was her only hope for survival. Although a few other surgeons had previously attempted a lung transplant without a survivor, no one had ever tried to transplant the heart and both lungs. About this time, Dr. Bruce Reitz, working in Shumway's lab, had some success with heart-lung transplantation in monkeys but never tried it in humans. Our own heart-lung procedure was the first one in a human.[4] The operation was especially challenging because of the baby's size. The procedure worked well, but she developed complications unrelated to the operation and died within twenty-four hours. Today, heart-lung transplants are fairly standard. The operative technique that I used in 1968 is the one still being used.

By September 1968 I had transplanted ten hearts, and six of the patients were alive (up to four months after their procedures). Although I was pleased with these results, the situation soon began to change. Two more patients died of tissue rejection in October. That same month, my first transplant patient, Everett Thomas, was readmitted with acute tissue rejection.

After more than a month of treating Mr. Thomas for rejection, I decided that the only option was another heart transplant, and he agreed. Nobody had ever undergone a second transplant before. The procedure was problem-free, but Mr. Thomas died two days later of infection. He had formerly done so well that his death hit me especially hard. Because he survived the operation and was discharged from the hospital, his operation is considered to be the first *successful* heart transplant in the United States.[5]

I now had only one surviving patient of my original ten transplant recipients.

Other transplant surgeons were encountering similar problems. The initial euphoria associated with heart transplants was beginning to fade, less than a year after Chris Barnard's groundbreaking sur-

---

[4] The baby had a complete atrioventricular canal defect and severe pulmonary hypertension. You can read the scientific report of this case in *The Annals of Thoracic Surgery*, vol. 8 (1969), pp. 30–46.

[5] The scientific report of my first four heart transplant procedures can be found in *The Journal of the American Medical Association*, vol. 205 (1968), pp. 479–486.

gery. Since that first operation, more than one hundred transplants had been performed in almost fifty centers throughout the world. I had the single largest experience. By January 1969 only twenty-nine of the first one hundred patients were still alive. The others had lived for an average of twenty-nine days, but most died by the eighth postoperative day.[6] However, there did still seem to be hope. Chris's second transplant recipient, Philip Blaiberg, was still alive at sixteen months and was leading a fairly normal life, even swimming in the surf off Cape Town. Sadly, three months later, he died of complications resulting from chronic tissue rejection. He was the longest-surviving patient from those early transplants. Only one of my own patients lived for longer than a year, and that patient was never discharged from the hospital. He also died of chronic tissue rejection.

Finding a way to control rejection of a transplanted heart would remain a challenge for more than a decade. To the patient's immune system, the transplanted tissue was a "foreign" invader that had to be attacked. The only way to prevent the body from rejecting the heart was to suppress the immune response. Unfortunately, in the late 1960s the only immunosuppressants available were powerful drugs, such as azathioprine, antilymphocyte globulin, and corticosteroids, which shut down the immune response of the entire body. As a result, the immune system could no longer carry out its usual task of fighting infection. Even the mildest infection could prove fatal. The antirejection drugs were also associated with a number of serious side effects. Because of these problems, most heart transplant surgeons had stopped their programs by the early 1970s. Shumway was the only one who persisted throughout that decade, and he almost single-handedly kept the program alive until better antirejection drugs were developed.

In looking back, I have no regrets about my transplant experience in the late 1960s. I did my last transplant in that series on September 29, 1969. By then I had done twenty transplants, but only two of the first nineteen patients were still living. Like other transplant surgeons, I was disappointed with the results. However, we did prove that the operation itself worked, and our experience laid the foundation for a later successful resurgence of the procedure. Our experience also

---

[6] Harris B. Shumacker Jr., *The Evolution of Cardiac Surgery* (Bloomington: Indiana University Press, 1992), p. 333.

caused laws to be passed sanctioning the concept of brain death, which ultimately facilitated organ procurement and allocation.[7]

In the late 1970s a serendipitous discovery stimulated a new interest in heart transplantation. Scientists at the Sandoz pharmaceutical company were working to develop an antifungal agent from a fungal compound that naturally occurs in the soil. They called the derivative agent "cyclosporin A." It's now called cyclosporine. In their animal experiments the researchers were surprised to find that the drug didn't work for treating fungal infections. In fact, the infections got even worse in the animals that received cyclosporine. This made the researchers theorize that cyclosporine was an immune system suppressant. Further animal experiments indeed proved this theory. When the drug was finally used for immune suppression in liver and kidney transplant patients, the results were vastly better than those obtained from traditional drugs. Cyclosporine suppressed the portion of the immune system directly responsible for tissue rejection while sparing the rest of the immune system and preserving an adequate white blood cell count. Used in combination with other drugs, it was far more effective than any previously used antirejection drug regimen. Ultimately, cyclosporine made it possible for heart transplantation to fulfill its earlier promise.

In 1982 the Texas Heart Institute became one of the first centers to use cyclosporine for heart transplantation. Although we did not have an active transplant program at the time, Dr. O. H. (Bud) Frazier, a heart surgeon on my staff, had a connection to Dr. Barry Kahan, a kidney transplant surgeon at the University of Texas Medical School at Houston. Bud was on the staff at the medical school and directed our research lab at the Heart Institute. Kahan had found that cyclosporine worked well in his kidney transplant patients. He and Bud felt that the new drug was such an improvement over the old ones that we should consider renewing our heart transplant program. When Bud came to me with this proposal, I thought it seemed promising and told him to proceed. I offered him whatever help he needed. He did proceed, and that's how we got back into heart transplants.

---

[7] In 1974 the state of California passed an act that allowed a still-beating heart to be removed for transplant if the potential donor had no evidence of brain function. Other states would follow suit.

Bud had trained at Baylor, completed his cardiothoracic residency with me at THI, and remained afterward as part of my surgical staff. He had a unique perspective: during medical school at Baylor, he'd worked with both me and Mike DeBakey. Bud was also interested in academic medicine. Under his direction, our transplant program flourished and became a leader in the field. As of 2011 Bud has performed more than 1,200 heart transplants. I was proud to be asked to help with one of these procedures, which was done in an eight-month-old girl—at that time, the youngest successful heart recipient. She led an active, normal life, even being a cheerleader at her school. Sadly, she developed blockages in the coronary arteries of her transplanted heart and died of a heart attack at age fourteen.

Currently, eighty-seven of our heart transplant patients have lived for more than twenty years, and twelve of these patients have lived for more than twenty-five years with their donor hearts. Many of them received their new hearts in mid life and have been able to live out a full lifespan. One of our first patients is still alive and well twenty-eight years after his transplant. These gratifying results make up for some of the harsh criticisms that were leveled at the pioneers of the procedure.

Although transplantation is now a widely accepted option for patients with otherwise untreatable heart failure, it is not an ideal solution. Rejection has yet to be completely conquered, and even the best antirejection drugs are associated with serious side effects. Patients who develop blocked coronary arteries in their transplanted hearts may need a second transplant. Probably the most serious problem, however, is the lack of enough donor hearts. Since the mid-1990s the supply has remained constant at about two thousand per year in the United States. For the many thousands of additional patients who could use a donor heart, a different solution was needed.

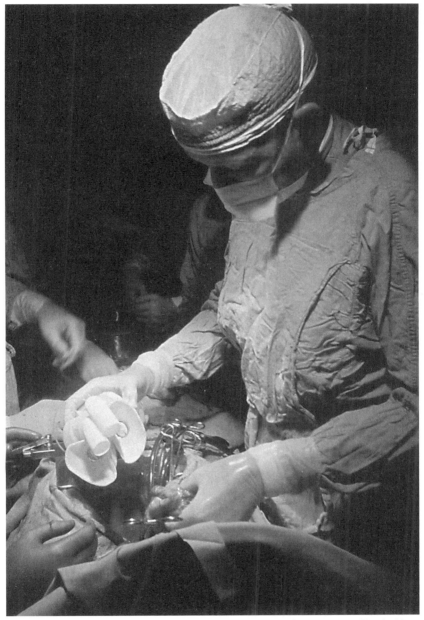

Implanting the first total artificial heart in a human on April 4, 1969. I'm holding Haskell Karp's diseased heart in my left hand and the total artificial heart in my right hand. I was assisted by Domingo Liotta (not pictured), who was across from me.

CHAPTER 13

The Total Artificial Heart

EVEN BEFORE HEART TRANSPLANTATION BEGAN to be done in humans, researchers were exploring another option for patients with terminal heart failure: the use of a partial or a total artificial heart. In the late 1960s many of us believed that a total artificial heart, or TAH, would be the next major breakthrough in cardiac surgery.

Much of the initial work on the TAH was done in the 1950s by Dr. Willem Kolff at the Cleveland Clinic and by a few other researchers, including Dr. Domingo Liotta, a surgeon at the National University of Córdoba in Argentina. In 1957 Kolff and his associate Dr. Tetsuzo Akutsu were the first to implant a TAH in a dog. By the early 1960s they had dogs that were living for more than a day with a TAH. In Argentina, Domingo and his brother, Salvador, were developing an implantable artificial heart made of materials they had obtained from an airplane factory. Domingo and Salvador conducted experiments on dogs and calves, finalizing a prototype TAH by 1959.

In March 1961 Kolff asked Domingo to come to the United States to present the results of his work at a meeting of the American Society for Artificial Internal Organs in Atlantic City.[1] Domingo was invited by Kolff to return to Cleveland with him afterward to observe the work in his lab. Meanwhile, Mike DeBakey had heard about Domingo's presentation in Atlantic City and offered him a surgical fellowship at Baylor. Domingo thought that he would be developing his TAH, but, in fact, Mike was more interested in developing a workable partial artificial heart, or left ventricular assist device (LVAD). In Mike's view,

[1] After the 1961 meeting, Dr. Liotta published his early results in the *Transactions of the American Society for Artificial Internal Organs,* vol. 7 (1961), pp. 318–323.

it made more sense to concentrate on the LVAD, because it could provide temporary support for patients who developed potentially reversible cardiac failure after heart surgery.

In 1964 Mike received a grant from the National Heart Institute (NHI) for a collaborative Baylor-Rice artificial heart program. Although Domingo hoped this would finally allow him to work on his TAH, Mike told him that his main focus should remain LVAD research. By 1967 Mike had used LVADs successfully to support two patients.[2] He also implanted LVADs in several other patients, none of whom survived. Those cases were never reported.

Under the circumstances, Domingo became concerned that his TAH would never be used in humans. Although he contacted Mike repeatedly, requesting his support and permission to refocus efforts on the TAH, Domingo never got a response. Thinking that a face-to-face meeting might help, he finally went to see Mike and showed him the prototype of the heart. Barely glancing at it, Mike said not to bother him about it again.

In December 1968 Domingo came to my basement office in St. Luke's Hospital. He knew that I needed a way to keep patients alive while they waited for a transplant. And he also knew that almost all of our transplant patients had died of tissue rejection. The TAH could potentially solve both problems. Initially, it could keep patients alive while awaiting a transplant. Because the TAH wasn't living tissue, it also would not be subject to rejection. He asked whether I would be willing to work with him to further develop his artificial heart. Ultimately, it might serve as a permanent heart substitute.

I understood Domingo's frustration and agreed that the device could be useful in my transplant program. That is how I first became involved with the TAH. Domingo said that we would need to fabricate a new heart, as well as a new console to power it, to keep our TAH from being confused with any device he had been working on at Baylor.[3] I agreed to pay for the remaining development with funds from my foundation and a couple of small grants. I made it clear to Domingo that we would use the TAH only in an emergency as a

[2] Dr. DeBakey's two successful cases are described in *The American Journal of Cardiology*, vol. 27 (1971), pp. 3–11.

[3] This heart was Dr. Liotta's design from his research in Argentina. It was never Baylor's design.

"bridge" to transplantation. It would be used to keep the patient alive until a suitable donor heart could be found. Neither of us felt a need to ask Mike's permission to proceed. After all, he'd already said that he wanted Domingo to work on the LVAD project.

Over the next few months, Domingo worked intensely to perfect his TAH. It was larger than the human heart and was made of Dacron embedded in a rubbery substance called Silastic. This gave its two chambers a rigid exterior. At my suggestion, the new heart was redesigned to include Wada-Cutter tilting disc valves, which had a larger opening than the valves in his earlier version and would improve blood flow in and out of the device. As testing proceeded, Domingo and I regularly discussed its progress. I also met with William O'Bannon, an engineer at Rice University, who built the console that we would use to power the air-driven device. The console was about the size of an upright piano. To build it, Bill received approval from his department head, Dr. J. David Hellums, who was a collaborator of Mike's in the Baylor-Rice artificial heart program. The only requirement was that building the console not interfere with Bill's normal work, so he did it in his home workshop.

By the end of March 1969, Domingo and I had performed extensive bench tests on the artificial heart and had implanted it in seven calves, the last of which survived for forty-four hours. We believed that our TAH was ready for human use in a desperate situation, so we fabricated a duplicate one specifically for use in a patient. That device was bench-tested in our basement laboratory at St. Luke's Hospital.

I had several patients who were awaiting cardiac transplantation at St. Luke's. Among them was forty-seven-year-old Haskell Karp, a printing estimator from Skokie, Illinois. Mr. Karp had diffuse atherosclerotic disease that affected all of his major coronary arteries. By his early forties, he'd already had several heart attacks, which had left much of his heart tissue scarred and useless. He also had severe angina and complete heart block, for which he had received a pacemaker. In early 1969 his condition began to deteriorate rapidly, and he was referred to me for a transplant. His wife, Shirley, accompanied him to Houston, where he was admitted to St. Luke's. Our cardiologists performed an intensive evaluation and concurred with the referring physicians. His enlarged heart was so weak that it was barely pumping enough blood to sustain his life.

At first, Mr. Karp had reservations about undergoing a heart transplant, but later he began to plead with me to find a donor. After nearly a month in the hospital, he was losing hope. His breathing was becoming more labored, and he could hardly even brush his hair. Whenever he heard an ambulance, he would ask, "Is that my donor?" I felt considerable pressure to save his life.

On April 3 I told Mr. Karp and his wife that the only option other than a transplant was to remove a wedge of tissue from his diseased left ventricle,[4] thereby decreasing its size and allowing it to pump more efficiently. I explained that his heart had so much diseased tissue, he had only a 30 percent chance of surviving the operation. If the procedure failed, the only way to save his life would be to use the TAH as a "bridge" to a transplant. I explained how the TAH worked and stressed that we could not predict how long it would take to locate a donor heart. I also promised to do whatever I could to ensure his well-being and keep him alive. Mr. Karp and his wife agreed to the plan. He signed a special consent form, which was witnessed by his wife and Mr. Henry Reinhard Jr., one of our hospital administrators. Rabbi Nathan Witkin, of the Jewish Community Council of Houston, was also present for additional confirmation of the conversations and the Karps' approval.

The operation was to be done the next day, April 4, 1969, which happened to be Good Friday. That afternoon Mr. Karp was wheeled into the surgical ward. Though receiving oxygen, he was pale, sweaty, and breathing with difficulty. His blood pressure had fallen to half its normal level. Dr. Arthur Keats, chief of anesthesiology, called and told me to come right away. My patient was about to die.

I got to the operating room as quickly as possible and opened Mr. Karp's chest. I'd never seen a worse-looking heart. The inside wall had been almost entirely replaced by fibrous tissue.[5] It was amazing that this heart had been keeping Mr. Karp alive at all. I had to remove about 35 percent of his left ventricle—a much larger portion than anticipated. When the clamps were released to let blood back into the heart, it beat erratically. We tried for more than fifteen minutes

---

[4] This operation is called a ventriculoplasty, or ventricular remodeling procedure.

[5] The scientific report of this operation can be read in *The American Journal of Cardiology*, vol. 24 (1969), pp. 723–730.

to restore a regular rhythm with electric shocks and manual massage but were unsuccessful. I'd reached a crucial point in the procedure. Was I going to let Mr. Karp die on the operating table or try to save his life by whatever means? I decided to proceed with implanting the TAH, as we'd agreed beforehand. I asked that the device and console be brought to the operating room immediately. Meanwhile, I removed Mr. Karp's lifeless heart.

Implanting the artificial heart was an arduous task. The TAH was so stiff that a normal surgical needle was hardly sharp enough to do the job. I implanted one side of the device at a time, beginning with the left atrial connection. I was able to do the whole procedure, including the wedge operation, in less than two hours of pump time. "Okay, Domingo, let's see how well this thing works in a human being." As the heart was turned on and began to fill with blood, my team members and I held our breath. A few of us were silently praying. We were immediately relieved when the TAH began to pump blood, almost like a natural heart. Soon the blood pressure monitors revealed a steady pulse, almost identical to normal.

We turned the operating room into an intensive care unit and kept the patient there for privacy. Within fifteen minutes after the incision was closed, Mr Karp regained consciousness, responded to verbal commands, and moved his hands and feet. All of his organs were being maintained by the normal circulation provided by the TAH. He had been so close to death that my team and I were gratified, even exuberant. After the breathing tube was removed from his throat about 1:30 a.m. on April 5, he was able to speak a few words. Mainly, he just smiled.

Soon after the procedure, I had called Willem Kolff and Adrian Kantrowitz, whom I considered to be true pioneers in artificial heart research. I told them about the operation and the patient's status. They both conveyed their warm congratulations and hailed my operation as a milestone in the history of medicine. I recall that Willem was vacationing at Zion National Park at the time. He told me, "Denton, you need to beware of Mike DeBakey's reaction." Then he said that he would ask some of his Navajo friends there to do a ritual dance to protect Domingo and me. "I'm afraid you're going to need it," he added. He later told me that the Indian dance went on for more than two hours. I also called Dr. Ted Cooper, director of the NHI, but could not reach him. I wanted to get his reaction to the use of the TAH.

The search for a donor heart began immediately. Because Mike would no longer allow donor hearts from Baylor-affiliated hospitals to be used for my patients, our chances of getting a heart in Houston were slim. Mr. Karp was conscious and comfortable, but we didn't know how long he would remain that way. We needed to move quickly. I made a public appeal through the news media in an informal press conference held right after the procedure. Showing a model of the TAH, I explained that the device wasn't designed for permanent use. I told the reporters, "We have taken a desperate measure to save a man's life. What's important now is finding a donor."

That night we received a telephone call about a prospective donor in East Texas, who had developed a brain embolism while giving birth. She was unable to breathe without a respirator, and her brain waves were flat. We made arrangements for her to be brought to St. Luke's via ambulance. Because we believed we had a donor, we began to give Mr. Karp large doses of immunosuppressive drugs to prevent rejection after the transplant. When the donor arrived, I was extremely disappointed to discover that her heart had stopped beating en route. The ambulance personnel hadn't dealt with a heart donor before and didn't realize that they had to keep the heart beating for it to be usable.

The next day, Mrs. Karp herself appeared on a national television network to request a donor to save her husband's life. "Someone, somewhere, please hear my plea for a heart for my husband. I see him lying there, breathing, and knowing that within his chest is a man-made implement where there should be a God-given heart. How long can he survive? . . . Maybe somewhere there is a gift of a heart for my husband. *Please*." After Mrs. Karp's statement, I told the press that whereas Domingo had created the artificial heart, I was solely responsible for deciding to use it in Mr. Karp.

While we waited for a donor, several well-intended individuals called to offer their own hearts. One elderly woman who was crippled with arthritis said that she would be happy to exchange her healthy heart for the TAH, since she was confined to a nursing home anyway. Sadly, we also had a number of mentally and emotionally disturbed people who called. A couple of individuals even told us that they would kill themselves in the hospital parking lot, after which we could take their hearts.

By Easter Sunday, April 6, Mr. Karp's kidney function was deteriorating. Fortunately, that night a call came in from Lawrence, Massachusetts, from a family who had seen our televised appeal the day before. The potential donor, a forty-year-old widow, had been in a coma for nearly a month after having a stroke, and her brain waves were flat. The family wanted to donate her heart. In Houston, pilots and a Learjet were standing by, ready to transport a donor. Our medical team, comprising a registered nurse and a technician, was soon on its way to Massachusetts. After picking up the donor and her adult daughter, they took off for Texas. On the way, the Learjet lost hydraulic control, and the pilot was forced to make an emergency landing without functioning brakes or flaps at Barksdale Air Force base near Shreveport, Louisiana. Because they were going about 200 mph, it took the full length of the mile-long runway for the plane to stop.

At the air base, the donor and team were transferred to another Learjet and flown to Houston's Hobby Airport, where an ambulance met them for the thirteen-mile trip to St. Luke's. During the ambulance's harrowing dash through busy streets to the hospital, the donor's heart began to fibrillate. Cardiac massage was required to keep it "alive." As soon as the donor arrived at our emergency room, defibrillator paddles were applied to the heart, and it started beating feebly again. A cold saline solution was poured over the heart to help preserve it.

Sixty-four hours after receiving the TAH, Mr. Karp was prepared for the transplant. His incisions had not yet healed, so I simply had to clip the wires that held his sternum together. The TAH was easily removed by dividing the sutures that attached it to Mr. Karp's atria and vessels. I took out the two chambers one at a time and put them on the table. I then sewed in the donor heart. After only one countershock, it started beating with a regular rhythm.

The transplanted heart worked well at first. Unfortunately, the large doses of immunosuppressant drugs that Mr. Karp had received to prevent rejection seriously weakened his immune system. He soon developed renal failure and acute pneumonia in his right lung. His compromised immune system couldn't fight the infection, and he died on April 8, just thirty-two hours after the transplant. Had we known then what we know now, we never would have kept giving him those large doses of immunosuppressants. Although Mr. Karp lost his heroic struggle, he proved that a TAH could work as a bridge to transplantation.[6]

For a week, I'd had little sleep, had hardly eaten, and had faced a constant barrage of difficult decisions. I had gone home only once, briefly—to help Louise hide eggs for our children on Easter morning, a family tradition. Mr. Karp's case was a supreme test not only of my skill as a surgeon but also of my judgment as a physician. I was now trading the bright lights of the operating room for the glare of public opinion. My critics were eager to pounce, seeing this operation not as an attempt to save my patient but as a bid for the surgical limelight.

A number of scientific and clinical groups hailed our effort at cardiac replacement as a major milestone in medical history. Many of my professional peers, especially Chris Barnard, praised my decision to move forward with the artificial heart. In July 1969 Willem Kolff wrote in *The Hospital Tribune*, "The implantation of an artificial heart in Houston, Texas . . . was a step forward in medical history. . . . While the patient eventually died of complications following the second operation, the important fact is that the Houston doctors proved that an artificial heart can indeed replace a natural one in man." Others, however, were sharply critical, claiming that the operation was premature and unjustified.

At first, the media were quite supportive, reporting the event as another major breakthrough in a decade of stunning technical accomplishments. They were later just as negative as they had originally been positive and seemed to feast on the situation. It was a trying time for me, but I kept on with my busy practice and ignored my detractors as best I could.

News of the TAH implant led to my complete break with Mike DeBakey, who was irate that I had not requested his permission to do the procedure. On the day we implanted the TAH, Mike was on his way to a meeting at the NHI in Washington, D.C. He learned of the procedure when he opened the morning paper and saw the headline.

---

[6] I am extremely proud that, in 1978, the TAH that Domingo and I used in Mr. Karp was selected by the Smithsonian Institution's National Museum of American History to be part of its permanent collection, further validating the device's importance.

Later, in a newspaper interview, he claimed that the operation was a "stunt" that had no useful research purpose. According to Mike, the only reason I had performed the operation was because I wanted to be the first. Both statements were false.

Although Baylor had a grant from the NHI to develop mechanical cardiac devices, Mike himself had never intended to implant an artificial heart. The controversy that ensued centered on whether the specific device that Domingo Liotta and I used was the product of NHI research, as Mike was claiming, or whether it had been created with private funds. If it had been developed under NHI auspices, I would have been required to get Mike's and the NHI's permission before I could use it. But because Domingo and I funded our device privately, the only criteria governing its use were medical ethics and the patient's willingness to receive the device.

Mike immediately launched a major attack against me. He acted as if he had been personally wounded and his own heart stolen. He went through the Baylor lab and confiscated everything relating to Domingo's and my work, including the notes on our calf experiments. He embarked on an aggressive international campaign to have the medical profession chastise me. With the help of his two sisters, Lois and Selma, who were medical writers at Baylor, he prepared a package of documents indicating that I had exceeded my medical authority and had used "his" device without permission. He sent these documents to almost every major department of surgery in the United States and Europe. A package was even mailed to one of Mr. Karp's sons. Mike also tried to prevent my publishing a scientific manuscript about the use of the TAH. Ultimately, the paper was published by a scientific journal.[7]

As a result of Mike's accusations, a number of investigations were launched, most notably by the American College of Surgeons, the NHI, and Baylor. Ultimately, the investigatory committees of the NHI and the American College of Surgeons agreed that in a situation as desperate as the Karp case, any physician should feel obligated to take whatever reasonable steps might save the patient's life. The fact that something hadn't been done before didn't mean that it

---

[7] The full report can be read in the *Transactions of the American Society for Artificial Internal Organs*, vol. 15 (1969), pp. 252–263.

shouldn't be tried. Both committees issued only mild censures. Baylor's investigation was led by a panel of faculty members that Mike had handpicked. Not surprisingly, I received a censure from Baylor for not requesting permission from the Baylor Committee on Research Involving Human Beings.

In June 1969, two months after Mr. Karp's death, Mike DeBakey persuaded the trustees of Baylor University College of Medicine to distribute an agreement that all faculty members had to sign as a requirement for continued employment. The agreement required the faculty to follow NHI guidelines for research and to submit research protocols to the Committee on Human Research for approval before proceeding with any clinical trials, including surgical ones. This new regulation was a direct result of the Karp case. Obviously, the committee, which Mike controlled, would prevent me from continuing my work on the TAH. In addition, I could not accept any rule that might prevent me from taking whatever medical or surgical steps I felt were necessary to save a human life in the operating room. In my opinion, my patients themselves granted me all the permission I needed.

I could not in good conscience sign the agreement, so I resigned from the Baylor faculty and concentrated all of my efforts on developing the Texas Heart Institute, where I was already surgeon-in-chief. Domingo also resigned from Baylor and joined me at THI full-time to continue our work.[8]

In the months after the TAH implant, I called Mike several times and left messages but never got a response. In December 1969 I tried once more to make peace. I told Mike's secretary that I wanted to talk to him and at least declare a truce, so that we could discuss the future of our respective institutions. After all, even in the Vietnamese conflict, the soldiers would declare a Christmas truce. Mike still didn't return my telephone calls. In fact, he would not speak to me again for nearly forty years. If we happened to attend the same medical meeting, he would act as if I didn't exist.

After Mr. Karp's death, I stayed in touch with his wife, Shirley. She was very supportive, giving statements to the news media in praise of

---

[8] In 1971 Domingo returned to Buenos Aires, where he became surgeon-in-chief of the Cardiovascular Service at the Italian Hospital there. His fellow Argentinians greeted him as a national hero.

my efforts on her husband's behalf. On one occasion, she wrote me, "Be assured that I know you did everything that was humanly possible. . . . My husband did not know he was being so courageous when he consented to surgery—he only wanted to live a useful life. At least he had a chance." Somewhat later, after hearing of Mike's reaction, she wrote a statement that she asked St. Luke's to release to the press, "What kind of a world do we live in? Why the condemnation? . . . A man is drowning—grasps a life preserver—does he examine it for flaws? No he does not! . . . Dr. Cooley, in my opinion, did everything in his power, using his ability and whatever facilities at hand to save my husband's life."

In April 1971, however, with the strong encouragement of a plaintiff's attorney, Mrs. Karp and her three sons filed a $4.5 million malpractice lawsuit against Domingo and me. She later claimed that she started thinking about filing the suit after viewing a documentary called "The Heartmakers," which was broadcast on National Educational Television. Mrs. Karp herself had participated in the documentary, which aired in the fall of 1969. Although she was aware beforehand that the film showed her husband's heart being removed, she said that seeing it on television shocked her. She wrote me a letter stating that she wished she had been more prepared for the viewing. However, she still didn't mention any other concerns. So you can imagine my surprise to learn of the lawsuit, in which she accused me not only of negligence resulting in her husband's death but also of improper experimentation and lack of informed consent.

The case was filed in the U.S. District Court in Houston, and the trial was presided over by Judge John Singleton.[9] It began in late June 1972, after a jury was selected. Tom B. Weatherly, a senior trial lawyer with Vinson, Elkins, Searls & Smith, assisted by Paul Stallings, served as my legal counsel. We argued in my defense that malpractice didn't occur because Mr. Karp's life was actually prolonged, and the TAH was not the cause of his death. Also, Mr. and Mrs. Karp had agreed to the procedure.

Mrs. Karp's attorneys expected to have Mike DeBakey serve as an expert witness, but he was not willing to do so. Although he gave a

___

[9] In 1978 the Public Broadcasting Service series *Nova* aired an episode called "The Trial of Denton A. Cooley," which was based on testimony from the Karp trial.

deposition, he never testified in open court. Judge Singleton did question him in his chambers about the TAH. Mike made it clear that he would not give his medical opinion on the Karp case to the court, nor would he answer any hypothetical questions about the case. Because Mike said he lacked any direct knowledge of the case, Singleton felt that his testimony would serve "no useful purpose," and he would not compel Mike to testify. Mike was also asked whether he'd said that my actions were unethical. He claimed not to remember saying anything of the sort. "Where are you quoting that from?" he asked. "A magazine article?"

After nine days of testimony and proceedings in the federal court, the attorneys for Domingo and me asked for a "directed verdict." In this type of verdict, the judge decides that there aren't enough facts for a jury to make a reasonable decision. Judge Singleton granted our motion. He ruled that the plaintiffs had not presented sufficient evidence to warrant a jury trial, that their accusations were unsubstantiated, and that, without Mike, there was no expert testimony to the contrary. On April 26, 1974, the U.S. Court of Appeals upheld Judge Singleton's decision. The U.S. Supreme Court later refused to consider the Karps' appeal.

I have never regretted using the TAH to prolong Mr. Karp's life. What the court found, and what was often forgotten in the controversy, is that Mr. Karp was dying of his heart disease long before I ever saw him. He came to me because he'd heard of my surgical reputation, and he was so sick that no other surgeon was willing to try to save him. He and I both had high hopes that he would eventually return to normal life.

People tend to think of the physicians who make important breakthroughs as the real pioneers and to underestimate the contribution of the patients, who take the ultimate risk. Mr. Karp should be remembered as a true medical pioneer, and he will always be a special hero to me. When I think about those days, I see his face—framed by the dark-rimmed glasses he always wore—and am reminded of the trust and hope he put in me and in medical science. I've seen that look on the faces of many patients since, and I'll never stop believing that it's my responsibility not to betray their trust.

The furor over the TAH implant caused the NHI to redirect funding in the early 1970s toward the development of long-term, implantable LVADs, which were likely to be developed more quickly and, therefore, could potentially benefit more patients than a TAH. In 1971 I established a laboratory at the Texas Heart Institute devoted specifically to developing and testing such systems. Dr. John Norman was its first director. In 1978 he and I were the first to use an LVAD as a bridge to transplantation.[10] In July 1981, twelve years after the Karp operation, I performed the world's second TAH implant, again as a bridge to transplantation. This time, I used a heart designed by Tetsuzo Akutsu, who had been working in the THI lab since 1974.[11] After those transplants, both patients died of infection related to immunosuppression—the same problem as occurred in Mr. Karp and all the early transplant patients.

I have always been a strong advocate for the use of innovative medical procedures and devices. I've tried to speak to the public in understandable terms about why operations, techniques, and devices should be developed, even if they seem futuristic. I've always tried to be forthright and to never overstate the importance of a new technique or product. And I have insisted that each new development is often but a single step on the way to routine clinical use. Without such advocacy by me and other surgical pioneers, LVADs, the TAH, and cardiac transplantation might not have become what they are today.

Obviously, no one can predict when the TAH will become a routinely used device, but I do think we're getting closer. At THI, Bud Frazier has made incredible progress toward this goal. He has helped develop a new, small LVAD that is available off the shelf both for bridging to transplantation and for long-term support. He's now working on TAHs that combine two of the small devices as the pumping chambers. One of those devices is composed of two MicroMed DeBakey LVADs.

But I'm getting ahead of my story. Although the 1969 TAH implant was dramatic, it would soon be overshadowed by another procedure—coronary artery bypass grafting—which would bring many thousands of new patients my way.

[10] You can read the details of this case in *Lancet*, vol. 1 (1978), pp. 1125–1127.

[11] The details of the second artificial heart implant are in the *Texas Heart Institute Journal*, vol. 8 (1981), pp. 305–319.

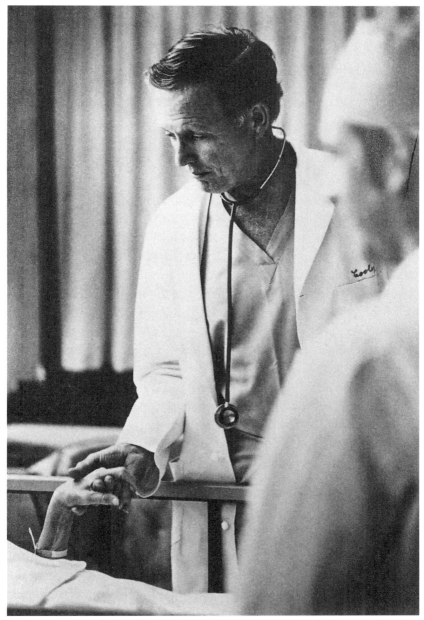
With a patient in the ICU during the 1970s.

CHAPTER 14

The "Cooley Hilton" and Beyond

By THE LATE 1960s, surgeons had developed procedures to repair most heart problems. But the most common heart condition—coronary artery disease—could not be effectively treated, and many people with severe coronary disease died of heart attacks.[1] Vascular surgeons had shown that it was possible to bypass blockages in the large vessels of the legs and arms by using a Dacron graft to route blood around obstructions. In contrast, the coronary arteries are so small—about the size of a wooden matchstick—that surgeons were hesitant to operate on them. Grady Hallman and I did so in several pediatric patients who had congenital coronary artery defects. In those cases, we chose to use a Dacron graft to bypass the defect.[2] We showed that a bypass of this type could be done, but the material and technique weren't optimal.

In adults with coronary disease, some surgeons tried to remove blockages by opening the arteries and reaming them out in a procedure called an endarterectomy. Bill Longmire, my friend from Hop-

---

[1] In a heart attack part of the heart is cut off from the blood supply and doesn't receive enough oxygen. The affected area becomes scarred and weakened. In most cases, the underlying problem is atherosclerosis, which causes fatty plaques to build up in the coronary arteries. This condition does not generally cause symptoms until middle age, when the plaques have become large enough to block the flow of blood through the arteries. What actually causes the heart attack in most cases, is rupture of a fatty plaque. At that site, a blood clot then forms, which blocks blood flow and causes the heart attack. Ironically, the clot formation is an example of the immune system's attempts to repair an injury.

[2] In 1963 Grady Hallman and I reconstructed the arterial system in an eight-year-old girl with a single, anomalous coronary artery by using a Dacron bypass graft to connect the aorta and the coronary artery. You can read about this case in *Circulation*, vol. 32 (1965), pp. 293–297 Subsequent cases were reported in *The Journal of Thoracic and Cardiovascular Surgery*, vol. 52 (1966), pp. 798–808.

kins, was one of the first to do this. In 1964 one of Mike DeBakey's colleagues, Dr. H. E. Garrett, was performing a coronary endarterectomy at Methodist Hospital and had trouble removing the heavily calcified plaque. His only option was to take a portion of the saphenous vein from the patient's leg and use the vein for a bypass graft. The procedure was successful, but it wasn't reported at the time.

Much of the pioneering work in coronary artery bypass grafting was done by René Favoloro and Donald Effler, at the Cleveland Clinic, and by Dudley Johnson and Derward Lepley, in Milwaukee, beginning in late 1968. The first bypass procedures were tedious because of a lack of optimal suture material. Ideally, the vessels would have been joined with a continuous "running" suture. However, at the time, only silk or polyethylene sutures were available. Neither of these suture materials slid easily through the tissues, so surgeons had to tie each stitch before going on to the next. With the introduction of polypropylene suture, which was smooth and frictionless, surgeons were able to use a running stitch, so the procedure became easier and quicker to do. At that time, most of the bypasses were done with saphenous vein grafts. The surgeon would take a section of the saphenous vein from the patient's leg, cut an appropriately sized piece, and sew one end of the graft to the aorta and the other end to the diseased coronary artery beyond the site of the blockage. Blood would then flow through the graft, bypassing the blocked artery. It was later found that an artery in the chest wall, known as the internal mammary, made a more durable bypass graft than the saphenous vein.

Coronary artery bypass grafting soon became the most frequently performed cardiac operation. I was deluged with patients who needed the procedure. Many were so ill that they had been turned away by other surgeons. Houston's Hobby Field was dotted with chartered planes bringing patients to our city. Jokingly, the Shamrock Hilton Hotel, situated two blocks from the Medical Center, was dubbed the "Cooley Hilton" because many of my patients and their families stayed there. We were getting so busy that I decided we needed to add an official medical director for the Institute. Dr. Robert J. Hall agreed to accept this position. He had just retired as chief of cardiology at Walter Reed Army Hospital in Washington, D.C., where he had been responsible for the care of President Dwight D. Eisenhower before his death.

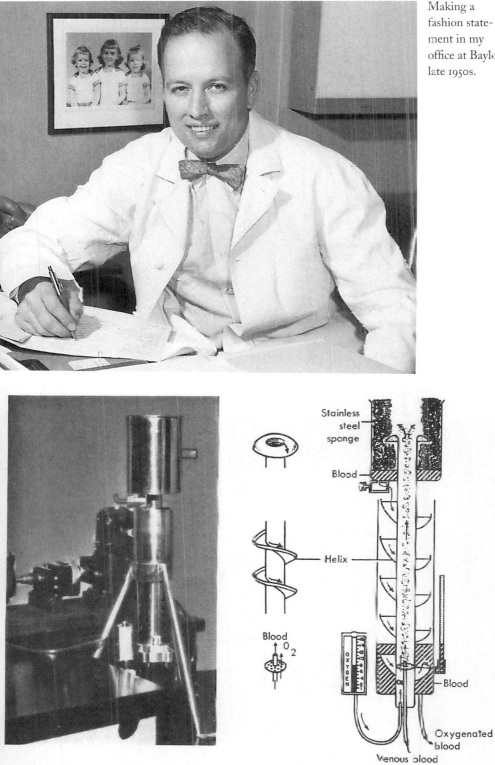

he Cooley "coffeepot" oxygenator and diagram showing how it worked. The original coffeepot is in the allace D. Wilson Museum at the Texas Heart Institute.

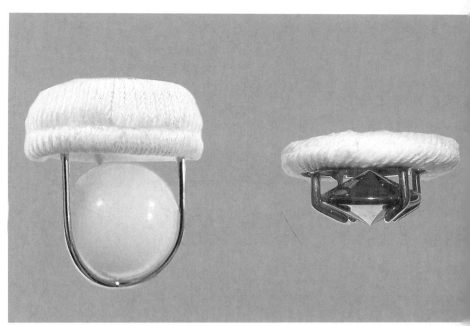

The Starr-Edwards caged-ball valve, which became available in the early 1960s for commercial use. Shown next to it is the Cooley-Cutter biconical disc valve, which I designed with engineering colleagues. The Cooley-Cutter was introduced commercially in 1971.

King Leopold and Princess Lilian of Belgium. Princess Lilian was an early supporter of open heart surgery.

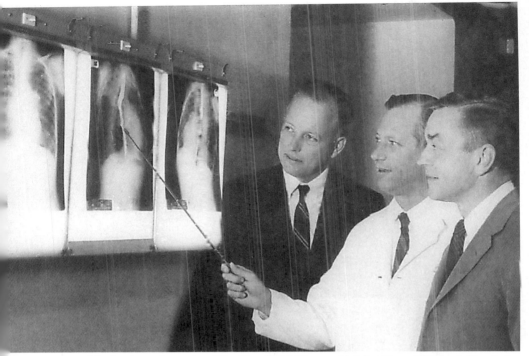

With Dr. Edward B. Singleton (center) and Dr. Dan G. McNamara (right) at Texas Children's Hospital in the early 1950s.

he four-story expansion of the southern wing (foreground) of the hospitals, which gave more space to H, ca. 1985.

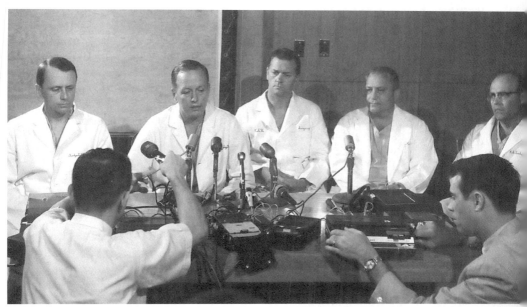

At a press conference with my colleagues at St. Luke's Episcopal Hospital after Everett Thomas's transplant operation, which was the first successful heart transplant in the United States. Left to right: Grady Hallman, me, Robert Bloodwell, Arthur Keats, and Robert Leachman.

With Christiaan Barnard in Washington, D.C., during the early days of the transplant era.

n Cape Town, South Africa, for the First International Human Heart Transplant Conference in July 968. Sixteen pioneers in cardiac surgery were invited. Chris Barnard gave each of us a gift of an ostrich gg with a personal message from him. The conference participants signed additional eggs for each other.

y ostrich eggs from the Cape Town meeting, which are now displayed in the Wallace D. Wilson useum at THI. Chris wrote, "To Denton, with best wishes to a wonderful friend and the best surgeon I ow. Chris Barnard, Cape Town, July 16, 1968."

Included in this 1968 photo at a press conference during the Cape Town meeting are transplant pioneers (front row, left to right) C. Walton Lillehei, me, P. K. Sen, Adrian Kantrowitz, Edward Stinson and (back row, left to right) James Pierce, Christiaan Barnard, Miguel Bellizzi, and Jean-Paul Cachera.

Waterskiing with the "aid" of Chris Barnard at Cypress Gardens, Florida, in 1970.

verett Thomas, the first successful heart transplant recipient in the United States, working in the trust epartment of a bank in the Texas Medical Center after his transplant.

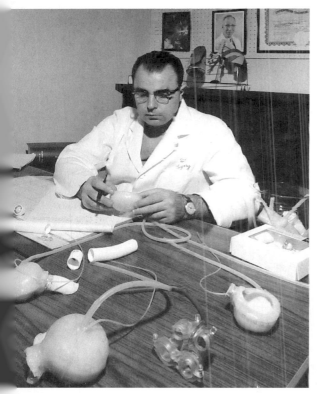

Dr. Domingo Liotta shown with the various parts of the artificial heart.

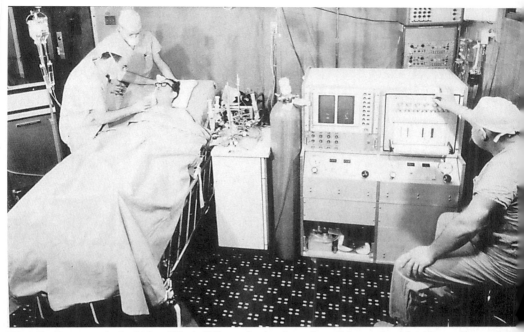

With Dr. Liotta at the bedside of Haskell Karp after implantation of the total artificial heart. Biomedical engineer John Jurgens sits at the control console and regulates the artificial heart's function.

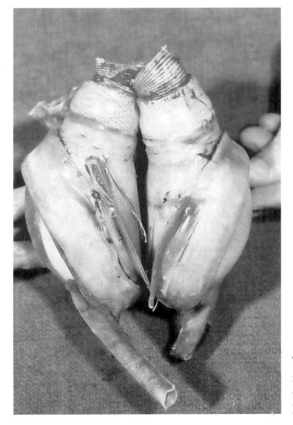

The Liotta artificial heart used in the historic 1969 operation. This heart is now displayed in the Smithsonian Institution in Washington, D.C.

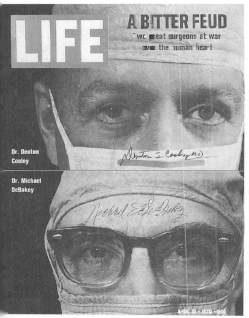

ife cover, April 10, 1970. The magazine featured
story about the feud with Mike DeBakey that
esulted from the implant of the artificial heart.
9 1970 Time Inc. *Life* is a registered trademark of
ime Inc.

Life cover September 1981. The magazine story
described my implantation of the world's second
total artificial heart implant in a human. The
Akutsu III heart was implanted at the Texas
Heart Institute in July 1981. *Life* is a registered
trademark of Time Inc. Artificial heart photograph by Enrico Ferorelli. © Ferorelli 2011.
Soldier photograph by Dennis Brack, used with
permission.

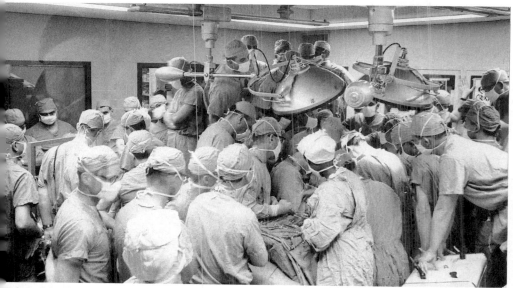

yday of the Cooley Hilton era. Visiting surgeons crowded the THI operating rooms to observe coro-
y artery bypass surgery. This image inspired the painting by Mary Cooley Craddock on the back cover
this book.

Dr. Helen Taussig and Dr. Dan McNamara at the Texas Heart Institute in March 1970. Dr. Taussig was attending a conference at THI.

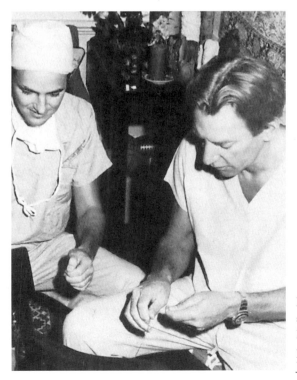

Dr. Jim Livesay, when he was a resident, showing actor Donald Sutherland how to tie knots in surgical sutures, 1980. Sutherland w preparing for his role in the movie *Threshold* Jim Livesay is now one of my associates.

Reaching a major milestone with my associates at THI: 100,000 open heart operations, January 10, 2001. Standing, left to right: Charles Hallman, Grady Hallman, George Reul, O. H. (Bud) Frazier, Jim Livesay, Mike Duncan, and David Ott.

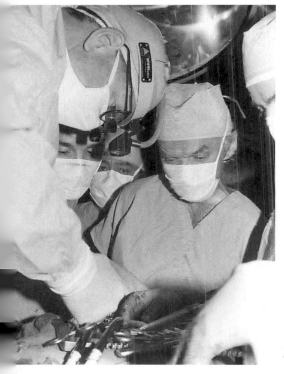

Dr. C. Walton Lillehei observes an operation at THI. I am on the left.

In my office between surgical cases. The office was just a few steps away from the operating room.

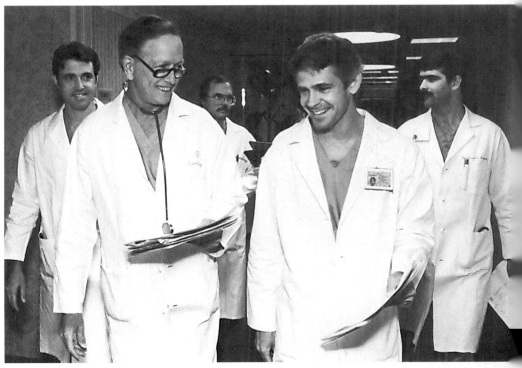

With a few of my trainees on daily rounds. Left to right: O. Jay Chastain, me, William Wallace, John R. Garrett, and Bill Johnson, ca. 1986.

With Princess Grace in Monaco at the first international DAC Society meeting in 1979.

At the DAC Society meeting luau on Maui, 1986.
One of my former residents, Dr. Doug Grey, and
his daughter, Emily, are in the background.

With Princess Anne and Dr. Bud Frazier at the 1984 DAC Society reception at the Café Royal
London.

Pioneers in Cardiac Surgery dinner at the Fairmont Hotel in San Francisco, 1980. Seated, left to right: Me, C. Walton Lillehei (Minneapolis), Dwight Harken (Boston), Conrad Lam (Detroit). Standing, left to right: Charles Hufnagel (Washington, D.C.), Viking Björk (Stockholm), Frank Gerbode (San Francisco), Henry Swan II (Denver), Charles Bailey (New York), Wilfred Bigelow (Toronto).

Founding members of the Senior Cardiovascular Surgical Society. Left to right: James A. DeWeese, me, Richard J. Cleveland, Mortimer J. Buckley, James W. MacKenzie, Paul A. Ebert, John L. Ochsner, Jay L. Ankeney, George J. Magovern Sr., John E. Connolly. Not shown are Harvey W. Bender and Norman E. Shumway.

With Susan, our neighbor Carolyn "Honey Bear" Wolters, Louise, and Mother in 1958 at the Fat Stock Show parade in downtown Houston.

With my family in 1960 (clockwise: Me, Weezie, Susan, Louise, Mary, Florence, and Helen on my lap).

Playing my bass with the Heartbeats in 1965. Grady Hallman, leader of the band, is in the back row, third from left. I'm at the far right.

With Louise and Pope Paul VI.

Aerial view of Cool Acres on the Brazos River, Orchard, Texas.

Watching a softball game at a Texas Heart Institute picnic at Cool Acres.

With grandsons John Plumb and William Walker on "Muscle Beach" during a weekend at our Galveston beach house, the "Cooley Bunkport," in the mid-1980s.

With the family at Helen's wedding to Chuck Fraser in December 1983. Back row, left to right: Me, Mary, Weezie, Susan, and Louise. Front row: Helen and Florence.

Rafting the Salmon River with the Frasers. We had been attending the OAC Society meeting in Sun Valley, Idaho, in 1996. From the front (left to right): Chuck Fraser, Helen Cooley Fraser, a friend, Louise, me, Will, Gracie, Laura, Charlie, and our guide.

With Louise and our sixteen grandchildren (eight boys and eight girls).

With the family on the occasion of our fiftieth wedding anniversary celebration in 2008.

Giving tennis my best shot.

Golfing with Paul Marchand, the pro at the Houston Country Club; Greg Norman, the famous Australian golfer; and Don Houchin, the husband of my clinical coordinator, Dena. I am the one with the "great" swing.

With golfing buddies Johnny Ochsner, George H. W. Bush, and James Baker III at the Seniors Golf Tournament, River Oaks Country Club, Houston. Johnny asked me who would fill out our foursome, and I honestly did not know. We were both astounded when we learned that George and James would be joining us. I found a photographer in the club to record the event.

Thanksgiving at Cool Acres, with family and friends at the treehouse overlooking the Brazos River.

With Mike DeBakey after the ceremony on April 23, 2008, in Washington, D.C., where Mike received the Congressional Gold Medal. Mike's invited guests included (left to right) Dr. Charles McCollum, Dr. George Noon, Dr. Matthias Loebe, me, Dr. O. H. Frazier, Dr. Charles Brunicardi, and Dr. Tony Herring

With Mike DeBakey on May 2, 2008, at the Michael E. DeBakey International Surgical Society meeting. I was given an honorary membership in the society and a Lifetime Achievement Award. Dr. George Noon, who helped in our reconciliation, is at the table directly behind us. Dr. Charles Fraser is in the next row back, slightly to the right.

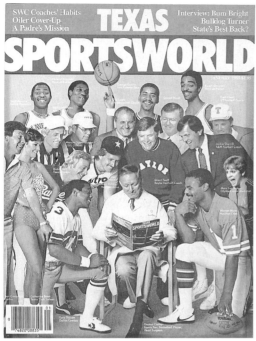

Cover of *Texas Sportsworld*, January 1985—proving to me that I could be both "a good doc and a good jock."

At the dedication of the Denton A. Cooley Center at Johns Hopkins in 1981.

Dedication of the Denton A. Cooley Pavilion at the University of Texas, Austin, February 19, 2004. Left to right: Rick Barnes, men's basketball coach; Louise; Jody Conradt, women's basketball coach; me; and Mack Brown, football coach.

Shooting a basket at the UT Cooley Pavilion dedication.

2nd Annual Memorial Park Conservancy Golf Tournament

May 22, 2007

Memorial Park
Conservancy, Inc.

With some "Garden Club" members: Ed Turley, John Cook, and Richard Andrassy.

The Texas Medical Center (looking north), ca. 2011. The largest healthcare complex in the world, it is soon expected to surpass the area of downtown Houston (in the distance). This photo is quite a contrast to the size of the medical center in 1951 when I first came to Baylor University College of Medicine. The arrow marks the location of the Texas Heart Institute at St. Luke's Episcopal Hospital.

The Denton A. Cooley Building (dedicated in 2002) at the Texas Heart Institute at St. Luke's Episcopal Hospital.

With Dr. James T. Willerson, who took over from me as president of the Texas Heart Institute in 2008.

With the addition of Dr. Hall, THI's reputation continued to grow and brought more attention to Houston as a cardiovascular center.

However, in one instance we didn't get the attention we thought we deserved. In 1972 THI had its 10,000th open heart case, a number that included about 1,900 coronary artery bypasses. Not only was this number of overall cases huge, but our survival rate of 98 percent was also amazing for the time. The story was offered to the medical editor of *Life* magazine, who said that another story about heart surgery was already scheduled, so a second one wasn't needed. "Call us back if you do something exciting," he said. As we later found out, the article that bumped our story from *Life* was about my trainee Ted Diethrich and his recent founding of the Arizona Heart Institute.

In 1980 we had our busiest year ever. My associates and I performed more than five thousand open heart procedures in that year alone! No other center could ever begin to compete with this number. As the senior surgeon, I oversaw as many as thirty operations a day and typically did about eight or ten of the most difficult ones myself. The others were done by my associates. We were able to maintain such a high volume of cases because the junior surgeons did the routine parts of the operation, such as opening the patient's chest, establishing the connections to the heart-lung machine, and later closing the chest. When it was time for the actual heart operation, I or one of my associate surgeons took over. Although this approach reminded some visiting physicians of an assembly line, it enabled us to benefit the most patients in the time available.

We had so many patients that we did our 50,000th open heart operation in 1982. Until the advent of computerization in the 1990s, our statistician, Mary McReynolds, kept track of all procedures by recording the data on three-by-five–inch index cards. She kept separate lists for each type of procedure we might do. When I wanted to write a paper, I'd ask Mary to compile the data for me. If I needed something especially complex, she would have to sort through all the cards and copy the information. I am still amazed that, with just a pencil, she could provide everything we needed.

So many people wanted bypass surgery that countries without heart centers couldn't begin to handle the volume. As a result, many of my patients came from overseas. Two European countries even organized airlifts to transport heart patients to Houston. In 1976 THI signed an agreement with the government of the Netherlands to repair the hearts of a large group of Dutch citizens who would otherwise have had to be on a long waiting list for surgery. At that time, the Netherlands had a backlog of about five thousand heart patients. We agreed to do the procedures at a modest, fixed cost that would be paid by the Dutch government. We called the program the Dutch Airlift. Even with airfare and accommodations for the patients and their families, we could still do the procedures cheaper at THI than they could be done in Holland. Every two weeks for nearly three years, the airlift brought about fifteen patients to THI via a KLM-contracted flight. The patients were often accompanied by a physician and, in most cases, a family member also came along. Every time a new group arrived, the previous group would be flown back, so most patients were home within two weeks of their operation. Ultimately, 1,500 Dutch patients were involved. While it lasted, the airlift was a boon to both THI and the Dutch people. By 1980 a government-sponsored heart program had become active in the Netherlands, so the airlift was no longer needed. About that time, THI established a similar airlift with the Yugoslavian government that brought about ten heart patients a month to Houston.

The airlifts were formal arrangements, but many other patients from around the world were referred to me by physicians I had trained. As early as 1965 I had begun to accept heart surgeons from other countries as "fellows." The term "fellowship" was used to differentiate this training program from our thoracic residency program. The fellows were qualified surgeons in their own countries but sought an opportunity at THI to see rare heart cases and complex repairs that they would seldom have had a chance to observe otherwise. They learned new surgical techniques and ways to apply them in their own practices, which may have involved conditions that were far from ideal. We sometimes had as many as thirty foreign trainees a year. With so many different cultures represented here, THI was like a mini United Nations. This has always been one of our special strengths. The fellows were also another important reason why our case load increased in the 1970s and 1980s. Once they returned home, cases that they couldn't handle were often referred to me and my associates.

• • •

My work with foreign patients and surgeons led to some of my more memorable overseas trips. One of the strangest trips I took was to the Philippines. Some of the young surgeons from there who had trained at THI had begun to send Filipino patients to me for heart surgery. Imelda Marcos, the wife of Philippine president Ferdinand Marcos, knew of THI's program and became interested in creating a similar one in the Philippines. She led the effort to establish the Philippine Heart Center for Asia, supposedly as a surprise for the president. In February 1975 she and the president invited Louise and me to be their honored guests at the opening of the center. I agreed to go, though I was somewhat reluctant because of the political climate in the Philippines at the time. Three years earlier, Marcos had imposed martial law in reaction to a Communist guerilla movement, so security was tight. At the time of my visit, Marcos hadn't been tarnished by the extensive corruption and other controversies that would eventually cause his downfall.

In Manila, Louise and I stayed in the historical Malacañang Palace, in quarters that had been used by General MacArthur. The palace was partly surrounded by a high wall with machine-gun posts and armed sentries on top. We attended the festivities, parades, and conferences for the opening of the heart center. I also remember rushing from one athletic activity to another—all arranged by President Marcos, who was an avid sportsman. He first invited me to play golf. There was a nine-hole course laid out on the other side of the Pasig River from the main palace. But the first tee was on the palace side, so the ball had to clear the river to the fairway on the other side, more than a hundred yards away. Thankfully, my drive reached the fairway. After teeing off, we were ferried across the river by a military launch, where we finished the game. I was relieved that the president was no better a golfer than I was. As we played, guards with machine guns patrolled the high wall around the course.

We then went back to the palace and played pelota, which is sort of like American handball or paddleball. I'd never played pelota before but managed to win a few games. The next day, we moved to the president's seaside home, where we played yet more pelota. Afterward, we went aboard the presidential yacht, and President Marcos asked if

I could water ski. I water skied a lot back in Texas so was confident I would do well. He insisted that I go first, so I got into the water, put on the skis, grabbed the line attached to the ski boat, and took off. I made a number of passes around the yacht, then let the president have his turn. While he was getting ready, several frogmen dove into the water and swam around, obviously looking for something. "What are they doing?" I asked a nearby official. "Before the president jumps into the water, they want to make sure that you didn't attract any sharks," he replied.

The following day, Louise and I boarded the president's private jet to go to a picturesque mountain area for a picnic. On the way, we stopped at Baguio City to watch a graduation ceremony at the Philippine Military Academy. We were leaving for home right after the picnic and were dressed for the flight back to the United States. As the cadets marched past the viewing stand, the president leaned over and whispered, "Shall we play another game of golf this afternoon before you get away?" With that, he summoned a two-star general, who raced up and saluted, probably expecting some critical order. "We need some appropriate clothing and golf shoes for Dr. Cooley," Marcos commanded. I was amazed that they could find anything to fit me on such short notice. After the whirlwind of sporting events and banquets, I was ready to get back to the operating room.

• • •

I went to India several times during these years. Once, while I was in New Delhi, one of my former trainees scheduled me to perform a difficult coronary bypass operation on a critically ill woman at the All India Medical Center. At first, I declined because I didn't have my surgical magnifying glasses, called loupes, or my headlamp with me. I finally agreed to do the operation after much pleading by my trainee. The surgery was successful but, without my loupes and headlamp, extremely difficult. Later, I was scheduled to meet with Indira Gandhi, the Indian prime minister. At our meeting, I was shocked to learn that my surgical patient was a close relative of hers. I wondered why I hadn't been told beforehand.

In 1982 I did a bypass operation at THI on Giani Zail Singh, the president of India. He was grateful, warm, and friendly and invited me to visit him in the presidential palace in Delhi. It happened that I was going to Bombay for a meeting several months later, so I arranged to visit President Singh after the meeting. My flight from Bombay to Delhi was delayed, and I landed several hours late. The president was hosting a formal dinner in my honor, which was in progress by the time I arrived. A funny thing happened during the dinner. My hosts had gone to a lot of trouble to sculpt a replica of the THI *Symbol of Excellence* from an enormous chunk of ghee, or Indian butter. It was really hot in the room. About halfway through dinner, I noticed that the sculpture had melted down and was now one big, buttery lump. Among the dinner guests were high-ranking members of the Indian government, including the Indian secretary of state—none of whom mentioned the melted sculpture.

The secretary of state did ask me if I would enjoy a round of golf the next morning. I was rather surprised that important members of the government would be playing golf on a work day, but I accepted the invitation. I learned that they frequently played golf during the week on a course laid out on the palace grounds. Eight of us met there at 8:00 a.m.—most of the group had been at the dinner the evening before. Bets on the game were modest, but competition was brisk. Fortunately, I played well. At the end of nine holes, we broke for tea, which was served under a large banyan tree. After that, the officials moved on to their daily duties. I have a treasured memento from that Indian trip: a carved ivory blotter that I "borrowed" from the desk in my suite. The blotter is now on display in the museum at THI.

• • •

I recall one humorous moment that occurred during a press conference in Madrid, Spain, around that time. One of the reporters asked me what famous people I had performed surgery on. I thought for a moment and then answered that I had recently operated on President Giani Zail Singh of India. That information was met with no response. So I named Alexander Haig, U.S. secretary of state. No interest. Hoping to name someone the reporters might think famous, I mentioned the great opera star Gladys Swarthout, who was renowned for playing Carmen—but again no interest. Finally, I mentioned Whitey Ford, the famous New York Yankees baseball pitcher. Their faces immediately lit up. "You operated on *Whitey*!!" For the rest of the conference, we discussed the successful operation I'd performed months earlier to fix a blocked subclavian artery that had caused numbness in Whitey's left arm and hand. The reporters couldn't get enough of Whitey. They were even interested in my view of the upcoming U.S. baseball season.

I have many other stories from my travels—too many to mention in this book. I've been invited to operate and lecture throughout the world, have received countless medals from heads of state, and have gotten gifts from important foreign physicians, as well as ordinary people. These trips have been highlights of my career.

When foreign patients come to THI for surgery, they also often bring me gifts—small religious statues, women's perfume, caviar, and a varied assortment of other things. My office sometimes resembles an eclectic museum. A Middle Eastern patient showed up with a paper bag containing opium, which he said he'd used regularly since adolescence. He did not offer me any, but gave me candy instead. Once, a *New York Times* reporter spent two days interviewing me. Afterward, he said, "Dr. Cooley, I'm grateful that you gave me so much of your time. I have been trying to think of the perfect thank-you gift, but I see that you already have a jeweled, wooden peacock, and I'm not sure that you need two of them." The jeweled peacock, a gift from a grateful patient from Bombay, sits proudly at the entry to my office.

In 1981 the famous movie actor Donald Sutherland arrived at THI to learn how to "perform" heart surgery. He was to star in a movie called *Threshold*, which featured a surgeon doing a daring artificial heart operation against the orders of hospital authorities. Sutherland shadowed me and observed procedures in the operating room. My associate Jim Livesay, who was a resident at the time, showed him how to tie knots in sutures. Sutherland was tall and slender, like me. At one point, he was watching one of my associates operate, when a circulating nurse approached him from behind and said, "Dr. Cooley, may we get started in Room 3?" As soon as Sutherland looked around, she realized her mistake. Later, I played a minor part in the movie. On another occasion, I was shadowed by Chad Everett, who played the part of a surgeon in the TV series *Medical Center*.

• • •

In 1978 a catheter-based procedure called percutaneous transluminal coronary angioplasty, or balloon angioplasty, revolutionized the treatment of coronary artery disease and paved the way for other so-called interventional procedures—most of which are performed by cardiologists rather than surgeons. In balloon angioplasty, cardiologists use a catheter that has a small, expandable balloon on its tip to open coronary arteries blocked by plaque deposits. The catheter is inserted through a peripheral vessel and, under fluoroscopic vision, is advanced to the site of the blockage. The balloon is then inflated to flatten the plaque against the artery wall and restore blood flow. This procedure can be performed without general anesthesia and also has the advantage of avoiding cardiopulmonary bypass. Patients can recover much sooner than after bypass surgery. Cardiologists quickly became excited about this new procedure and began to recommend angioplasty over surgical bypass, when appropriate. It soon became clear, though, that restenosis could be a problem. To help keep the artery open, cardiologists developed a device called a stent—a small, metal scaffold—that is placed at the newly unblocked site. This has improved the results but hasn't completely solved the problem. Cardiologists and surgeons still disagree about whether a catheter-based procedure or a conventional bypass gives the best overall results. What started out as a rivalry between these two groups of physicians has settled down into a healthy "competition." Certainly, for uncomplicated coronary disease, angioplasty plus stent placement works well. As a surgeon, I still believe that coronary bypass is the gold standard, although at THI and most other heart centers, patients with coronary disease now undergo more interventional procedures than direct surgical procedures. Because angioplasty is done by cardiologists, not surgeons, it doesn't count toward the numbers of surgical operations performed by my team and me.

As angioplasties increased and bypasses decreased, I turned my focus back to some of my earlier interests. I still did bypass operations but also began developing new, innovative procedures for treating ventricular and aortic aneurysms, the procedures that had begun my career. It seems as if I never stop thinking about how to make a procedure better. Even when I'm asleep, I sometimes dream that I am doing an operation and working out ways to improve it.

In the late 1970s, I decided to modify the technique used for repairing left ventricular aneurysms—aneurysms that occur after a major heart attack. I developed a way to cut out the dead tissue and reline the ventricle with a Dacron patch, which returned the ventricle to its normal shape, allowing it to pump better and thereby improving heart function.[3] This procedure is now the standard method for repairing these types of aneurysms.

I also developed a technique for repairing aneurysms of the ascending aorta and arch by using hypothermia and temporary circulatory arrest with cardiopulmonary bypass.[4] Randall Griepp, in New York, was the original pioneer of this technique. With the body cooled, circulation could be stopped for about an hour without damage to the patient's organs, especially the brain. Without blood circulation, it was easy to visualize the aneurysm, cut it out, replace the vessel with a Dacron tube graft, and secure the repair site. Because I treated so many aneurysms, I quickly established that this procedure worked very well. Other surgeons soon began to use this simplified technique, and it became the standard for repairing these challenging aneurysms. I later modified it for treating aneurysms in the descending section of the aorta.[5]

I am very proud of these advances in the surgical repair of ventricular and aortic aneurysms and pleased that I have been able to refine the procedures that began my career in the 1950s. In all, I've repaired about 12,000 aortic aneurysms.

Despite the advent of interventional cardiology, our surgical program at THI remains a very active one. My associates and I have probably performed more open heart procedures than any other group of surgeons in the world. In 2001 we reached a huge milestone: *100,000 hearts*. It's hard to grasp how many hearts that is. If all of the patients were grouped together at once, their numbers would equal the population of Wichita, Kansas, or Peoria, Illinois, or Berkeley, California. This number doesn't include the thousands of operations we've performed that didn't involve open heart surgery. On the peripheral vessels alone, we've done more than 45,000 operations.

A small number of our patients were famous, but most of them were ordinary people—the girl down the block with congenital heart

---

[3] This procedure is called an endoaneurysmorrhaphy. It is explained in the *Texas Heart Institute Journal*, vol. 16 (1989), pp. 72–75. Although I started doing it in the late 1970s, I didn't publish anything about it at that time.

[4] This procedure is described in the journal *Circulation*, vol. 66 (1982), pp. 122–127.

[5] The technique of open distal anastomosis for repair of descending thoracic aortic aneurysms is explained in *The Annals of Thoracic Surgery*, vol. 54 (1992), pp. 932–936.

disease, the retired postmaster with heart failure, the college professor with an aortic aneurysm, the plumber with coronary disease, the corporate executive with a faulty valve. I consider all of them heroes, especially the ones who were willing to take the risk of being the first human being to undergo a new procedure.

Over the years, I have received thousands of letters from my patients. I've read all of them and kept many of them. I've done my best to respond to specific questions, and I still do. Some of my patients have thanked me, then given me suggestions for helping to prevent heart disease—some of them quite imaginative. I've gotten a lot of dietary advice. I still remember a recipe for okra gumbo that was suggested as a much better protein source than a beefsteak. There were suggestions for improving various devices used in heart surgery. One idea came from a young boy I'd operated on who dreamed of designing an artificial heart that could be sold for five dollars so that poor people could afford it. There were suggestions for curing cancer, halitosis, and other medical conditions unrelated to heart surgery These people seemed to be so grateful that they wanted to pass on advice to help others.

Not everyone was grateful, though. During the early days of heart transplantation, I received a few letters accusing me of violating a patient's soul or identity. I've also received some angry letters from loved ones of patients who had died. I always wrote back and acknowledged the writer's feelings. Some of the patients who died had been so sick that no other surgeon would have even considered operating on them. There was probably nothing anyone could have done to save these patients. I've always felt a sense of personal defeat whenever one of my patients has died. Some who I thought were doing well would develop complications in the recovery room or later during their hospital stay. Those cases have always haunted me, and I've gone over them in my head and tried to learn from each one.

One of the hard parts of being a surgeon is that once the operation is over and the patients leave the hospital, you seldom get to see them again. That's the desired result, of course, but I do often wonder how their lives turned out. One of the most dramatic and unusual stories was that of a patient who escaped from East Berlin to come to me for a valve replacement operation. He wrote me a letter in 2009, on the twentieth anniversary of the fall of the Berlin Wall. I remembered his case well. When he was a child, he had rheumatic fever that weakened his aortic valve, leaving it susceptible to infection. After numerous infections, his valve was so damaged that he was given less than five years to live. He was twenty-two at the time. In 1967 he was listening to a radio program from the American Sector in West Berlin that happened to mention my work. In his 2009 letter, he said:

> *I knew that very moment that I wanted you to repair my heart! I was very excited: there was hope after all. . . . I was ready to do anything to get to Houston. After three tries, I was able to climb over the wall in 1969. With the help of a cardiologist in West Berlin, I was able to arrange a date for you to operate on me. You even agreed to waive your professional fee. My friends paid for the travel, and I arrived in Houston on a hot, humid July night. My English was very poor, so it happened that my cab driver drove me to Methodist Hospital—where I ended up in Dr. DeBakey's office. I knew there was something wrong, as I'd seen a picture of you. It did not take very long to find a German-speaking person who realized that I wanted to be at St. Luke's. My surgery was a success, and two weeks later I stood on the shore of the Gulf of Mexico, in Galveston, and breathed the fresh air of a new world.*

Eventually, this man became a U.S. citizen, took a job with a technology company in Florida, got married, and had a family. In his letter to me, he said, "My 40-year-old Cooley-Cutter heart valve is still clicking happily ever after."

Other, more typical letters, which I keep in a special file, have brought me much pleasure. One was from a woman whose valve was replaced.

> *I'm pleased to tell you that my St. Jude #19 [valve] seems to be doing a fine job. I can hear it faintly clicking along like a best friend. I'm able to walk a mile or more without stopping, something I was unable to do before the surgery. I've also gone on marathon girlfriend shopping sprees without tiring. My housecleaning skills have improved (yuck), since I have so much more stamina and energy. I'm back on schedule working at my part-time job. Who could ask for more? So Dr. Cooley, all is well and progressing nicely. I will always be eternally grateful for your skill.*

Another letter was from a thankful man:

On September 9, 1962, when I was 12 years old, my mom and dad walked with me into Texas Children's Hospital. That was the day I met you—the doctor who was going to give me a "chance." I had been diagnosed with supravalvular aortic stenosis, and my surgery was set for September 12th. All went well, and I was home in Carmi, Illinois, on September 23rd. In high school, I participated in basketball and golf. I also played golf at Eastern Illinois University, and I still love to play the game.

My mother was a collector of anything that had information about your career. I have Time *magazines from 1968, newspaper articles from around the United States, and even a* Grit *newspaper that carried a story about you. I have followed your many accomplishments in newspapers, magazines, and now on the Internet. I have seen you recognized at professional sporting events. Recently, I was watching the PGA Tournament when they aired a segment sponsored by Buick that honored you.*

I know that I am one of 100,000 surgeries that you and your team have performed. Your talent gave each of us a gift—a chance to have a life. In my case, it also gave me the chance to walk my daughter down the aisle many years later. Dr. Cooley, you made that and so much more possible for me. I am forever grateful.

I also received a note recently from a patient who had come from Mexico: "After 43 years, I want to say thank you. Often I look at a picture of you and me taken in my hospital room. And I still feel your hug. Thank you, Doc, with all my repaired heart."

• • •

For an hour or so on the operating table, each of my patients had my total attention. Then another patient took precedence. In most cases, we were nearly strangers, yet all of these people put their hearts in my hands for a brief period. At the same time that I touched their hearts, they also touched mine.

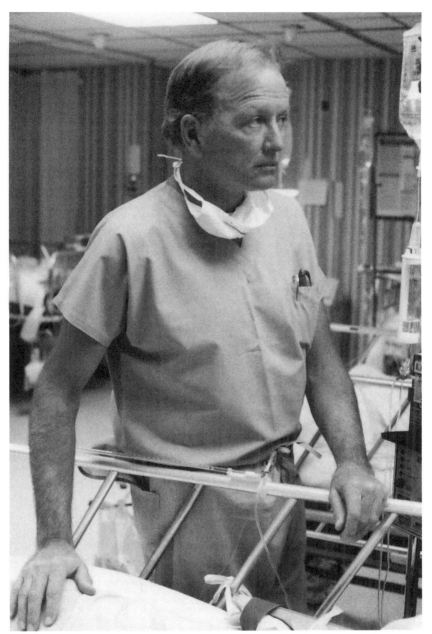

At a patient's bedside in the ICU, observing monitors of vital status, around 1980.

CHAPTER 15

On Being a Surgeon

O NCE WHEN I WAS A DEFENDANT in a medical liability trial, the plaintiff's lawyer asked if I considered myself the best heart surgeon in the world.

"Yes," I replied quietly.

"Don't you think that's being rather immodest?" the lawyer asked me.

"Perhaps," I responded. "But remember, I'm under oath."

The case was soon dismissed.

I do think that surgeons may be a little more egotistical than other doctors, perhaps because the public perceives surgery as involving dramatic, often life-or-death situations and surgeons as superheroes. Physicians in other specialties certainly accomplish as much, but the results may not be as immediate or obvious.

Combined with good mental and physical skills, excellent training, and solid experience, a strong ego can make the difference between a good surgeon and a great one. When I say ego, I mean a robust self-confidence and deep faith in one's ability to get the job done, whatever the situation. When an unexpected crisis occurs, self-confidence can be critical to a surgeon's ability to remain calm and cool, which may make the difference between success and failure. I often tell my trainees, only *half* jokingly, that a successful heart surgeon should be a physician who, when asked to name the three best surgeons in the world, would have trouble naming the other two.

An ego should never manifest itself in temper tantrums. I've already mentioned how I was often disappointed by Dr. Blalock's and Dr. DeBakey's behavior in difficult situations in the operating room. Such behavior may reveal a lack of self-confidence. A good team needs harmony and has no room for temperamental surgeons. I have visited many operating rooms around the world and have seen many celebrity surgeons, and others have visited me. Those I admire the most are even-tempered. They treat their assistants and nurses well and don't abuse their team members.

I've always tried to choose associates who were not temperamental and whose behavior I admired in the operating room. Currently, I have ten associates in my practice, which is called Surgical Associates of Texas. They joined me in the following order: Grady L. Hallman, George J. Reul, O. H. (Bud) Frazier, David A. Ott, J. Michael Duncan, James J. Livesay, Charles H. Hallman (Grady's son), Igor D. Gregoric, Ross M. Reul (George's son), and Jennifer Del Prete. George has served for many years as my associate chief of surgery at THI. In 2004 we were also able to recruit William E. (Billy) Cohn to join our surgical, transplant, and mechanical circulatory support service. Former associates are E. Ross Kyger (deceased), John C. Norman (retired), Frank M. Sandiford (deceased), William E. Walker (retired), and Don C. Wukasch (retired).

In the operating room, I have always been proud to be not only the captain but also an integral part of the team. A good captain understands his teammates, including their skills and limitations. He must encourage his team and not be overly critical of misdeeds or mistakes. I've heard that in World War I, when soldiers followed their second lieutenants out of the trenches, the officers were sometimes shot in the back rather than in the chest. I hope my team knows that I am always there not only to lead them but also to back them up, even when they make mistakes.

People have told me that I am a good leader. If they're right, then my style of leading by example, not by force, has been successful. I believe there are different ways, small and large, in which a person can show leadership. For instance, punctuality is important to me. I come to work every morning at the same time. My staff members always know exactly when I'll arrive. I remain until I complete my work for the day. When I get up in the morning, I appreciate the fact that people are waiting for me to show up and that I might be able to help them. I think being able to help people is a great privilege.

At the height of my surgical career, I would set my alarm for 5:00 a.m. every day. Even on Sundays, when I didn't have cases scheduled,

I had difficulty sleeping past 5:00 or 6:00. On regular days, I usually left home just before 6:00, arrived at the hospital fifteen minutes later, and did paperwork until patient rounds began—at 6:30 or 6:45. During rounds, I conferred with the residents about the day's scheduled surgery and visited patients who had recently been operated on. Occasionally, I attended lectures that were held before the schedule began. By the time my first patient was ready for me in the operating room, it was 7:45. I stayed in the operating room most of the day, often for six-hour stretches or even longer if necessary. At lunch, I returned to my office and had a bowl of soup or cup of yogurt. As I got older, I might spend twenty or thirty minutes napping on my couch afterward. Generally, I finished my operating room schedule by about 4:00 p.m., after which I attended to administrative duties or staff meetings. I made rounds with my residents again around 6:00 and saw the postoperative patients and those listed on the next day's surgical schedule. I usually got home about 8:30, but sometimes it was later. After chatting with Louise and checking on my daughters, I might watch a little television or read the newspaper while eating dinner, often from a TV tray.

One thing that I looked forward to at the end of a busy day was having some time to write, which has always been important to me. Academically oriented surgeons have to publish to stay competitive. I have written half a dozen textbooks on surgical techniques and have contributed chapters to many others. Since 1947 I have authored or coauthored about 1,400 scientific articles. At the height of my career, I had to do my writing between 9:00 p.m. and midnight, or even later, if I wanted to avoid interruptions. That reminds me of a few lines from one of my favorite poems, "The Ladder of St. Augustine" by Henry Wadsworth Longfellow, a copy of which hangs on a wall near my desk.

> The heights by great men reached and kept
> Were not attained by sudden flight,
> But they, while their companions slept,
> Were toiling upward in the night.

When I was up late working in my ground-floor study, Louise would often call down from the bedroom and ask what I was doing. I'd reply, "I'm toiling upward in the night."

I learned many of the skills that have been important to me throughout my surgical career by participating in team sports. In surgery, as in basketball, it is imperative to perform well under pressure. When an unexpected problem arises during an operation, I always tried to remain composed, which helped my team stay cool and confident. My exposure to competitive sports taught me to make decisions quickly and to act on them. In addition, I learned endurance, which later helped me, as a surgeon, to work fifteen-hour days with very few breaks.

When I played basketball, tennis, or golf, I enjoyed winning, but I also sometimes had to accept loss. In heart surgery, loss is also inevitable but on a much more tragic scale. I have generally made it a policy to avoid operating on a friend, but occasionally someone has insisted. One of the saddest cases of my career involved a routine heart procedure that I performed on one of my closest friends. Ninety minutes after the procedure, my friend died in the recovery room. It was a freakish turn of events. Another close friend died suddenly when his coronary artery became blocked by a clot two days after I had performed a straightforward operation on his lung. Whether it involves an old and dear friend or someone who has just been referred to me, the death of a patient affects me deeply. Different people have different ways of handling such tragedies. For me, the best way has always been to continue working.

Throughout my career, I've also had to deal with the business side of surgery. I'll always be grateful to Gerald A. Maley, who was the administrator for the Cardiovascular Surgical Service at Baylor and who came with me to THI in 1969, when I resigned my Baylor position. Jerry was the first president of THI and was a long-standing member of the board of trustees.

Many people who grew up during the Great Depression, as I did, have a keen awareness of the value of money and the folly of waste. Today, too few doctors seem to worry about how much things cost. I have always tried to save costs in the operating room. If I considered something too high-priced, I looked for a safe, less-expensive alternative. Sometimes, I would even create my own version at a much lower cost. In 1973 I started a company called Texas Medical Products, which manufactured disposable equipment for open heart surgery at about 20 percent of the cost charged by some of the nationwide firms. Eventually, my company was so successful that it was bought out. Another example of my cost-cutting measures was the Cooley annuloplasty ring, which was used to reduce the size of an enlarged mitral valve opening. I created the rings by slicing segments from Dacron grafts[1] left over from other procedures. A large national company was selling a similar product for $1,800. Mine cost nothing to make, and the patient wasn't charged a dime for it.

The cost of health care was skyrocketing in the early 1980s, in part because medicine had become more high-tech. I had always prided myself on keeping my fees low, and I now had an idea for a plan that could help employers keep their healthcare costs down. Because of THI's large volume of patients, we'd learned to be very efficient yet provide exceptional care. One day, I was visiting with a friend of mine who was the medical director of Tenneco, a Houston-based multinational company that self-insured its employees. He mentioned that heart surgery costs varied widely from one hospital to another but said that THI's costs were always the lowest. I told him I was working on a plan that would "bundle" all the services involved in a heart operation and charge a fixed fee. He was interested in the concept. I talked to my surgical associates, some THI cardiologists, the head of anesthesiology, and the St. Luke's administrators about my idea for a packaged-pricing plan that we could offer insurers, companies that self-insured their employees, and even the Health Care Finance Administration, or Medicare.

Thus, in 1984, CardioVascular Care Providers (CVCP) was born It was the first-ever packaged-pricing plan for cardiovascular surgery, and it quickly became popular with many companies in Houston. Under this plan, which is still in effect, we offer cardiac care at a flat rate, which is lower than the sum of the individual charges from the separate physician groups and the hospital. So insurers or companies that sign up with CVCP get only one bill. If someone needs a bypass operation, the flat fee covers everything associated with that procedure. The plan lowers costs while maintaining a high quality of care. It also increases patient access to surgical procedures, avoids unnecessary diagnostic tests, allows payers to predict their expenses, and streamlines the billing process. The concept was later adopted by Medicare and is now the basis for many other similar types of plans. In the 1980s

---

[1] The annuloplasty ring is described in *The Annals of Thoracic Surgery*, vol. 55 (1993), pp. 185–186.

this was a radical, new approach to health care and was in contrast to insurance-based forms of managed care that were becoming popular, such as health maintenance organizations. When I explained the plan and its success to prominent heart surgeon Dwight Harken, of Boston, he laughed and said, "Denton, you are providing Tiffany quality at Woolworth prices." Looking back from 2011, I can see that the plan was easily twenty years ahead of its time. I count it as one of my major accomplishments.

• • •

I have always tried to avoid letting my fees stand in the way of a desperately needed treatment. I created a special fund and have solicited donations from my more affluent patients to pay hospital costs for deserving, indigent heart patients. In every such case, I have deferred my fee. Some of my financial relationships with my patients have been rather humorous. For instance, I recall some years ago charging a modest $345 for closing a patent ductus arteriosus in the young daughter of a plumber. On receiving my bill, he was irate. He explained to my secretary that he was a master plumber and charged $38 an hour. He knew that the operation had lasted only about forty-five minutes, which meant that I was charging $460 an hour. "You're not that much better than I am," he complained. "Well, maybe you're *twice* as good, I'll grant you that, but no more." He sent me a check for $100, which I accepted with amusement.

In the earlier part of my career, barter was also sometimes used as a means of payment. One man paid for a family member's surgery by agreeing to build a carport onto my house. I provided all the materials, and the man was doing a satisfactory job—at least until he was halfway finished. He then asked for $75 in cash to buy groceries for his family, and I gave it to him. I never saw him again. Unfortunately, he left in the middle of August. Anybody who's ever been to Houston in August will know how sweltering that month is. So I'm not sure why I decided to continue the work myself. It seemed that every time I got up on the roof and started adding shingles, I'd get a call that I was needed at the hospital. I'll confess that I was thankful for those calls. Finally, I hired a carpenter to finish the project.

I also accepted an offer from a tree surgeon in exchange for my doing a mitral valve repair on his wife. He said that he was strapped for cash and asked whether he could work off my fee by trimming the three large pecan trees in my yard. I agreed to the arrangement. Several days later, I saw him leaving the yard after trimming only two of the trees. I asked why he hadn't finished the job. He replied, "Doc, I charge $250 to trim a large tree, and your bill was $500, so that makes us even. You know, tree surgery is expensive!" I told him that I'd once considered becoming a tree surgeon but "couldn't stand the sight of sap." That was my last experience with bartering for services.

· · ·

As I look back on my career, I'm grateful that I never departed from the academic side of surgery I believe that an institutional environment is essential to a successful surgical career. Although most physicians are encouraged to teach, those who aren't affiliated with academic institutions seldom do. At THI, the academic program has been a major success. I'm fortunate that my medical mentors ingrained in me an obligation to pass my knowledge on to others. One of my favorite activities is teaching residents and other trainees, many of whom are from foreign countries. I also *learn* through teaching, because it requires me to study, read, reflect, and organize my thinking. Surgery has traditionally been an art passed on from master to apprentice, and this method still works well today. Sometimes it works equally well in reverse. I also think that belonging to professional societies and participating in their programs is an important part of any surgical career.[2]

To me, the art of surgery involves doing everything as gracefully and efficiently as possible. Given a choice between two or more techniques, I have generally picked the one that is the most straightforward. "The secret is that the fingers never leave the hands," I've sometimes joked. Like accomplished pianists, surgeons need to use their sixth sense and develop "brains in their fingers." My guiding principle has always been "modify, simplify, and apply," which is the motto of the Denton A. Cooley Cardiovascular Surgical Society (DAC Society). This academic society was formed in 1972 by my trainees as a tribute to me. It now has more than 850 physician members represent-

[2] I belong to more than thirty such societies and hold honorary memberships in many more. (See Appendix F.)

ing forty-four states and forty-nine countries. I'm proud of the society and its symposia, which provide opportunities for education, scientific exchange, and camaraderie.

Although the scientific sessions have a serious purpose, I always encourage the DAC Society members to make the meetings a family affair, and my daughters and their families have enjoyed being included in these events. The society has chosen destinations where everyone could also vacation, and we have tried to make the meetings entertaining. Part of the fun has been to surprise the attendees during the informal family events. My trainees still kid me about the grass skirt I wore to the luau on Maui. Then there was the golf outfit that I wore in Bermuda—a red jacket, pink necktie, pair of black Bermuda shorts, and knee-length white socks. My favorite costume was a ringmaster's outfit. That was the year when the meeting was held in Colorado Springs and sported a circus theme. Dr. John Ochsner, our honoree[3] that year, dressed as a lion tamer.

A few other DAC Society meetings also stand out in my memory. Our first international meeting was held in Monaco in 1979. Princess Grace was an honored guest at a reception before the gala dinner. She was everything a princess should be—charming, beautiful, and regal. The next day, we attended a party at a private residence in the hills overlooking the city. Princess Grace and Prince Rainier came and brought their thirteen-year-old daughter, Stéphanie. Princess Grace was standing near me, visiting with the guests. When she and the prince were ready to leave, she turned toward the pool, where Stéphanie was swimming with the other children. She said quietly, "Your father and I are ready to go home now. Please get out of the pool, so we can leave." Stéphanie continued to swim. Princess Grace repeated her request a little more loudly. Stéphanie still kept swimming. At that point, Princess Grace went to the edge of the pool, put her hands on her hips, and shouted, "Stéphanie, we're not waiting any longer. Get out of the pool—NOW!" I was amused by this shift in her role from princess to mother. Our trip to the party took us along the same winding road that Princess Grace and Stéphanie would drive on the fateful day of the accident that claimed Princess Grace's life in 1982.

---

[3] Each year, the DAC Society honors a leader in the field of cardiovascular medicine or surgery. (See Appendix E.)

In 1984 the DAC Society held its meeting at the stately Grosvenor House Hotel in London. We convinced the hotel manager to fly the Texas Heart Institute flag along with the Union Jack at the hotel's entrance. One morning we woke up to a twenty-one-gun salute, which was *not* for us but was, rather, for announcing the birth of Prince Harry. The morning's headline read, "An Heir and a Spare." That evening, Princess Anne attended the reception held before our gala dinner at the Café Royal. She had previously visited THI so was familiar with our work. At the reception, Bud Frazier and I gave Anne a small, engraved THI *Symbol of Excellence*. Unfortunately, neither he nor I had brought our reading glasses, and we couldn't quite make out what was inscribed on the thing. So I peered at it and guessed at the words. As the princess accepted the *Symbol*, she quipped, "Well, it *almost* says that." For a short time afterward, she stayed to greet the guests. So many people wanted to meet her that a crowd quickly formed. Louise graciously guided people so that as many as possible could meet the princess. During the dinner, we were surprised by a muffled beat coming from behind the red velvet curtains at one side of the room. The sound grew louder, the curtains opened, and the Queen's Coldstream Guards marched out. They filed around our tables and gave an unforgettable performance.

In 1992 my previous residents joined together to form another society in my honor called the Cooley Hands. Membership is limited to residents who have completed their full two- or three-year training program at THI. The Cooley Hands are also all members of the DAC Society, but the objectives of the two groups are different. Through their dues and annual contributions, the Cooley Hands fund a variety of educational activities for the residents and support the residency program. Many of the Cooley Hands now lead cardiovascular surgery departments or surgical practices, so they also form an important network that can help graduating residents find positions in academics or private practice. Traditionally, the Cooley Hands have met in conjunction with the Society of Thoracic Surgeons. I am proud to say that I was president of the Society of Thoracic Surgeons in 1993.

* * *

Being a surgeon has been extraordinarily satisfying. I'm very fortunate to have found a profession that is suited not only for my personality and level of intelligence but also for my physical abilities. I am also especially fortunate to have become involved in cardiovascular surgery when it was a new field.

I've worked very hard at being a surgeon. If I weren't at the top of my game, patients could die, so I always played the game full tilt. Before each heart operation, I made a conscious effort to prepare myself, to psych myself up to a peak of readiness—just as I would do in a basketball game. I wanted my entire team to feel that no one in the world could handle the surgery any better. I'm known for my speed as a surgeon, but it wasn't simply a matter of being fast. The key was having a game plan: knowing what I wanted to do, then thinking through the easiest, best, and quickest way to do it. I've been described as a "no-wasted-motion" surgeon, and I do like to keep things simple. Even when I've occasionally had personal injuries, I've tried to carry on without a fuss. In the early 1990s, however, I went too far. I severely fractured my left wrist while playing tennis and immediately "set" the fracture myself before leaving the court. Afterward, I stayed out of the operating room for a day or two but couldn't stand not being there. So I removed the splint and went back to operating. The bone healed improperly, and I now suffer from arthritis in that wrist.

I've often been asked what advice I might give to young surgeons. I've always believed that success in any field starts with desire, persistence, and hard work. Surgery is both an art and a science. It depends on book knowledge and practical skill, as well as good judgment and the ability to handle the unexpected. I learned early in my career that time in the operating room is precious. Even just a few seconds can make the difference between the patient's life and death. When everything goes as it should, it's exhilarating to walk away from an operation and know you have done a good job—that the patient is going to do extremely well.

Dr. and Mrs. "Darl" and their Rolls Royce.

CHAPTER 16

Private Life

I AM FORTUNATE TO HAVE A WONDERFUL WIFE AND FAMILY. Like most other men, I always wanted a son. But all of *my* sons turned out to be daughters! Starting in 1950, a baby girl came along about every two years until there were five—Mary, Susan, Louise ("Weezie"), Florence, and Helen. I'd mostly been involved in male-dominated activities—especially sports, fraternities, and surgery. Nothing in my life had prepared me for dealing with so many girls at one time. Doing so gave me a new appreciation for the female sex.

As the daughter of a surgeon, Louise understood what our lives would be like when we married back in 1949. She has always been very supportive of me, and our partnership has been typical of married couples of our generation. The gender roles were fairly standard. As the husband, I was the breadwinner. Even though Louise previously worked as a registered nurse, her role in our marriage centered on raising the girls and ensuring that the household ran smoothly. As a result, my free time was unencumbered. When I was home, I could relax and enjoy my family. These days, "togetherness" is emphasized, but back in the 1950s and 1960s, fathers didn't participate in as many of their children's activities. My own father spent little time attending my school functions and athletic events. It just wasn't expected.

From 1951 until 1960, my family and I lived in a fairly small, two-story house on South Boulevard, within a few minutes of the Medical Center. This allowed me to spend as much time as possible with my family, while still being near the hospital and my patients. To outsiders, it might seem that my demanding work schedule caused me to neglect my family, but I honestly don't believe that is true. Although I wasn't able to be with my family much during the week, I made time for them on weekends. We enjoyed activities typical of the day. The girls had the usual pursuits—dance classes, piano lessons, and school sports. Louise let me know where and when I was expected to show up to see them perform. I remember one of Susan's ballet recitals. She looked adorable in her pink leotard and slippers. As she began a pirouette, she got dizzy and whirled into the wrong corner of the stage. Once she realized what had happened, she improvised a few steps and finished the routine. I was pleased by her composure.

For many of these recitals, Dr. Dan McNamara, head of pediatric cardiology at Texas Children's, was also in the audience, as he had children of his own the same age. Dan was amazed by my ability to predict exactly when my child was to take the stage. "Denton, how is it that you always show up at just the right time? No matter how hard I try, I end up sitting through the whole darn thing."

One of my favorite times with the girls was Halloween. For trick-or-treating with them, Louise and I sometimes dressed up in costumes. I was always amused when I encountered trick-or-treaters in surgical garb. I preferred to be something more "scary"—like a ghoul or Dracula.

• • •

On September 15, 1959, I was driving downtown to a business meeting. I had recently been kicked by a horse and was wearing a thigh-to-ankle cast for a broken kneecap, so it was challenging to drive at all. Suddenly, I heard on the radio that a bomb had gone off at Poe Elementary School, just a few blocks from our house. The radio announcer said that students had been killed. Three of my daughters—Mary, Susan, and Weezie—were enrolled at that school. I was stunned by the news. I was used to dealing with emergencies but never of this type. I turned the car around and drove to Poe as fast as I could.

When I arrived at the school, I was shocked at how its normally peaceful playground had been transformed into such a tragic site. Inside, the teachers had the children sitting in orderly lines in the hallways. Amazingly, the children all appeared calm. In contrast, the parents were frantic as they looked for their little ones. Louise was one of the first on the scene. Because of her nursing skills, she was tending the wounded. I tried to make myself useful, helping where I could. I then went to look for my girls, who had been inside the school at the time of the blast. I was relieved to find them unhurt but was saddened by the fatalities and injuries. Among the injured was the principal, Mrs. R. E. Doty, who had been a favorite teacher of mine at Montrose Elementary School. The dead included the school custodian, James Montgomery, and Susan's beloved second-grade teacher, Mrs. Jennie Kolter. One of the dead children was eight-year-old Johnny Fitch, a classmate of Susan's and the son of our friends Bobbie and Jack Fitch.

I later found out that Susan secretly thought she, herself, had caused the blast because she had flushed the toilet at the exact moment the bomb went off. She kept this to herself and grieved unnecessarily for weeks before finally telling her mother. As a second grader, Susan didn't understand that she couldn't possibly have been to blame. The man responsible for the tragedy was a forty-nine-year-old ex-convict named Paul Orgeron. That morning, he had tried to enroll his seven-year-old son, Dusty, in Poe school but didn't have the necessary paperwork, so was asked to return the next day. He had the bomb with him in a suitcase and set it off before leaving the school grounds. Both he and his son were among the dead.[1] The Poe school bombing is something none of us who were there will ever forget. It made us all realize how precarious life could be. The incident reminded me that my loved ones were not immune to tragedy.

In late 1960 Louise and I had our fifth child—another girl, Helen. Our South Boulevard home was soon running out of room. So in 1962 we decided to buy our present house, in the River Oaks subdivision. The new house doubled our living space and seemed quite grand to us. Compared with some other homes in the area, though, it is fairly modest. We live there to this day. I often say that when the time comes, I plan to be "carted out" of there. There will be no high rise or nursing home for me if I have anything to say about it.

Once Helen was old enough, she went to River Oaks Elementary School. When she was in second grade, in 1969, Domingo and I were working on the artificial heart project. We'd made several models of it, and I happened to have one of them sitting in my study at home. It was Helen's turn to take something to school for show and tell. She wanted to take something other than dead lizards or butterflies like

---

[1] The details of the Poe school bombing can be read in the September 28, 1959, edition of *Time* magazine.

the other children took, so she tried to think of something different and interesting. In scouring the house, she went into my study and found an artificial heart, which to her seemed like a toy with its hard-plastic ventricles. At school, she proudly pulled it out of the paper bag she'd taken it in. Everyone was in awe, even the principal. Helen was quite pleased that she'd found a "showstopper." Little did she know what a future impact that heart would have on the medical world.

With five teenagers, our house was always filled with laughter and music—usually rock and roll from the record players in every bedroom. One afternoon, a writer from *Life* magazine arrived to do an article about "Dr. Cooley's family life." He knew I played the upright bass in a band called "The Heartbeats,"[2] so he decided that a family musicale would make a good photo op. In the Heartbeats, I always stood in the corner with my bass. Nobody but my family and fellow band members knew that I could only play a few chords and kept a cheat sheet of chord fingerings taped to the side of the instrument.

For the *Life* photo, the girls and I gathered at the piano. We chose to play "Alley Cat," because it was one of Mary's favorites in her limited piano repertoire. Susan faked it by strumming the few simple chords she knew on the guitar, and I plucked several chords on my bass. Helen, Florence, and Louise looked on. Our Lhasa Apso, Koko Nor, and our mutt, Hansel, groaned along with the music. I am certain that the photographers realized we were *not* ready for prime time! Nonetheless, the photo ended up in the *Life* spread, and we all got fan mail from readers who believed we were just like the Von Trapp family in *The Sound of Music*.

By playing with the Heartbeats, I gained a much better reputation for being a musician than I deserved. In fact, some years ago, I received a letter on official-looking stationery from a music conservatory in

---

[2] In 1965 Dr. Grady Hallman organized a band composed mainly of physicians, called "The Heartbeats." We started with about twenty musicians. Grady, an outstanding trombonist, wanted me to be in the group and suggested that I learn to play the upright bass. So I bought an old bass for about thirty-five dollars. After playing around with it and talking to a couple of experienced bass players, I learned enough to follow a few chord changes and keep time. I enjoyed being in the group but obviously wasn't soloist material. The band played at charity events and medical meetings around Texas and as far away as New York. We made two records, and the proceeds were donated to the Mended Hearts, a volunteer organization that supports patients with heart disease. Our theme song was "Mercy, Mercy, Mercy!"

Albuquerque, New Mexico. The letter stated, "Dear Dr. Cooley, we have just completed building a new conservatory and are planning our fall schedule. You are being considered for presenting a solo cello concert." I looked at the letter and thought, 'They can't be serious—*a cello concert?* I don't even own a cello." I put the letter aside for four or five days. Then I picked it up again and thought, "Well, maybe they *are* serious." So I replied with a formal letter, saying that I had spoken to my agent, who confirmed that I was completely booked for the upcoming season. I suggested they contact the Spanish cellist Pablo Casals, who might have an opening. I never heard any more from the conservatory. To this day, I don't know whether the letter was a joke.

• • •

When the girls were out of school in summer, Louise and I took them with us whenever we could manage a trip that coincided with a meeting where I was invited to speak. We would stay over and see the sights of the area. Wherever we went, the five girls made quite a splash with the locals. During the height of the transplant era, I was invited to give a lecture at the Hospital San Camillo in Rome. The lecture was arranged by my friend Professor Dr. Guido Chidichimo, who was head of cardiac surgery there. While we were in Rome, he arranged for us to have a private audience with Pope Paul VI. The audience was to be at the pope's summer residence, Castel Gandolfo, just outside the city. We soon learned that Louise and the girls would have to be completely recostumed for the meeting. Their mini skirts were too short, their sleeveless blouses were not allowed, and they had not brought head coverings. A papal audience required a different look. Dr. Chidichimo's wife escorted Louise and all five girls to the high-fashion district of Rome for a shopping spree. When we saw the bill, we wished there had been a Roman version of Sears. The girls would never wear those dowdy outfits again.

The papal guards were surprised when *"Il Dottore"* and his family arrived at the gates in a rented Volkswagen van driven by fifteen-year-old Susan. When the pope walked into the room wearing a white robe, white cap, and red leather shoes, Florence whispered, "Look, the pope is wearing red Pappagallos." Pappagallos were *the* footwear coveted by teenagers at the time.

The pope was cordial and friendly. I was surprised that he was not

much taller than my girls. He had previously sent one of his bish-
ops to Houston to discuss the moral and ethical issues of transplants
with me. When I introduced the subject of brain death, His Holiness
seemed unwilling to accept the idea entirely. He seemed to feel that
these decisions were the province of medical science, not religion. He
was familiar with the Karp operation and was in favor of the artificial
heart because it avoided the brain death issue. Later, I was informed by
the monsignor, who hosted us at the audience, that I should not have
opened a topic of conversation for His Holiness. Protocol dictated
that the pope was to choose the subjects for discussion.

Toward the end of the audience, the pope reached toward the top
left-hand drawer of his desk. He paused and asked, "You *are* Catholic,
aren't you?" I replied, "No, Your Holiness, I am Episcopalian." He quietly shut the left-hand drawer and opened the right one. He handed
me a small certificate in Latin but no medal or memento. Ever since
then, I have wondered what was in that left-hand drawer. I guess I'll
never know.

Back in Houston, our family often spent weekends at our "ski
shack," which sat on the banks of the San Jacinto River just twenty
minutes south of downtown. The shack had three rooms with enough
bunk beds for eight children to sleep in. On these getaways, we could
water ski and visit with friends—the Schnitzers, Levins, and Jacob-
ses—who had more impressive dwellings. Being close to the Houston
Ship Channel, the water was polluted from ships and barges and was
home to water moccasins. But we didn't let those things spoil our fun.
One Sunday afternoon, I was invited by Jimmy Greer and his friend A.
J. Foyt to ski behind their boat. By accident, I skied over some fishing
lines out in the river. When I skied back by, the "beered-up" fisherman
shot at me with his hunting bow and arrow! Luckily, the arrow just
came close, so I wasn't hurt—only frightened. Had the arrow injured
me, it would have made quite a story for the ten o'clock news.

· · ·

Like many other men who grew up in a city, I thought it would be
good to own property in the country. One Sunday afternoon in 1958, I
found a newspaper ad for a 139-acre piece of land on the Brazos River
described as suitable for a club or golf course. I visited the site and
decided that it would provide an ideal getaway for my family and me.

Even at rush hour, it was just a fifty-five-minute drive from the hospital. The land was covered with grass, wildflowers, and large pecan trees. There was half a mile of frontage on the high side of the Brazos River. To buy the property, I took advantage of a partial loan offered by the state of Texas to World War II veterans. We named the place Cool Acres. Later, I acquired adjacent land, increasing the size of the present ranch to four hundred acres.

A patient who was a building contractor offered to construct a four-bedroom house for us with a porch overlooking the river. Once the house was finished, my family and I began to spend some weekends at the ranch. We always felt like we were on vacation there. I enjoyed trading my surgical garb for boots and a cowboy hat. That was a welcome relief from the pressures of my work. My original objective was to raise cattle, but this proved less lucrative than expected. So after thirty years of losses, I sold the cattle, leased the pasture land to a neighbor, and kept enough land for recreation. I still enjoy seeing cattle on my land.

The girls like to tell a story about something that happened shortly after we got the ranch. As we were leaving Cool Acres to go home, I stopped the family station wagon and loaded a calf in the back, behind the second seat. The calf mooed all the way home. The girls were thrilled at the thought of having a new pet. When they went out to the backyard the next morning, they found only a pile of hay—the calf was nowhere in sight. 'Daddy' had taken it to the hospital to be part of a research project. No more was said about the calf. They were happy to know that, over the years, some of THI's research animals were "retired" to the ranch after the projects were finished.

As a UT graduate, I have a fondness for longhorns. We've always had a longhorn steer named Bubba at Cool Acres. As one dies, the next appears. Last year, my grandsons, now mostly grown, presented me with a longhorn they bought "for a bargain" at auction—Bubba IV. On Thanksgiving weekend, the boys fetched me on a golf cart and took me to the corral, where we branded Bubba with "CA" for Cool Acres. While we were at it, I was tempted to add CA to the old UT brand on my chest.

Louise and I have greatly enjoyed watching the children and grandchildren play at Cool Acres. Throughout the years, we added playground equipment and other interesting things. I told myself that what we bought was "for the children," but I often got as much pleasure as they did. First, we bought playground equipment. Then we built a pool and two tennis courts. The *pièce de résistance* is a three-story treehouse in an old elm with branches that overhang the river. The treehouse has been the setting for many family photographs. I'm told it has also been the site of teenage spooning and even one marriage proposal.

We also had annual THI family picnics at the ranch. As the picnics grew, we added a pond—"Lake Louise"—a roller skating rink, a picnic pavilion, and basketball hoops. And we have what may be the world's only uphill baseball diamond. Making a home run is really difficult. No matter how far the ball is hit, the runner is always at a disadvantage. The incline is so steep that it is nearly impossible to run all the bases at one time.

After learning that a one-room post office was going to be torn down in Orchard, Texas, we had the building moved to our property. The girls and Louise converted the post office into a schoolhouse filled with antique desks. The children love to play school there among the mud daubers. Also, when Houston's famous Pin Oak Charity Horse Show was discontinued, I acquired the bandstand and moved it to the "shores" of Lake Louise. The bandstand is where we hang plaques to commemorate important family events, such as marriages and births. The playground is now complete with an old Texaco gasoline hand-pumper, an authentic railroad caboose, and Louise's beloved gypsy wagon, which she saw at an antique auction of items from the Roy Hofheinz estate at Hart's Gallery, in Houston, and simply had to have. She gave the wagon to me for a birthday present. My grandsons, all avid outdoorsmen, added a sunflower field to attract doves and stocked the ponds with fish. Because Cool Acres is so close to Houston, they can go to the ranch after work with friends for an evening of hunting, fishing, and burgers.

Cool Acres is the place where my girls and their children have learned to drive a car. You could tell which one was becoming a teenager because that child would abandon the family for the weekend in a trail of gravel dust. The older girls taught the younger ones, and I made sure they learned in cars that had a stick shift. I gave them each a car for their sixteenth birthday, because I wanted them to have the mobility that a car provided and that I had enjoyed with the Model T

Ford during my teenage years. I always said, "A girl should have her own wheels!" And my girls did.

. . .

I believe that it is not the amount but the quality of time spent with children that makes a lasting impression on them, and my family seems to offer proof of this. For most of my career, I've worked really long hours. There were many days when I barely saw my children, but they realized that I was responsible for the welfare of my patients and that my schedule was often beyond my control. The girls also knew how demanding it was for their mother to meet their needs in my absence. We must have been good role models because all five girls were excellent students and turned out to be responsible, hard-working adults. They all went to UT Austin for their undergraduate degrees and had good scholastic records.

Our oldest daughter, Mary, is an artist. She earned a master's degree in medical and biological illustration from Johns Hopkins. For many years, she worked as a medical illustrator. She also does beautiful fine art paintings. Lately, Mary has been painting commissioned portraits of children playing sports, of hunters in the field, and of pets and homes. She has six children of her own—Sarah, Blair, Denton, William, Jack, and Caroline—and is married to Dr. John Craddock Jr., an otolaryngologist. Louise and I have several of Mary's paintings on our walls at home. One of her works is on the back cover of this book. The painting shows an operating room scene from an especially busy day in 1970 during the Cooley Hilton era. Visiting surgeons had crowded the operating room to watch me perform a coronary artery bypass operation, which was a relatively new procedure at the time.

Our second daughter, Susan, is a nurse practitioner. She received her Ph.D. in nursing from Texas Woman's University in Houston. She seems to take after her great-grandparents, Daniel Denton and Helen Winfield Cooley, as she has always been dedicated to community service. Susan was on the faculty in the pediatrics department of the UT-Houston Medical School for thirty years before becoming vice president of clinical services for RediClinic, a Texas-based company that provides affordable health care. While at UT, she founded Reach Out and Read Texas, part of a national pediatric literacy program. She has also been involved with Lord of the Streets at Trinity Episcopal Church, which provides support for the homeless in Houston; Bo's Place, a bereavement center for children; and other community-minded programs. I'm pleased that Susan is also on the board of the Harris County Hospital District. She has four children—Louise, John, Robert, and Mary.

Our third daughter, Louise—known as Weezie—graduated with a medical degree from the University of Texas Medical School in Houston. She is an ophthalmologist with a busy practice in Los Angeles. She also serves on the board of Junior Blind of America, which helps visually impaired children and adults live independently. Weezie is the only one of our daughters who doesn't live within a mile of her parents. I remember taking her into the operating room during the early heart transplant days. Maybe that's when she decided to become a doctor. If so, she didn't tell me about it. I was actually surprised when she decided to go to medical school. Once launched into her medical studies, she would occasionally ask for my help. I remember one time when she was very impressed because I could answer her questions about neurobiology. Even today, I send her relevant articles about ophthalmology that I run across. Sometimes she jokingly refers to me as GOD for "Good Old Dad." Weezie is a natural athlete and low handicap golfer. She recently qualified and played in the U.S. Golf Association Senior Women's Amateur Championship tournament. She has two children—Susan and Peter—and is married to an attorney, Richard Davis, who is also a skilled golfer.

Our youngest daughter, Helen, married Charles Fraser, who is now chief of Congenital Heart Surgery at Texas Children's Hospital and one of the world's leading experts in the field of pediatric heart surgery. Like me, Chuck did his cardiovascular residency at Johns Hopkins. He and Helen met when they were schoolmates at UT in Austin. They now have four children—Laura, Charles, Grace, and William.

Our fourth daughter, Florence, was a tall, green-eyed beauty who was independent, artistic, creative, high-spirited, and sensitive. She had lots of friends. Wherever she went, there was always fun involved. After graduating from UT, Florence spent two years in New York City, living with friends and working at the Young & Rubicam Advertising Agency. At one point, she decided that she wanted to become a doctor, so she enrolled in premed courses and made good grades. She later changed her mind about medical school and took a job in a Houston retail shop. For a brief time, she was married to a fine young man, who had been a classmate at UT.

For much of her life, Florence experienced mood swings. The medical term for her condition was manic-depressive disorder, now known as bipolar disease. We did our best to get her help, but it was not enough. In 1985 Florence took her own life. What a tragedy! She was the apple of so many people's eyes, including mine. She was adored by all who knew her. For her to believe that life was not worth living breaks my heart to this day

The afternoon of her death, I was performing an extremely difficult open heart procedure, which required my utmost concentration, when one of my colleagues came into the operating room and told me the terrible news. It took all of my self-control to be able to finish that procedure. Just the day before, I'd had a long, unusually warm talk with Florence. She was under a psychiatrist's care, but nobody realized how desperate she had become.

Florence's death was the worst tragedy of my life. The sadness was overwhelming. Not only do I miss her terribly, but I feel like I failed her. I continue to ask myself whether I could have done more to help her—maybe somehow treated her differently, so that she wouldn't have taken that final, desperate step. Maybe I just wasn't there enough for her. Her death drew our family even closer, reminding us how dear we are to each other.

• • •

In the late 1980s and early 1990s, Houston's economy headed south. During this period, I experienced a very difficult time in my business life, when I was forced to file for bankruptcy. Although I knew a few people who had declared bankruptcy, I never thought it could happen to me. In fact, I was doing so well financially in the 1970s and early 1980s, when Houston's oil economy was booming, that I decided to invest in real estate. I remembered my grandfather's telling me that land in Houston was like 24-karat gold.

Property was appreciating in value in the 1980s, and there seemed to be no end in sight. Many of my investments were undeveloped property close to Houston's city limits—most of it near freeways and intersections. I also invested in some commercial buildings downtown and obtained loans to build Travis Centre, a hotel and an office complex close to the hospital.

In 1978 I bought perhaps my most satisfying investment, the historic Galvez Hotel on Galveston Island. This *grande dame* had been built in 1911 as part of the City of Galveston's effort to revive tourism after the devastating hurricane of 1900. A major landmark on the beachfront of the island city, the Galvez once attracted heads of state and other famous guests. My parents spent their wedding night there. By 1970 the Galvez had seriously deteriorated. I felt that it should be saved, so I bought it and arranged for the Marriott Corporation to manage it.

My investments did reasonably well until 1987, when the price of oil fell overnight, the stock market crashed, and banks were strapped for cash. Property values in Houston were hit especially hard. One day, I got a call from the bank that held the note for Travis Centre. The bank wanted $18 million by the following Monday. I hadn't known that a bank could "call" a loan like that. I'd thought I had forty years to pay it off. Now I was expected to pay it off overnight, and my assets, mostly real estate holdings, had suddenly become worth less than half of what I owed.

After careful deliberation with my lawyer and accountants, I decided to file for Chapter 11 reorganization. The whole idea of bankruptcy was totally opposed to everything I had ever believed in. When I was growing up, bankruptcy was considered a disgrace that couldn't easily be lived down. But when Chapter 11 was explained to me, it was different from what I'd envisioned. I would be able to reorganize my assets in a bankruptcy estate, which would allow court protection from creditors and time to sell the assets and raise money. The court accepted my reorganization plan about five months after it was submitted. Unfortunately, the Galvez became part of the estate holdings, and I lost it. But I was pleased that it was eventually sold to Galveston native and real estate developer George Mitchell, who continued to restore it to its former glory.

The media exploited my situation. It was disconcerting to see my private financial affairs discussed in newspapers and talked about on the radio. I was embarrassed and felt especially bad for my family. The Texas homestead law, however, allowed me to keep my home and the income from my medical practice, and I was eventually able to buy back two automobiles and a Galveston beach house that had been put into the bankruptcy estate. I had no delinquent taxes. Fortunately, I had given Cool Acres to my daughters ten years earlier and had paid the gift tax, so the ranch wasn't involved in the filing. It was tough starting over, but I think that I met the challenge with honesty and dignity. Ultimately, my debts were resolved.

• • •

I have always believed in having a proper balance between work, rest, and recreation. At times, I haven't been able to achieve that balance and have felt the effects. So even when I have not gotten enough rest, I've tried to find time for exercise—usually tennis or golf—which has relieved the stress of the operating room. Getting away for even an hour can rejuvenate me.

In my senior years, I enjoy nothing more than a golf outing with friends or family. My eldest grandson, Denton, is an accomplished golfer who played on his university team and was a pro for several years. At age seventeen, he was junior golf champion at the Houston Country Club. One day, I was invited to play golf with my friend Bert Magill and his family, including Brett, his twelve-year-old son. Bert asked his son, "Do you know who Dr. Cooley is?" "Yeah, he's *Denton's granddaddy.*" I was pleased that my grandson was the hero. Denton is a much better golfer than I. However, the handicap system allows even a mediocre player like me to think he can compete with a champion if given the strokes. After seventy years of playing the game, I made my first hole-in-one on a 165-yard hole at the Grand Cypress Golf Club, in Orlando. That was a lifelong dream come true!

In recent years, our family has expanded to include two more generations. My wife, Louise, is still at its heart, communicating with everyone (now by e-mail) and making sure that we all get together regularly. For birthdays, anniversaries, and other celebrations, we prefer to keep it simple—people just drop by the house. Togetherness is what we covet, not fancy occasions. We've found that by keeping the tone casual, everyone feels at ease.

When Louise and I were courting and first married, we befriended Jack Handelsman, the other chief resident at Hopkins, and his wife Shirley, whom everyone called "Shirl." Louise and I liked the sound of it, so we began to call each other simply "Darl," short for darling. I don't believe Louise has called me Denton ever since. When the girls became too old to call me Daddy, they and their friends started calling me Darl. Louise and I together are referred to as the Darls, now the GrandDarls. And my nonsurgical business affairs company is DARLCO. My sons-in-law have installed a plaque at the Cool Acres cattle guard that reads, "Welcome to DARL WORLD." Jack and Shirl may have no idea how much of a mark they left on our lives.

It gives me immense pleasure that my daughters and their children are close and have a strong sense of family pride. As my work life has become less active, I have had more time to spend with my sixteen grandchildren, who call me Grandaddy or GrandDarl, depending on their mood. I feel a strong bond to each of my grandchildren and get great pleasure from being included in their activities. I am proud of them. Most have followed the Cooley tradition of going to UT for their undergraduate degrees. A number have gone into medical fields. So far, we have a doctor, a nurse, and a chiropractor. Two more grandchildren are in medical school. By the time this book is published, Louise and I will have four great-grandchildren.

In 1994 I celebrated my fiftieth year in medicine and received numerous congratulatory letters. Probably the most special one came from my teenage granddaughter Sarah, writing for all of the grandchildren. She said,

> *Considering our number, it is no small achievement to stay involved in all our activities. . . . To each child, you have given equal enthusiasm. Even the babies feel it when they bounce on your knees. . . . In addition, there has been a special benefit in having a famous grandfather with an outstanding career. We always have a topic for school assignments, such as "Write a paragraph about a famous American (or Texan), or a person you admire, or someone who helps other people." I'm sure that among our lot, we have produced over 50 essays, poems, and pictures concerning you. Thank you for being such a convenient and worthy subject. You are the most wonderful grandfather. We love you and are proud of you.*

Recently, at Cool Acres, Louise and I decided to build a replica of the bungalow at 908 W. Alabama Street where I was born and grew up. Whenever we drove past that small house in Montrose, the girls would point it out, calling it "the manger." The Cool Acres replica is called "The Manger by the Brazos" and has 9-0-8 in brass above the door. Building the replica was especially fun for me because I worked on it with my grandson John Plumb. He was the general contractor on the project and finished it just in time for the first Annual Cool Acres Catfish Cup Tennis Tournament, an event dreamed up by the grandchildren. All of their friends came for a weekend of tennis, swimming, and other fun activities.

Thanks to my wife and helpmate, Louise, I am one of those fortunate people who has been able to "have it all." I have been able to create a satisfying professional life while maintaining some semblance of balance. In retrospect, buying Cool Acres and marrying Louise Thomas were the best decisions of my life, not necessarily in that order.

With Mike DeBakey after he accepted an honorary membership in the DAC Society on October 27, 2007.

CHAPTER 17

Reconciliation with Mike

M Y RIFT WITH MIKE DEBAKEY had always been distressing to me, but the more I thought about our relationship, the more I realized that our personalities were simply incompatible. For instance, we had very different leadership styles. I believed in creating a pleasant working environment, which fostered harmony and productiveness among my staff. If a simple mistake was made, I didn't make a big deal out of it. I didn't scream or shout. I simply fixed the problem and went on with the matter at hand, whatever it might be. In contrast, Mike was stern and abusive toward his residents and staff. He required that the residents work excessively long hours, and he frequently reprimanded or fired them for minor infractions. People were so busy worrying about possible repercussions that they sometimes ended up making the very mistakes that they were trying to avoid. His attitude and behavior created an unpleasant professional climate at Baylor. Mike also needed to be in complete control of every situation. When something didn't go his way, he could be extremely vindictive. On the other hand, he could be quite kind—especially to his patients—and was revered by many people throughout the world for his scientific contributions.

To be fair, our ambitions and egos also got in each other's way. When two men with strong ambition are put together, conflict is almost inevitable. Mike and I were both intensely ambitious, hard-driving individuals who were not satisfied with a few achievements, no matter how large. For this reason, I wondered if reconciliation between us would ever be possible. In the end, some of our colleagues, especially Bud Frazier and George Noon, would have to play an integral role in bringing Mike and me back together.

Our initial contact came in 2004. Bud had organized a conference called "The Implantable LVAD: From Concept to Clinical Reality," which was to be held May 21–22. Many of the pioneers in the field, including John C. Norman, Bud's predecessor as our laboratory director, were going to be present. Bud hoped that Mike would attend, but because the conference was being held at the Texas Heart Institute, he thought it unlikely that Mike would even consider it. Bud extended an invitation to Mike to speak on the history of LVADs, but this was not publicly known. Much to our surprise, Mike accepted. We weren't sure, though, that he was actually going to show up until he entered the auditorium. At ninety-three years old, he still had the sharp wit I remembered. He gave an excellent talk. I wanted to approach him afterward but thought it best not to make this event about him and me. He didn't acknowledge me, and he left the conference right after his talk. However, his mere presence at THI had been a start in the right direction.

Around Christmas of 2006, I read astronaut Eugene "Gene" Cernan's memoir, *The Last Man on the Moon*. Gene, who flew on NASA missions Gemini 9A and Apollo 10 and 17, had heart surgery at THI after his retirement. In his book, he described the space race between the Soviets and the Americans. In the early years of that race, the Russians seemed to preempt us at each turn, beginning with the launch of Sputnik—the first satellite to orbit the earth. With the advent of manned space flight, the rivalry between U.S. astronauts and Russian cosmonauts became personal. Once the astronauts reached the moon, however, the race was all but over. Gradually, the Russians and the Americans began to collaborate on joint space projects. With time, the astronauts and cosmonauts even became friends—sharing vodka and trading stories. Gene came to realize that the cosmonauts were "regular guys," and he couldn't understand why we'd ever considered them enemies. This was a lesson to him about the folly of continuing pointless feuds.

Gene's book got me thinking again about taking steps toward ending the animosity between Mike and me. By that time, we'd both retired from active surgical practice, so further developments in cardiovascular surgery were in the hands of a new generation. Mike had always publicly denied the existence of our rivalry. I think that's because he was my senior and, in his eyes, regardless of my achievements, I would always be his junior. For him, the idea of granting me equal status—even as a rival—would have been intolerable.

In early January 2007, I was driving home from the hospital one day when I acted on impulse and stopped by Mike's house. It was just off my usual route. Not quite a year earlier, he'd had surgery for an aortic dissection.[1] His recovery had been slow, and he'd only recently come home from the hospital. He was ninety-eight years old, and I was eighty-five. It was time to make peace. As I approached Mike's front door, I had mixed emotions but knew it was a good thing to do. His wife Katrin answered the doorbell.[2] I said, "Good afternoon, Mrs. DeBakey. Would it be possible for me to see Dr. DeBakey and say a few words to him?" She replied, "I wish that were possible, Dr. Cooley, but Mike has had a bad day. He's just been given a sedative, and now he's asleep." So I told her, 'Well, I'll try again later. Next time, I'll make an appointment."

I waited for several days before trying again to contact Mike. On January 16 I wrote him a note on my personal stationery.

> *Dear Mike: Congratulations on your miraculous recovery from illness and surgery. As time passes, I have a growing desire to meet with you and express my gratitude for the influence you have had on my life and career. Especially, I am grateful for the opportunity you provided me more than 50 years ago to become established at Baylor and to be inspired by your work ethic and ambition. Those years remain in my memory. I appeared at your house about 10 days ago for this purpose. Mrs. DeBakey graciously received me but said that you were sleeping. If you are willing to receive me, I am available at your convenience. Yours truly, Denton*

As the weeks passed and no reply arrived from Mike, I began to believe that none ever would. Finally, a solution was suggested by some of our colleagues—mainly Bud, George, Dr. Barney Barrett, and Dr. Ken Mattox—who were aware of my desire to make peace. Years ear-

---

[1] It was an extensive procedure and, to my knowledge, no one his age had ever undergone, much less survived, such an operation. Ironically, the technique for repair of an aortic dissection was one that he and I had developed together in the early 1950s.

[2] His first wife, Diana, died of a heart attack in 1972.

lier, our former trainees had honored Mike and me by establishing two separate surgical societies—first the Denton A. Cooley Cardiovascular Surgical Society and then the Michael E. DeBakey International Surgical Society. Why shouldn't the members of the Cooley Society recognize Mike for his lifetime achievements in surgery and present him with an honorary membership? We extended the offer, but I had doubts whether Mike would respond. To my surprise, he accepted the invitation and agreed to participate in a ceremony with me. It would be held on October 27, 2007, at the Society's Fifteenth International Symposium. Despite his acceptance, I wasn't absolutely certain he would attend. For that reason, only a few people were even told that he had been invited. Everyone in attendance was astounded when they saw Mike DeBakey enter the THI auditorium in a motorized wheelchair. He received an immediate, spontaneous standing ovation. Some attendees even jumped onto their chairs to get a better view.

As I gave Mike the award, we smiled at each other, shook hands, and enjoyed a moment that no one had ever believed would happen. I said, "I hope this is not just a temporary truce or a cease-fire but a permanent treaty between us." Mike responded, "I'm glad to be here for two reasons. One is, I'm alive. And the other, of course, is to get this award. Denton, I am really touched by it. I'm going to put it in my library."

I was relieved that we'd finally declared peace and could enjoy our remaining days without animosity toward each other. And as a result of the reconciliation, our two institutions could work together on mutual projects. Two months later, Mike would come to the THI animal laboratory to watch Bud Frazier implant a TAH into a calf. The device was composed of dual MicroMed DeBakey LVADs.[3] Bud, who had begun his career in this field as a medical student in the Baylor laboratory under Mike's direction, wanted to honor both Mike and me by performing this research at the Texas Heart Institute.[4] By creating a workable TAH, he hoped to bring the early research to fruition.

---

[3] In the 1990s Mike had begun development of this new LVAD in conjunction with engineers at NASA.

[4] On June 12, 2008, the Texas Heart Institute at St. Luke's Episcopal Hospital was awarded a $2.8 million grant from the National Institutes of Health to support the development of a pulseless TAH comprising the two MicroMed DeBakey LVADs.

Mike's presence in the THI lab was another sign that he and I once again had a positive relationship.

This fact was confirmed a few months later when Mike was awarded the Congressional Gold Medal in Washington, D.C. At his personal invitation, I sat in the audience that gathered in the rotunda of the U.S. Capitol on April 23, 2008, to witness the ceremony. After the congressional leaders of both parties made speeches praising Mike for his accomplishments, President George W. Bush presented the Gold Medal to him.

A few days after we returned to Houston, I attended a luncheon arranged to honor Mike and enjoyed having the opportunity to visit with him in a more informal setting. I was touched that he promised to send me a replica of his Congressional Gold Medal. With his usual close attention to detail, he sent me the package a few days later. In the accompanying letter, he wrote,

Dear Denton: I am enclosing herewith a replica of the Congressional Gold Medal given to me last week. I would like to share it with you, since I think you deserve a part of this award. Our pioneering work in cardiovascular surgery was jointly done by us, and the "first" successful clinical cases that were reported helped to usher in the specialty of cardiovascular surgery. We can take pride in that observation. With kind regards, Mike

In writing him a thank you letter, I ended with the following thoughts,

Please know that I am comforted by the events of the past few months, which have restored our former relationship. Let me join so many others in congratulating you upon your life and accomplishments.

On May 2, 2008, Mike's surgical society recognized me with an honorary membership and a lifetime achievement award. At that ceremony, Mike gave me a leather-bound copy of the first scientific article the two of us had coauthored, which symbolized our work together. He said, "Denton, it's a great pleasure for me to acknowledge the pioneering contributions you have made." Later, he said, "I don't think I could have made it without Dr. Cooley. In fact, I know I couldn't."

I would again honor Mike by choosing him for the Denton A. Cooley Leadership Award, which he agreed to accept. This award, presented annually by the Texas Heart Institute, was established to recognize leadership and meritorious contributions to the advancement of society. Over his lengthy career, Mike was responsible for saving countless lives, either directly or indirectly. He was probably best known for his work in vascular surgery, especially the repair of aortic aneurysms. During World War II, he conceived of stationing medical personnel closer to the front lines, which greatly improved treatment of battlefield injuries. These mobile hospitals would eventually become known as MASH units.[5] He also was instrumental in establishing the U.S. National Library of Medicine—the world's largest medical library. Perhaps his most important accomplishment was developing Baylor into a world-class medical school. Sadly, Mike would not live to accept the Cooley Leadership Award. He died on July 11, 2008, only two months before his hundredth birthday. After funeral services in Houston, he was interred at Arlington National Cemetery. On January 21, 2009, he posthumously became the fourteenth recipient of the award.

A little more than a year later, in June 2010, the Denton A. Cooley Cardiovascular Surgical Society and the Michael E. DeBakey International Surgical Society came together at the Barton Creek Conference Center in Austin, Texas, for a landmark joint session. This symbolic union was an important tribute to both Mike and me.

Looking back, I will always be indebted to Mike for giving me a faculty position at Baylor and the opportunity to continue my academic career. During the early years, we were close, and I usually enjoyed being his colleague. As a mentor, he was generous with his time, and I learned a great deal from him that shaped my career. Ironically, I think that our historic rivalry enhanced his reputation as well as mine, serving both of our careers well. Most of all, our competitiveness benefited the Texas Medical Center and its patients. For me, that is the greatest good that could have come from it all.

---

[5] MASH stands for mobile army surgical hospital.

Giving the commencement address at the Johns Hopkins Medical School in May 2009.

Summing Up

MY ADVANCING AGE causes me to reflect on the revolutionary changes that have occurred during my career. Most of the early pioneers and contributors to heart surgery have died, and I am one of the few still standing. I like to say that I knew everyone doing cardiac surgery in those early years on a first-name basis. The field was wide open and ready for any surgeon bold enough to seize the opportunity. Almost every operation involved exploring new ground, and the possibilities seemed unlimited. Those were exciting times that allowed for the kind of superhero status that is now much more difficult to achieve in cardiovascular surgery. The emphasis is currently on a multidisciplinary approach to cardiac disease, and many of today's pioneers are working at the cellular level. I don't believe the conditions that helped create a Denton Cooley or Mike DeBakey will ever exist again in heart surgery, though the field will continue to evolve in new ways.

What formative influences and twists of fate led me to achieve what I did? Often, opportunities just seemed to come my way: being called off the bench and scoring the winning points in a varsity basketball game, suturing wounds in the San Antonio emergency room, transferring to Hopkins from UTMB, attracting Dr. Blalock's attention during a "stolen" tennis match, happening to be the intern for the historic blue baby operation, being assigned as an army doctor to Austria rather than to Walter Reed Hospital (thanks to Mike), meeting a cute nurse named Louise, accepting Lord Brock's invitation to train in London for a year, working with Mike at Baylor, being approached by Domingo Liotta about the artificial heart, and even feuding with Mike, which was painful but also important to my career. These are just a few of the happenings that turned me into the Denton Cooley the world seems to know and that led me and my team to operate on 100,000 hearts.

I've always believed the key to my success was that I recognized the opportunities put in front of me and acted on them. And acting on them usually involved really hard work. In fact, one of my favorite aphorisms is "the harder you work, the luckier you become." Everybody has innate talents of some kind. Luckily, I found a career that suited my natural abilities and also benefited other people. I am humbled that my surgical talent has kept many people alive, given them another chance to fulfill their dreams, and enabled families to remain together longer.

Throughout my career, I have received many honors for my achievements. Nobody will want to read the entire list here, so I'll mention only a few—in case anyone *is* interested. I deeply treasure two medals that I received from presidents of the United States. In 1984 President Ronald Reagan honored me for my contributions to medicine and surgery with the Presidential Medal of Freedom, the nation's highest civilian award. In 1998 President Bill Clinton awarded me the National Medal of Technology and Innovation. I've also received the Gifted Teacher Award from the American College of Cardiology; the René Leriche Prize, the highest honor of the International Surgical Society; the Distinguished Service Award of the American Medical Association; and the American Surgical Association's Medallion for Scientific Achievement. In May 2011 I received the Bakoulev Premium, Russia's highest award for cardiovascular surgery, bestowed by the Russian Academy of Medical Science. The award had never before been given to a non-Russian surgeon. Just naming these honors doesn't begin to convey the pride I feel from having received them. Some of these awards are even more special because they were also given to my mentors—Drs. Blalock, Brock, and DeBakey. Additionally, I have been named a distinguished alumnus of my alma maters, the University of Texas and Johns Hopkins. Also, in 1979 the National Collegiate Athletic Association chose me for its highest honor: the Theodore Roosevelt Award, which is given annually to a varsity athlete who has achieved national professional recognition. With this award, I like to tell people, "I finally got recognized for being a good 'jock' as well as a good 'doc.'"

I've always been an avid fan of UT sports, especially basketball. In 2003 DeLoss Dodds, the university's athletic director, and Rick Barnes, the head basketball coach, visited me at THI and asked my permission for UT to name its new basketball practice facility in my honor. I said, "Well, give me a little time to think about it." After two seconds, I said, "Time's up. The answer is yes!" Overwhelmed, I asked, "But why did you select me? I wasn't the greatest basketball player or athlete who attended the university."

"No, but you showed that athletic participation and academic achievement are not mutually exclusive. We think your accomplishments might inspire our varsity athletes to do something else with their time at UT besides just pursuing athletics." So the new practice facility for men's and women's basketball teams became the Denton A. Cooley Pavilion. The pavilion is located near the special-events center named for my good friend and fraternity brother Frank Erwin.

All of these honors are certainly gratifying, but I believe, like Teddy Roosevelt, that "far and away the best prize that life has to offer is the chance to work hard at work worth doing."

Two of the early values my parents instilled in me were the importance of education and of giving back to the community. My education was essentially free. I went to Houston public schools. Because of my basketball scholarship, my college expenses were minimal. Most of my medical school expenses were paid by the United States Army. I have always felt obligated to repay these debts by giving to institutions that support education in some way, including my own Texas Heart Institute. At UT Austin, I've donated to a number of building projects and have funded academic professorships and scholarships, including ones in zoology, nursing, and basketball. There's also a surgery professorship at the UT Medical School at Houston and a cardiothoracic professorship at the UT Medical Branch at Galveston.

When I played basketball on the Student Book Store team at Johns Hopkins, the only place we could practice was at a small church whose court was tiny and had a single basket. By 1980 Johns Hopkins still did not have a recreational facility, so I decided to donate money toward building one next to the hospital. The university named the facility the Denton A. Cooley Recreation Center, and it opened in 1982. It not only includes a full basketball court but also squash and handball courts, tennis courts, and a swimming pool. Louise and I have also funded a nursing scholarship in her honor at Hopkins and an English professorship in her honor at William and Mary, her alma mater.

I have always loved animals and felt grateful to them because of the vital role they play in medical and surgical research. That is one reason why I provided funds to build a hospital at the Houston Zoo, in Hermann Park, even though my research never involved zoo animals. The facility, which opened in 1985, is named the Denton A. Cooley Animal Hospital.

Most recently, I have had a chance to show my pride and affection for my father. The older I've gotten, the more grateful I've become for his influence on my life. To honor him, I made a donation to the UT Health Science Center that will establish the Ralph C. Cooley, D.D.S., Distinguished Professorship in Biomaterials at the School of Dentistry. Part of the gift will also help build a multipurpose University Life Center that will serve as a place for professional conferences, meetings, and other events for the entire UT Health system. I have just learned that the center will be jointly named for me and my father. It will be gratifying to share this honor with him.

One of the perks of my job has been getting to meet famous people, many of whom come to visit me and tour THI. A number of them have been mentioned in stories throughout this book. I certainly can't mention all of the rest, but they include heads of state and presidents, diplomats, writers, musicians, artists, television and film personalities, businessmen, athletes, and scientists. One of my most memorable visits was from Charles Lindbergh, who was very interested in heart surgery and once developed an oxygenator for organ preservation. On several occasions, I've played golf in charity tournaments, including Bing Crosby's Clambake at Pebble Beach. I've thrown out the first pitches at baseball games and have even played tennis with Wimbledon champion Bobby Riggs in Houston's Astrodome.

When people ask me to name what I'm most proud of, I always reply, "My family." To have my beloved wife for more than sixty years, with whom I enjoy a comfortable life and companionship, is a blessing. I am also blessed to have my daughters, grandchildren, great-grands, and sons-in-law. If I am asked to name my greatest achievement, however, the answer is "the Texas Heart Institute." Of course, I'm also proud of the first artificial heart implant, the first successful heart transplant in the United States, and my other surgical firsts. Although these procedures changed the course of medicine, they were isolated events performed by one man. The Texas Heart Institute is my legacy and has a much wider impact than I alone ever could. When I first envisioned THI back in the late 1950s, I could never have foreseen how it would evolve into what it is today. Through the work of its cardiologists, surgeons, researchers, and trainees, THI has affected millions of lives. The newest part of it, the Denton A. Cooley Building, was dedicated in 2002. The ten-story building houses everything from research labs to surgical suites and educational facilities. These resources are allowing THI to broaden its fight against heart disease, which remains the leading cause of death in the United States. For the twenty-first consecutive year (2011–2012), THI has been ranked by *U.S. News & World Report* as being among the top ten heart centers in the nation. It is now ranked fourth from the top.

A key element in THI's success has been its outstanding board of directors. The board was originally chaired by Robert Herring, who served until his death in 1981. The position was then held by Isaac Arnold Jr. until 1993, when he became chairman emeritus, a title he continues to hold. Meredith Long became chairman in 1993 and still remains in that capacity. To ensure that THI would endure, I knew that it would need a strong, talented leader to follow me as president. So when I was eighty-four years old, I recommended to the board that Dr. James T. Willerson be appointed president-elect. At that time, Jim was the president of the UT Health Science Center in Houston. He is a leader in the treatment of cardiac disease at the clinical and cellular levels and is considered one of the finest cardiologists in the world today. I first met Jim in San Antonio when he was fourteen years old and I was speaking at a conference there. He accompanied several physicians who were responsible for meeting my plane. I was impressed that a young person of his age would be interested in me. Even then, Jim's drive, intelligence, and determination were evident. He also spent time with me when he was a medical student at Baylor. I followed his career and was happy when he came back to Houston and ultimately ended up at THI. He took over as president in 2008, and I now serve as president emeritus.

I continued to operate until I was eighty-seven years old. At that point, it seemed time to put down the scalpel. As I pondered my decision, I was reminded of an old surgical adage that says, "It's better to quit a month too soon than a minute too late." Of course, I do miss operating. I even used to joke about having withdrawal symptoms but have now gotten past that.

After enjoying a remarkably healthy life, I've had to slow down in the last couple of years because some health problems have reduced my stamina. It all started with a small carcinoma of the colon, which thankfully was caught early and responded well to surgery. About the same time, I developed atrial fibrillation, which was treated by cardiac ablations and a pacemaker. I ended up with pulmonary emboli and now have a protective filter in my inferior vena cava. Whew! But I still had not finished being on the receiving end of the scalpel. After about sixty-five years of bending over an operating table, I had a pinched nerve in my lower back, and the pain was seriously limiting what I could do. I had to admit at age ninety that I needed back surgery. The surgery was successful, and I was back in my office five days later.

As for my professional life, I think it's "til death do us part." I expect to keep coming to my office until I'm too old or infirm to do so. Other than operating, I still do nearly everything else I've always done. I see patients occasionally, visit the operating room, drop into the research laboratories, give lectures, make rounds with the residents, write papers, attend conferences, and keep up with the medical literature. As an avid reader, I'm glad that I now have time to read more than just surgical journals. On Fridays, I sneak away from the office to play golf. I tell everyone, "I'm off to my 'Garden Club.'"

• • •

Sometimes I still wonder how that shy boy who was planning to be a dentist ever ended up as a "legendary heart surgeon." In this book, I have tried to describe that transformation. I hope to have conveyed a broader picture of me than has been portrayed in the news media and popular press. I've read a lot of inaccurate statements over the years and decided that it was time to set the record straight from my point of view.

I hope that this book will not only correct the record but also be a source of inspiration for others. If my story inspires just one reader, I'll consider it a success. At the beginning of the book, there's a favorite poem of mine, by R. L. Sharpe, that talks about the "bag of tools" we each receive when we come into this life. With those tools, we can make either stumbling blocks or stepping stones. I've always tried to use my tools constructively. Hopefully, the stepping stones I have made will endure long after I'm gone and I will be remembered as a "builder for eternity."

Postscript

At a recent Phi Beta Kappa meeting, someone asked me. "Dr. Cooley, have you spent your entire life in Houston?"

I could have simply answered, "Yes," but I somewhat mischievously responded, "Not yet."

With that, I think it's time for me to end these memoirs and get on with the rest of my life.

The Cardiovascular System

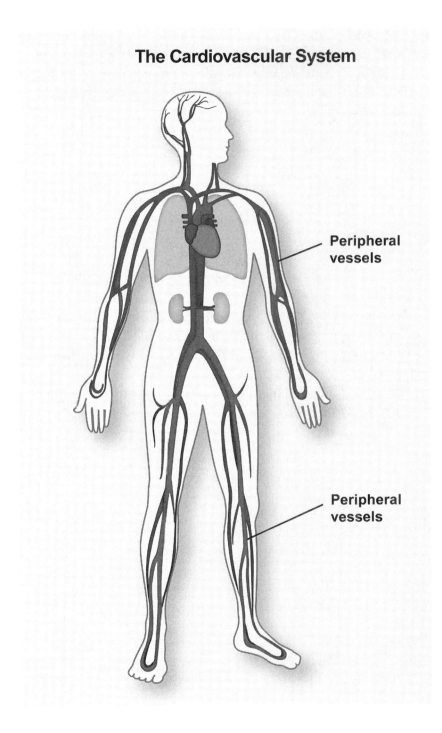

Peripheral
vessels

Peripheral
vessels

Appendix A

Glossary

See the end of the Glossary for illustrations.

ABDOMINAL AORTA. See **AORTA, ABDOMINAL.**

ACQUIRED HEART DISEASE. Heart disease that arises after birth, usually from infection or through the accumulation of fat deposits in key arteries that feed the heart muscle.

ANASTOMOSIS. Connection of two structures, such as blood vessels.

ANESTHETIC. A medication that causes loss of feeling or sensation. Because anesthetics combat pain, they make modern surgery possible.

ANEURYSM. A condition in which the wall of a vein, an artery, or the heart becomes weak and balloons outward. See drawings of aneurysms on p. 219. See also **FUSIFORM ANEURYSM; SACCIFORM ANEURYSM.**

ANEURYSMECTOMY. Removal of an aneurysm. Also a procedure in which a weakened section of an artery (aneurysm) is removed and replaced with a synthetic graft. See the drawing entitled Aneurysm Repair on p. 219.

ANGINA PECTORIS. Chest pain that occurs when the heart muscle does not receive enough blood.

ANGIOGRAPHY. X-ray studies of the heart and great vessels, made visible by intravenous injection of a solution that highlights the vessels. X-ray photographs that result from these studies are called *angiograms*.

ANGIOPLASTY. A technique for treating diseased arteries by briefly inflating a tiny balloon inside an artery.

ANNULOPLASTY. A surgical technique for repairing or reinforcing the annulus, the ring around a heart valve where the valve leaflet merges with the heart muscle.

ANTICOAGULANTS. Chemicals that prevent blood from clotting. Anesthesiologists use them in surgery, and cardiologists prescribe them to prevent clots when patients receive artificial heart valves.

AORTA. The largest artery in the body, which arises from the left ventricle and is the main trunk of the body's system of arteries. Blood pumped from the left ventricle begins its path through the body in the aorta. See the drawing entitled Vessels of the Torso on p. 220.

AORTA, ABDOMINAL. The portion of the aorta in the abdomen.

AORTA, THORACIC. The portion of the aorta in the chest.

AORTA, THORACOABDOMINAL. The long, straight portion of the aorta that stretches from the aortic arch to the abdomen.

AORTIC ARCH. The curved portion of the aorta.

AORTIC VALVE. A valve with three cusps, located between the left ventricle of the heart and the aorta. The aortic valve directs blood from the left ventricle into the aorta.

ARRHYTHMIA. Abnormal rhythm of the heart, also called *dysrhythmia*.

ARTERIES. The blood vessels that move blood away from the heart. All arteries except the pulmonary artery carry oxygen-rich blood.

ARTERIOGRAPHY. Studies of the arteries in which a dye is injected into the bloodstream to highlight the structure of the arteries as X-ray pictures are taken.

ARTERIOSCLEROSIS. Usually called *hardening of the arteries*, this term refers to a number of conditions that cause the walls of the arteries to thicken and lose their elasticity.

ARTIFICIAL HEART. A manmade heart. See also TOTAL ARTIFICIAL HEART (TAH).

ARTIFICIAL HEART VALVE. A metal, plastic, or tissue device that replaces a human heart valve.

ATHEROSCLEROSIS. A form of arteriosclerosis that involves the inner layers of the artery walls, which thicken and lose their shape as fats are deposited in them. If an artery becomes lined with fat layers, blood flow is reduced.

ATRIA. The upper two chambers of the heart. See the drawing entitled The Heart and Great Vessels on p. 221.

ATRIAL. Relating to one or both of the upper chambers of the heart.

ATRIAL SEPTAL DEFECT. A hole in the dividing wall between the atria, the upper chambers of the heart.

ATRIAL SEPTUM. The dividing wall between the atria of the heart.

ATRIOVENTRICULAR CANAL DEFECT. A large hole in the septum, the wall that separates the right and left sides of the heart. Also known as *atrioventricular septal defect*.

ATRIOVENTRICULAR VALVES. The tricuspid and mitral valves of the heart, located between the atria and ventricles.

ATRIUM. One of the two upper heart chambers; a site where blood collects before being pumped to the ventricles.

BALLOON ANGIOPLASTY. A technique used to open blocked coronary arteries. A special balloon catheter is threaded into the artery; inflating the balloon compresses fat deposits (plaque) against the wall of the artery, reestablishing blood flow.

BLALOCK-TAUSSIG PROCEDURE. Creation of a shunt between the subclavian and pulmonary arteries to increase the supply of oxygen-rich blood in "blue babies."

BLOOD PLASMA. A yellowish liquid that is 90 percent water but also contains salts, glucose, proteins, and other substances. The main component of blood.

BLOOD PRESSURE. Pressure exerted by the heart in pumping blood; also the pressure of the blood in the arteries.

BLUE BABY. An infant whose skin appears blue because of cyanosis, or inadequate oxygenation of the blood. The blue tinge is a warning sign of a heart defect.

BRIDGE TO TRANSPLANTATION. A mechanical circulatory support device that is implanted to keep heart failure patients alive until a donor heart becomes available.

BRONCHOSCOPY. Insertion of a bronchoscope through the nose or mouth to visualize the inside of the airways.

BRONCHUS. Either of the two main branches from the trachea (the windpipe) that lead to each of the lungs.

CARDIAC. Referring to the heart.

CARDIAC ARREST. Stoppage of all heart function.

CARDIAC CATHETERIZATION. A technique used to examine the heart by threading a thin tube (catheter) into a vein or artery and guiding it into the heart.

CARDIOLOGIST. A doctor who specializes in the study of the heart and its function in health and disease. Cardiologists diagnose heart disease, prescribe medications, and perform interventional treatments but do not do operations that involve opening the chest.

CARDIOLOGY. The study of the heart and its vessels.

CARDIOPULMONARY BYPASS (CPB). See HEART-LUNG MACHINE.

CARDIOPULMONARY RESUSCITATION (CPR). A technique that involves massaging the chest and breathing into the mouth to keep oxygenated blood flowing to the brain when the heart is beating erratically or has stopped.

CARDIOVASCULAR. Referring to the heart and blood vessels.

CAROTID ARTERY. One of the main arteries found in the neck.

CATHETER. A hollow, flexible tube inserted through a tiny incision in the body and advanced into a cavity, duct, or vessel.

CATHETERIZATION. See CARDIAC CATHETERIZATION.

Circulatory system. The heart, arteries, veins, and capillaries that carry blood through the body. The body has two such systems: respiratory circulation and systemic circulation.

Closed heart surgery. Procedure in which a small incision is made but the chest is not opened.

Coarctation of the aorta. A congenital heart defect in which the aorta, the largest artery in the body, is narrowed. Also called *aortic coarctation*.

Congenital heart defect. Malformation of the human heart or its blood vessels that is present at birth.

Congestive heart failure. A condition that arises when the heart is unable to pump out all the blood returning to it. As a result, blood backs up in the veins and other parts of the body, sometimes causing clots to form.

Coronary arteries. The arteries that branch from the aorta and deliver blood to the heart muscle. See the drawing entitled The Coronary Arteries on p. 222.

Coronary artery bypass grafting. A procedure in which an artery or a vein (from the leg or the chest) is removed or dissected surgically, then grafted to a coronary artery above and below a blockage to increase the blood supply to the heart muscle. See the drawing entitled Coronary Artery Bypass Grafting on p. 222.

Coronary occlusion. Blockage of one of the coronary arteries that provide blood to the heart muscle.

Coronary thrombosis. A clot that forms in one of the arteries that lead to the heart muscle. Sometimes called a *coronary occlusion*.

Corticosteroids. Synthetic steroids that resemble a hormone produced by the adrenal glands in the body. Steroids decrease inflammation in the body.

Countershock. An intense, brief shock applied directly to the heart to restore normal electrical activity.

Cross-circulation. A historic technique developed by Dr. C. Walton Lillehei in which a child's parent served as a living oxygenator during heart surgery. Blood flow was routed from the child to the parent, where it was oxygenated by the parent's lungs, then pumped back into the child.

Cyanosis. Blue appearance of the skin, resulting from insufficient oxygen in the bloodstream.

Cyclosporine. A medication used with other drug agents to prevent tissue rejection in patients who receive a kidney, lung, liver, or heart transplant.

Defibrillator. A device that restores the natural contraction of a heart that is beating erratically.

DEXTROSE. The natural form of glucose.

DIAPHRAGM. The dome-shaped muscle that separates the abdominal and thoracic cavities.

DISSECTION. A condition in which the layers of an artery separate or are torn, causing blood to flow between them.

DUCTUS ARTERIOSUS. See PATENT DUCTUS ARTERIOSUS.

ECHOCARDIOGRAPHY. Use of high-frequency sound waves to map the structure of the heart.

ELECTROCARDIOGRAPHY. A method for recording the electrical impulses produced by the heart.

EMBOLISM. Sudden blockage of a blood vessel by an embolus.

EMBOLUS. A detached blood clot or other object that travels through the bloodstream, becomes caught in a vessel, and blocks blood flow in that vessel.

ENDARTERECTOMY. Surgical removal of plaque from an artery, especially the carotid arteries of the neck.

ENDOANEURYSMORRHAPHY. A technique for repairing left ventricular aneurysms that involves cutting out the dead tissue and relining the ventricle with a Dacron patch to return the ventricle to its normal shape.

ENDOSCOPY. A technique for examining internal tissues by inserting an instrument called an endoscope, which has a fiberoptic camera, into a body opening. This approach is used for the diagnosis and treatment of diseases.

EXTREMITY. The arm or leg.

FIBRILLATION. Chaotic rhythm of the heart muscle.

FLUOROSCOPY. An imaging technique that provides real-time moving images of the internal structures of the body. The images are obtained with a fluoroscope, which basically consists of an X-ray source and a fluorescent screen.

FUSIFORM ANEURYSM. A type of aneurysm that is often located along an extended section of the abdominal aorta and that involves the aorta's entire circumference.

GLUCOSE. A simple sugar that is a basic energy unit in the body.

GRAFT, VASCULAR. A healthy piece of vessel that is removed from one part of the body and used to replace a diseased or injured vessel at another site. Also a manmade fabric tube or other alternative used to replace a faulty vessel.

GREAT VESSELS. The primary blood vessels of the heart: the vena cavas (inferior and superior), the pulmonary artery, the pulmonary veins, and the aorta. See the drawing entitled The Heart and Great Vessels on p. 221.

HEART ATTACK. Death of myocardial tissue, usually resulting from blockage of the coronary arteries that feed the heart. Also called a *myocardial infarction.*

HEART BLOCK. A rhythm disturbance of the heart that occurs when electrical signals are not transmitted normally along their pathways through the heart.

HEART-LUNG MACHINE. Sometimes called "the pump," this machine takes over the functions of the heart during open heart operations; it supplies the patient's blood with oxygen, then pumps the blood through the body while the heart is stopped.

HEPARIN. A compound used to prevent blood from clotting.

HIGH BLOOD PRESSURE. Higher than normal pressure in the arteries. Also called *hypertension.*

HOMOGRAFT. A graft made of tissue from a human cadaver.

HOUSE STAFF. Surgical trainees.

HYPERTENSION. Persistently high arterial blood pressure. Also called *high blood pressure.*

HYPOTHERMIA. An abnormally low body temperature.

IMMUNE RESPONSE. The cellular response to a presence that the body does not recognize as part of itself.

IMMUNOSUPPRESSION. Suppression of the body's immune response to a foreign tissue, for example, a donor heart.

INFERIOR VENA CAVA. The large vein that returns blood from the legs and abdomen to the heart. See the drawing entitled The Heart and Great Vessels on p. 221.

INNOMINATE ARTERY. An artery that arises from the aortic arch and divides into the right subclavian and right carotid arteries. See the drawing entitled The Heart and Great Vessels on p. 221.

INTERN. A recent medical school graduate receiving supervised training in a hospital.

INTERNAL MAMMARY ARTERY. A durable artery in the chest wall often used as a bypass graft in coronary artery bypass surgery.

INTERVENTIONAL TREATMENT. Any of the noninvasive procedures usually performed in the cardiac catheterization laboratory.

ISCHEMIA. Lack of sufficient blood flow to an organ or extremity of the body. Ischemia is caused by obstruction in a blood vessel.

LEFT VENTRICULAR ASSIST DEVICE (LVAD). A mechanical device used to assist the heart in pumping blood from the left ventricle to the aorta for distribution throughout the body.

LOUPES. Magnifying lenses mounted on a surgeon's eyeglass frames or headband.

MECHANICAL ASSIST DEVICE. Any artificial mechanical device that relieves the work of the heart by assisting the heart's pumping function; these devices include the artificial heart, the intraaortic balloon pump, and left or right ventricular assist devices.

METABOLISM. The chemical processes that occur in living cells or organisms to sustain life.

MITRAL STENOSIS. Narrowing of the mitral valve that frequently results from scarring associated with rheumatic fever. This condition reduces the flow of blood through the heart and causes blood to pool in the lungs.

MITRAL VALVE. The heart valve that links the left upper chamber of the heart (atrium) to the left lower chamber (ventricle). See the drawing entitled The Heart and Great Vessels on p. 221.

MYOCARDIAL INFARCTION. See HEART ATTACK.

MYOCARDIUM. Muscle of the wall of the heart, located between the outer and inner layers of the heart.

NON-BLOOD PRIME. Liquid used in the heart-lung machine to prime the pump for open heart surgery. The liquid consists of a 5 percent solution of sugar (dextrose) and dilute saline solution.

OPHTHALMOLOGY. The branch of medicine concerned with the eye.

OTOLARYNGOLOGY. The branch of medicine concerned with the ear and throat.

OXYGENATION. Addition of oxygen to a liquid, such as blood.

OXYGENATOR. An apparatus that introduces oxygen into the blood as it is circulated through the heart-lung machine during open heart surgery.

PACEMAKER. A mechanical device that is implanted into the body and connected to the wall of the heart to regulate the heartbeat.

PARAPLEGIA. Paralysis of the lower half of the body.

PARATHYROID GLANDS. Four small glands in the neck that control the amount of calcium in the blood.

PATENT DUCTUS ARTERIOSUS. The ductus arteriosus is a small blood vessel that links the aorta and the pulmonary artery before birth and that permits blood to detour around the unused fetal lungs. When the duct fails to close after birth, the result is a congenital heart defect known as patent ductus arteriosus. See the drawing entitled Patent Ductus Arteriosus on p. 223.

PERCUTANEOUS TRANSLUMINAL CORONARY ANGIOPLASTY (PTCA). See BALLOON ANGIOPLASTY.

PERFUSION. Passage of fluids through blood vessels and organs.

PERFUSIONIST. The technologist who operates the heart-lung machine during open heart procedures.

PERIPHERAL ARTERIES. The arteries farthest from the heart. These include arteries in the head, arms, and legs.

PHRENIC NERVE. A nerve that originates in the neck area and controls the movement of the diaphragm.

PLAQUE. A fat deposit in the inner lining of an artery.

PLATELET. An element in the blood that causes clotting.

PRIME. Liquid used in the heart-lung machine to prime the pump for open heart surgery.

PROSTHESIS. A manmade device designed to replace a missing part of the body.

PULMONARY ARTERY. The artery that sends blood to the lungs to be oxygenated; it is the only artery that carries deoxygenated blood. See the drawing entitled The Heart and Great Vessels on p. 221.

PULMONARY EMBOLUS. Blockage of an artery in the lungs by a blood clot (embolus) that has traveled from another part of the body. Also *pulmonary embolism.*

PULMONARY HYPERTENSION. High blood pressure in the arteries of the lungs.

PULMONARY STENOSIS. Narrowing of the pulmonary valve, which opens into the pulmonary artery from the right ventricle.

PULMONARY VALVE. Valve located at the juncture of the pulmonary artery and the right ventricle. The valve directs blood from the right ventricle to the pulmonary artery. See the drawing entitled The Heart and Great Vessels on p. 221.

PULMONARY VEINS. The only veins that carry oxygenated blood. These veins route blood from the lungs to the left atrium. See the drawing entitled The Heart and Great Vessels on p. 221.

PUMP OXYGENATOR. See **OXYGENATOR.**

PUMP TIME. The amount of time a patient is connected to the heart-lung machine.

REJECTION. See **TRANSPLANT REJECTION.**

RESIDENT. A doctor receiving specialized training in a hospital after completing an internship.

RESTENOSIS. Reclosing or renarrowing of an artery after treatment.

RHEUMATIC FEVER. A childhood infectious disease that causes high fever. It can occur when strep throat is not treated promptly with antibiotics and can scar heart valves and inflame cardiac tissue.

SACCIFORM ANEURYSM. A sac-like, asymmetrical aneurysm that forms on the side of the aorta.

SALINE. A solution of salt in water.

SAPHENOUS VEIN. A large vein in the leg.

SEPTUM. The wall of muscle that divides the heart into right and left halves.

SHOCK. A condition in which body function is impaired because the volume of fluid circulating through the body is insufficient to maintain normal metabolism. Shock may be caused by blood loss or by a disturbance in the function of the circulatory system.

SHUNT. A connector that allows blood to flow between two locations.

SINOATRIAL NODE. The heart's natural pacemaker, found at the juncture of the superior vena cava and the right atrium.

SQUAMOUS-CELL CARCINOMA. The most common form of skin cancer.

STENOSIS. A narrowing, oftentimes of a vessel in the body or a valve in the heart.

STENT. A device made of expandable, metal mesh that is placed at a narrowed site in an artery to keep that artery open.

STERNOTOMY. An incision made down the center of the chest to separate the sternum (the breastbone) and allow access to the heart.

STERNUM. The breastbone.

STROKE. A condition in which blood supply to the brain is suddenly restricted. Also called *cerebrovascular accident*.

SUBCLAVIAN ARTERIES. Two major arteries (right and left) that receive blood from the aortic arch and supply it to the arms. See the drawing entitled The Heart and Great Vessels on p. 221.

SUPERIOR VENA CAVA. The large vein that carries blood from the upper part of the body to the right upper chamber of the heart. See the drawing entitled The Heart and Great Vessels on p. 221.

SYPHILITIC. Pertaining to syphilis, a chronic, sexually transmitted infectious disease caused by a spirochete (*Treponema pallidum*).

TACHYCARDIA. Rapid heartbeats, usually more than 100 per minute.

TETRALOGY OF FALLOT. A combination of four congenital heart defects, which causes oxygen depletion. The defects include a narrowed pulmonary valve, a ventricular septal defect, an enlarged right ventricle, and a transposed aorta and pulmonary artery. See drawing entitled Tetralogy of Fallot on p. 224

THORACIC. Relating to the chest.

THORACIC AORTA. See AORTA, THORACIC.

THORACOABDOMINAL AORTA. See AORTA, THORACOABDOMINAL.

THORACOTOMY. A surgical incision in the chest wall.

THROMBOEMBOLISM. Embolic obstruction of a blood vessel by a thrombus.

THROMBOSIS. Formation of a blood clot inside a blood vessel or in the heart cavity.

THROMBUS. A blood clot inside a blood vessel or in the heart cavity.

THYROIDECTOMY. Surgical removal of the thyroid gland.

TOTAL ANOMALOUS PULMONARY VENOUS DRAINAGE. A rare congenital condition in which the pulmonary veins are connected to the heart's right atrium instead of the left atrium.

TOTAL ARTIFICIAL HEART (TAH). A manmade pump designed to replace the natural heart.

TRANSPLANT REJECTION. Attack of a transplanted organ or tissue by the recipient's immune system.

TRANSPLANTATION. Implantation of a tissue or organ from one person into another.

TRICUSPID ATRESIA. A congenital condition in which the tricuspid valve is missing.

TRICUSPID VALVE. The heart valve that links the right lower chamber of the heart to the right upper chamber.

VALVE, CARDIAC. A structure consisting of two or three cusps held together by a muscular ring. The valves open and close in response to blood flow, causing blood to move through the heart in only one direction.

VALVE PROSTHESIS. An artificial valve used to replace a severely damaged natural valve.

VALVOTOMY. An incision made into a narrowed cardiac valve to open the valve.

VEINS. Vessels in which blood is transported from various parts of the body to the heart. All veins except the pulmonary vein carry oxygen-poor blood.

VENTRICLES. The two lower chambers of the heart. See the drawing entitled The Heart and Great Vessels on p. 221.

VENTRICULAR. Referring to the ventricles of the heart.

VENTRICULAR FIBRILLATION. Chaotic beating of the ventricles.

VENTRICULAR SEPTAL DEFECT. A hole in the dividing wall between the ventricles. The defect allows blood to flow back and forth between the two lower chambers of the heart.

VENTRICULAR SEPTUM. The dividing wall between the ventricles of the heart.

VENTRICULOPLASTY. Surgical repair of the ventricles. Also *ventricular remodeling procedure*.

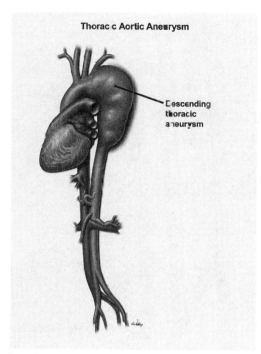

Thorac c Aortic Aneurysm

Descending
thoracic
aneurysm

Printed with permission from Baylor College of Medicine.

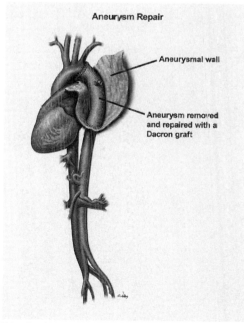

Aneurysm Repair

Aneurysmal wall

Aneurysm removed
and repaired with a
Dacron graft

Printed with permission from Baylor College of Medicine.

Vessels of the Torso

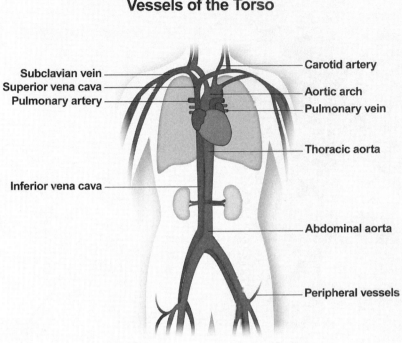

Subclavian vein

Superior vena cava

Pulmonary artery

Inferior vena cava

Carotid artery

Aortic arch

Pulmonary vein

Thoracic aorta

Abdominal aorta

Peripheral vessels

The Heart and Great Vessels

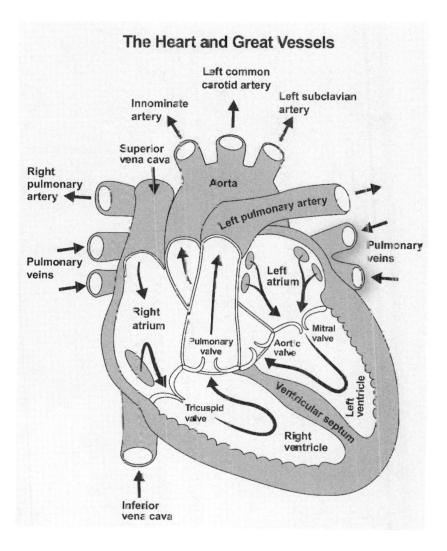

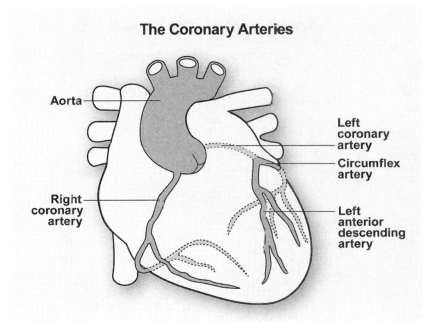

The Coronary Arteries

Aorta

Right coronary artery

Left coronary artery

Circumflex artery

Left anterior descending artery

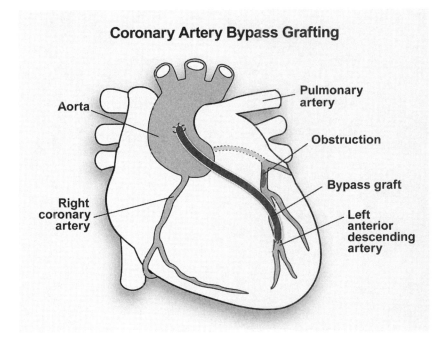

Coronary Artery Bypass Grafting

Aorta

Right coronary artery

Pulmonary artery

Obstruction

Bypass graft

Left anterior descending artery

Patent Ductus Arteriosus

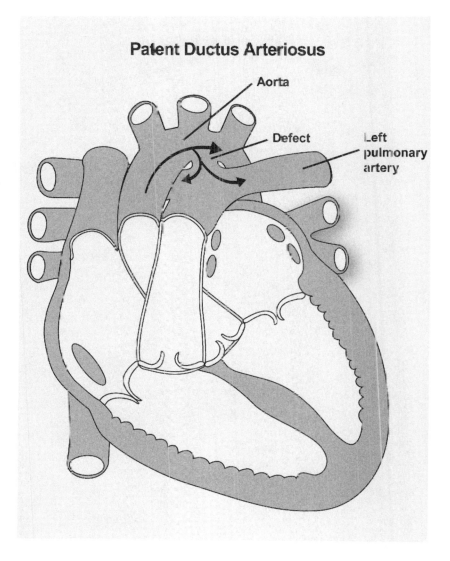

Aorta

Defect

Left
pulmonary
artery

Tetralogy of Fallot

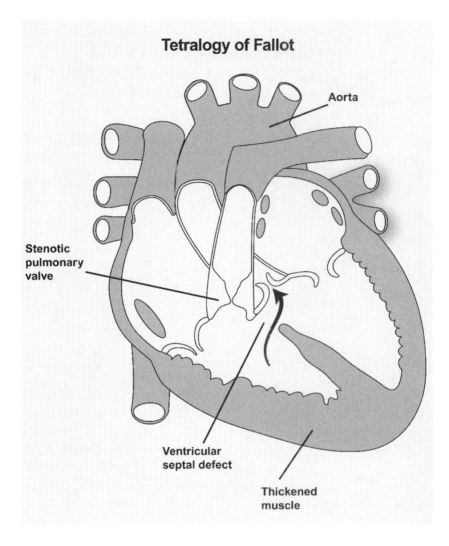

Aorta

Stenotic
pulmonary
valve

Ventricular
septal defect

Thickened
muscle

Personal Contributions to Cardiovascular Surgery

Denton A. Cooley, M.D.

1949   Excision of an aortic aneurysm*

1952   Homograft repair of a thoracoabdominal aneurysm*

1954   Excision of a ruptured abdominal aneurysm*

1956   First successful carotid endarterectomy*

1956   Repair of a post-infarction ventricular septal defect by using cardiopulmonary bypass*

1956   Repair of an aorticopulmonary septal defect by using cardiopulmonary bypass*

1956   Correction of total anomalous pulmonary venous drainage by using cardiopulmonary bypass*

1958   Excision of a left ventricular aneurysm by using cardiopulmonary bypass*

1959   Correction of congenital heart defects in newborns in 120 patients, a very large series at the time

1959   Report of 2,700 cases of arterial aneurysms

1960   Description of the relationship of spinal fluid pressure to the incidence of paraplegia after temporary aortic occlusion*

1961   Embolectomy for a massive pulmonary embolism*

1961   Open heart operations with a disposable oxygenator, 5 percent dextrose prime, and normothermia*

1962   Open heart surgery on patients of the Jehovah's Witness faith*

1962   Founding of the Texas Heart Institute

* Contributions considered "firsts" in the field of cardiovascular surgery

1963 Bypass to reconstruct the coronary system in a patient with a congenital defect of a coronary artery; this was an early type of coronary artery bypass*

1966 Intrapericardial aortic-to-right pulmonary artery anastomosis (called the Waterston-Cooley anastomosis)*

1968 First successful heart transplant in the United States*

1968 First heart-lung transplant in a human*

1969 First total artificial heart (Liotta) implantation in the world (the first bridge to transplantation)*

1970 Surgical treatment with a mitral valve prosthesis for idiopathic hypertrophic subaortic stenosis (a narrowing below the aortic valve of the heart)

1971 Commercial availability of the Cooley-Cutter artificial heart valve*

1972 Description of ischemic contracture of the heart (called "stone heart") and patients at risk for the syndrome, with a suggested preventive technique*

1972 Use of a contoured, knitted Dacron baffle for repair of transposition of the great vessels*

1972 Transaortic repair of a ventricular septal defect*

1975 Surgical treatment of left ventricular outflow tract obstruction by using a Dacron graft and valve combination (called a valved conduit)

1976 Report of a successful series of cases in which the Meadox-Cooley double-velour graft was used for arterial reconstruction*

1976 Surgical treatment of supraventricular tachycardia, a cardiac rhythm disturbance, in infants and children

1977 Delayed closure of the sternum, used to prevent tamponade or compression of the heart*

1978 Modified procedure for correction of truncus arteriosus, a congenital heart condition characterized by two main defects: a single vessel carrying blood from the heart and a hole in the ventricular septum*

1980 A method of preparing woven Dacron aortic grafts to prevent bleeding between the interstices, or spaces in the fabric, of the graft*

1981   Second total artificial heart (Akutsu-III) implantation in the world as a bridge to transplantation

1981   Report of "open" distal anastomosis for ascending and transverse arch resection in eighteen patients

1981   Comparison of hypothermic techniques in repair of aneurysms of the transverse aortic arch

1984   Cardiac transplantation in an eight-month-old female infant—at the time, the youngest-ever transplant recipient*

1984   Founding of Cardiovascular Care Providers, the first bundled services provider for open heart operations*

1987   Intravalvular implantation of a mitral valve prosthesis*

1989   Ventricular endoaneurysmorrhaphy, or intracavitary repair of a left ventricular aneurysm*

1992   Comparison of "open" distal anastomosis and the conventional two-clamp technique for repair of descending thoracic aneurysms

1993   Transmyocardial laser revascularization for ischemic coronary heart disease

1994   Repair of a post-infarction ventricular septal defect by a modified intracavitary method*

1995   Retrograde replacement of the thoracic aorta for aortic aneurysms*

1996   Myocardial revascularization by a less invasive, "limited-access" technique

1999   Selective hypothermia in the repair of aneurysms of the descending aorta*

1999   A new, transthoracic incision for implanting apico-aortic conduits*

2001   100,000 open heart operations (with Cooley team at the Texas Heart Institute)*

2002   Denton A. Cooley Building opens, with state-of-the-art diagnostic and surgical facilities for the Texas Heart Institute at St. Luke's Episcopal Hospital

Surgical Inventions and Products

Denton A. Cooley, M.D.

1949   Defibrillator (Johns Hopkins University School of Medicine)

1955   Reusable Stainless Steel Oxygenator

1956   Mark-Cooley Heart-Lung Apparatus (Mark Company)

1959   Cooley Mitral Valve Dilator (Pilling & Son)

1959   Mechanical Ventilator for Infants (with Dr. Arthur Keats)

1960s   Cooley Anastomosis Clamp (Pilling & Son)

1960s   Cooley Coarctation Clamp (Pilling & Son)

1960s   Cooley Jaw Serrations (Pilling & Son)

1960s   Cooley Pediatric Surgical Instruments (Pilling & Son)

1960s   Cooley Ring Handle Forceps, Offset Angle Forceps, Straight String-Type Tissue Forceps (These, among others, comprise a "matched set" of Cooley surgical instruments.) (Pilling & Son)

1960   Cooley Modified Dilator (for Smaller Adult Hearts) (Pilling & Son)

1960   Cooley Pediatric Modified Dilator (Pilling & Son)

1960   Cooley Pulmonary Valvulotome (Pilling & Son)

1962   Model 1500 Pump Oxygenator Console (Sarns, Inc.)

ca. 1962 Plastic Disposable Oxygenator (Travenol, Inc.)

ca. 1963 Cooley Patent Ductus Clamp (Pilling & Son)

ca. 1963 Cooley Renal Artery Clamp (Pilling & Son)

ca. 1963 Cooley Tissue Forceps (Pilling & Son)

1964   Cooley Atrial Retractors (Pilling & Son)

ca. 1964 Cooley Aortic Occlusion Clamp (Pilling & Son)

ca. 1966 Cooley Graft Suction Tube, Cooley Intracardiac Suction Tube, and
Cooley-Anthony Tip, Cooley-Crawford Tunneler (Pilling & Son)

ca. 1966 Cooley Left Ventricular Sump (Pilling & Son)

1969   Total Artificial Heart (with Dr. Domingo Liotta)

1970s   Cooley Sternotomy Retractors (V. Mueller)

1970   Cooley Knitted Graft (Licensing Agreement with Meadox Medicals, Inc.)

1971   Cooley-Cutter Heart Valve (Aortic and Mitral) (Cutter
Laboratories)

1975   Cooley Coronary Occluder, U-shaped (V. Mueller)

1975   Cooley Coronary Retractor, Straight (V. Mueller)

1975   Cooley Double Velour Guideline Graft[s] (Licensing Agreement
with Meadox Medicals, Inc.)

1975   Cooley Low Porosity Woven Graft[s] (Licensing Agreement with
Meadox Medicals, Inc.)

1976   Parallel "Y" Connectors: 16 Patented Products, Including Bifur-
cated Tubing Connector (U.S. Patent 3,944,261) (Surgimedics,
Texas Medical Products, Inc.)

1976   Saphenous Vein Cannula, Including Coronary Artery Bypass Graft
Testing Device and Method (U.S. Patent 3,958,557) (Surgimedics,
Texas Medical Products, Inc.)

1976   Veri-Soft Cooley Woven Vascular Graft[s] (Licensing Agreement
with Meadox Medicals, Inc.)

ca. 1976 Cooley Annuloplasty "C" Ring (Licensing Agreement with
Meadox Medicals, Inc.)

1976–78   Suction Systems: 23 Patented Products, Including:

1976, Suction Wand (U.S. Patent 3,963,028)

1977, Method of Making a Suction Wand (U.S. Patent 4,045,859)

1977, Surgical Suction Wand Assemblies (U.K. Patent 1,569,945)

1978, Surgical Suction Wand Assembly and Method (U.S. Patent
4,068,664) (Surgimedics, Texas Medical Products, Inc.)

1977   Air Aspirator Needles: 3 Patented Products, Including Air
Embolus Aspirator (U.S. Patent 4,002,174) (Surgimedics, Texas
Medical Products, Inc.)

1977   Disposable Surgical Instrument Tray (U.S. Patent 4,011,944)
            (Surgimedics, Texas Medical Products, Inc.)

1979   Blood Oxygenator (U.S. Patent 4,158,659—Not Produced)
            (Surgimedics, Texas Medical Products, Inc.)

1979   Multipurpose Disposable Needle for Open Heart Surgery
            (Texas Medical Products, Inc.)

1980   Blood Oxygenator Assembly Method (U.S. Patent 4,180,896—Not
            Produced) (Surgimedics, Texas Medical Products, Inc.)

ca. 1980   Cooley Knitted Graft with Guideline (Licensing Agreement with
            Meadox Medicals, Inc.)

1981   Method of Preparing Woven Dacron Grafts to Prevent Interstitial
            Hemorrhage

ca. 1982   Cooley Rigid Collar Prosthesis (Licensing Agreement with
            Meadox Medicals, Inc.)

1983   Cooley Sternal Boot (Texas Medical Products, Inc.)

1983   Pre-bypass Filters: 3 Patented Products, Including Blood and Per-
            fusate Filter (U.S. Patent 4,422,939) (Surgimedics, Texas Medical
            Products, Inc.)

ca. 1983   Cooley Flexible Collar Prosthesis (Licensing Agreement with
            Meadox Medicals, Inc.)

ca. 1983   Cooley Meadox Annuloplasty Tape (Licensing Agreement with
            Meadox Medicals, Inc.)

ca. 1984   Cooley Cold Light Projection System (Texas Medical Products,
            Inc.)

ca. 1984   Denton A. Cooley Fiber Optic Illumination Systems (Luxtec)
            (Headlamp and Gooseneck Floor Lamp)

1987   Bubble Oxygenator (U.S. Patent 4,637,917—Not Produced)
            (Surgimedics, Texas Medical Products, Inc.)

1987   Videolux Headset Camera (Luxtec)

1989   Collagen Graft[s] (Licensing Agreement with Meadox Medicals,
            Inc.)

1993   Dacron Annuloplasty Ring (Cost-effective Prosthesis Fashioned
            from Commercially Available Aortic Tube Grafts)

Appendix D

Selected Publications

Denton A. Cooley, M.D.

The 150 journal citations included here were selected from more than 1,400 publications so that readers could easily find references to my "firsts" and some other personal contributions to cardiovascular surgery. The twelve books I have authored or co-authored are at the end of this list. A complete list of my publications can be found at www.texasheart.org/cooley.

D. A. Cooley. "Cardiac Resuscitation During Operations for Pulmonic Stenosis." *Annals of Surgery*, vol. 132 (1950), pp. 930–936.

D. A. Cooley and M. E. DeBakey. "Surgical Considerations of Intrathoracic Aneurysms of the Aorta and Great Vessels." *Annals of Surgery*, vol. 135 (1952), pp. 660–680.

D. A. Cooley, M. E. DeBakey, and D. W. Chapman. "The Surgical Treatment of Mitral Stenosis by Commissurotomy: Report of Fifty Cases." *American Surgeon*, vol. 19 (1953), pp. 165–173.

D. A. Cooley and M. E. DeBakey. "Surgical Considerations of Excisional Therapy for Aortic Aneurysms." *Surgery*, vol. 34 (1953), pp. 1005–1020.

D. A. Cooley and M. E. DeBakey. "Subtotal Esophagectomy for Bleeding Esophageal Varices." *Archives of Surgery*, vol. 68 (1954), pp. 854–871.

D. A. Cooley and M. E. DeBakey. "Ruptured Aneurysms of Abdominal Aorta: Excision and Homograft Replacement." *Postgraduate Medicine*, vol. 16 (1954), pp. 334–342.

M. E. DeBakey, O. Creech Jr., D. A. Cooley, and E. Halpert. "Structural Changes in Human Aortic Homografts: Study of Ten Cases." *AMA Archives of Surgery*, vol. 69 (1954), pp. 472–482.

D. A. Cooley and M. E. DeBakey. "Resection of the Thoracic Aorta with Replacement by Homograft for Aneurysms and Constrictive Lesions." *The Journal of Thoracic Surgery*, vol. 29 (1955), pp. 66–104.

D. A. Cooley, J. R. Dunn, H. L. Brockman, and M. E. DeBakey. "Treatment of Penetrating Wounds of the Heart: Experimental and Clinical Observations." *Surgery*, vol. 37 (1955), pp. 882–889.

D. A. Cooley, G. L. Jordan, H. L. Brockman, and M. E. DeBakey. "Gastrectomy in Acute Gastroduodenal Perforation: Analysis of 112 Cases." *Annals of Surgery*, vol. 141 (1955), pp. 840–849.

D. A. Cooley and D. E. Mahaffey. "Anomalous Pulmonary Venous Drainage of Entire Left Lung: Report of Case with Surgical Correction." *Annals of Surgery*, vol. 142 (1955), pp. 986–991.

M. E. DeBakey, D. A. Cooley, and O. Creech Jr. "Resection of the Aorta for Aneurysms and Occlusive Disease with Particular Reference to the Use of Hypothermia: Analysis of 240 Cases." *Transactions of the American College of Cardiology*, vol. 5 (1955), pp. 153–157.

M. E. DeBakey, D. A. Cooley, and O. Creech Jr. "Treatment of Aneurysms and Occlusive Disease of the Aorta by Resection: Analysis of Eighty-Seven Cases." *The Journal of the American Medical Association*, vol. 157 (1955), pp. 203–208.

D. A. Cooley, Y. D. Al-Naaman, and C. A. Carton. "Surgical Treatment of Arteriosclerotic Occlusion of Common Carotid Artery." *Journal of Neurosurgery*, vol. 13 (1956), pp. 500–506.

D. A. Cooley and M. E. DeBakey. "Hypothermia in the Surgical Treatment of Aortic Aneurysms." *Bulletin de la Societe Internationale de Chirurgie*, vol. 15 (1956), pp. 206–215.

D. A. Cooley and M. E. DeBakey. "Resection of Entire Ascending Aorta in Fusiform Aneurysm Using Cardiac Bypass." *The Journal of the American Medical Association*, vol. 162 (1956), pp. 1158–1159.

D. A. Cooley, B. A. Belmonte, M. E. DeBakey, and J. R. Latson. "Temporary Extracorporeal Circulation in the Surgical Treatment of Cardiac and Aortic Disease: Report of 98 Cases." *Annals of Surgery*, vol. 145 (1957), pp. 898–914.

D. A. Cooley, B. A. Belmonte, L. B. Zeis, and S. Schnur. "Surgical Repair of Ruptured Interventricular Septum Following Acute Myocardial Infarction." *Surgery*, vol. 41 (1957), pp. 930–937.

D. A. Cooley, B. E. Castro, M. E. DeBakey, and J. R. Latson. "Use of Temporary Cardiopulmonary Bypass in Cardiac and Aortic Surgery: Report of 134 Cases." *Postgraduate Medicine*, vol. 22 (1957), pp. 479–484.

D. A. Cooley, D. G. McNamara, and J. R. Latson. "Aorticopulmonary Septal Defect: Diagnosis and Surgical Treatment." *Surgery*, vol. 42 (1957), pp. 101–120.

D. A. Cooley, D. G. McNamara, and J. R. Latson. "Surgical Treatment of Atrial and Ventricular Septal Defects: Results in 63 Patients." *Southern Medical Journal*, vol. 50 (1957), pp. 1044–1047.

D. A. Cooley and A. Ochsner Jr. "Correction of Total Anomalous Pulmonary Venous Drainage: Technical Considerations." *Surgery*, vol. 42 (1957), pp. 1014–1021.

J. P. Abbott, D. A. Cooley, M. E. DeBakey, and J. E. Ragland. "Storage of Blood for Open Heart Operations: Experimental and Clinical Observations." *Surgery*, vol. 44 (1958), pp. 698–705.

D. A. Cooley, H. A. Collins, J. W. Giacobine, G. C. Morris Jr., L. R. Soltero-Harrington, and F. J. Harberg. "The Pump Oxygenator in Cardiovascular Surgery: Observations Based Upon 450 Cases." *American Surgeon*, vol. 24 (1958), pp. 870–882.

D. A. Cooley, H. A. Collins, G. C. Morris Jr., and D. W. Chapman. "Ventricular Aneurysm after Myocardial Infarction: Surgical Excision with Use of Temporary Cardiopulmonary Bypass." *The Journal of the American Medical Association*, vol. 167 (1958), pp. 557–560.

D. A. Cooley, J. R. Latson, and A. S. Keats. "Surgical Considerations in Repair of Ventricular and Atrial Septal Defects Utilizing Cardiopulmonary Bypass: Experience with 104 Cases." *Surgery*, vol. 43 (1958), pp. 214–225.

H. A. Collins, F. J. Harberg, L. R. Soltero, D. McNamara, and D. A. Cooley. "Cardiac Surgery in the Newborn: Experience with 120 Patients under One Year of Age." *Surgery*, vol. 45 (1959), pp. 506–519.

D. A. Cooley and H. A. Collins. "Anomalous Drainage of Entire Pulmonary Venous System into Left Innominate Vein: Clinical and Surgical Considerations." *Circulation*, vol. 19 (1959), pp. 486–495.

D. A. Cooley, M. E. DeBakey, E. S. Crawford, and G. C. Morris Jr. "Surgery of the Aorta and Major Arteries: Experience with More Than 2700 Cases." *Proceedings of the Japanese Medical Congress*, vol. 15 (1959), pp. 491–494.

D. A. Cooley, W. S. Henly, K. H. Amad, and D. W. Chapman. "Ventricular Aneurysm Following Myocardial Infarction: Results of Surgical Treatment." *Annals of Surgery*, vol. 150 (1959), pp. 595–612.

D. A. Cooley, G. C. Morris Jr., and S. Attar. "Cardiac Myxoma: Surgical Treatment in Four Cases." *Archives of Surgery*, vol. 78 (1959), pp. 410–417.

F. W. Blaisdell and D. A. Cooley. "Relationship of Spinal Fluid Pressure and Incidence of Paraplegia Following Temporary Aortic Occlusion: An Experimental Study." *Surgical Forum*, vol. 11 (1960), pp. 153–154.

A. C. Beall Jr., G. C. Morris Jr., D. A. Cooley, and M. E. DeBakey. "Homotransplantation of the Aortic Valve." *Journal of Thoracic and Cardiovascular Surgery*, vol. 42 (1961), pp. 497–506.

D. A. Cooley, A. C. Beall Jr., and J. K. Alexander. "Acute Massive Pulmonary Embolism: Successful Surgical Treatment Using Temporary Cardiopulmonary Bypass." *The Journal of the American Medical Association*, vol. 177 (1961), pp. 283–286.

P. R. Ellis, D. A. Cooley, and M. E. DeBakey. "Clinical Considerations and Surgical Treatment of Annuloaortic Ectasia: Report of Successful Operation." *Journal of Thoracic and Cardiovascular Surgery*, vol. 42 (1961), pp. 363–370.

F. W. Blaisdell and D. A. Cooley. "The Mechanism of Paraplegia after Temporary Thoracic Aortic Occlusion and Its Relationship to Spinal Fluid Pressure." *Surgery*, vol. 51 (1962), pp. 351–355.

D. A. Cooley and A. C. Beall Jr. "Surgical Treatment of Acute Massive Pulmonary Embolism Using Temporary Cardiopulmonary Bypass." *Diseases of the Chest*, vol. 41 (1962), pp. 102–104.

D. A. Cooley, A. C. Beall Jr., and P. Grondin. "Open-Heart Operations with Disposable Oxygenators, 5 Per Cent Dextrose Prime, and Normothermia." *Surgery*, vol. 52 (1962), pp. 713–719.

D. A. Cooley, S. Berman, and F. A. Santibanez-Woolrich. "Surgery in the Newborn for Congenital Cardiovascular Lesions: Report of 400 Consecutive Operations." *The Journal of the American Medical Association*, vol. 182 (1962), pp. 912–917.

D. A. Cooley, H. E. Garrett, and H. S. Howard. "The Surgical Treatment of Ventricular Septal Defect: An Analysis of 300 Consecutive Surgical Cases." *Progress in Cardiovascular Diseases*, vol. 14 (1962), pp. 312–324.

J. L. Ochsner, D. A. Cooley, D. McNamara, and A. Kline. "Surgical Treatment of Cardiovascular Anomalies in 300 Infants Younger Than One Year of Age." *Journal of Thoracic and Cardiovascular Surgery*, vol. 43 (1962), pp. 182–198.

D. A. Cooley and D. M. Billig. "Surgical Repair of Congenital Cardiac Lesions in Mirror Image Dextrocardia with Situs Inversus Totalis." *The American Journal of Cardiology*, vol. 11 (1963), pp. 518–524.

D. A. Cooley and G. L. Hallman. "Criteria for Recommending Surgery in Total Anomalous Pulmonary Venous Drainage." *The American Journal of Cardiology*, vol. 12 (1963), pp. 98–99.

D. A. Cooley, E. S. Crawford, J. F. Howell, and A. C. Beall Jr. "Open Heart Surgery in Jehovah's Witnesses." *The American Journal of Cardiology*, vol. 13 (1964), pp. 779–781.

D. A. Cooley, G. L. Hallman, and W. S. Henly. "Left Ventricular Aneurysm Due to Myocardial Infarction: Experience with 37 Patients Undergoing Aneurysmectomy." *Archives of Surgery*, vol. 88 (1964), pp. 114–121.

G. L. Hallman, D. A. Cooley, D. G. McNamara, and J. R. Latson. "Single Left Coronary Artery with Fistula to Right Ventricle: Reconstruction of

Two-Coronary System with Dacron Graft." *Circulation*, vol. 32 (1965), pp. 293–297.

R. D. Bloodwell, G. L. Hallman, and D. A. Cooley. "Aneurysm of the Ascending Aorta with Aortic Valvular Insufficiency: Surgical Management." *Archives of Surgery*, vol. 92 (1966), pp 588–599.

L. T. Bowles, G. L. Hallman, and D. A. Cooley. "Open-Heart Surgery on the Elderly: Results in 54 Patients Sixty Years of Age or Older." *Circulation*, vol. 33 (1966), pp. 540–544.

D. A. Cooley, R. D. Bloodwell, A. C. Beall Jr., G. L. Hallman, and M. E. DeBakey. "Surgical Management of Aneurysms of the Ascending Aorta, Including Those Associated with Aortic Valvular Incompetence." *Surgical Clinics of North America*, vol. 46 (1966), pp. 1033–1044.

D. A. Cooley and G. L. Hallman. "Intrapericardial Aortic-Right Pulmonary Arterial Anastomosis." *Surgery, Gynecology and Obstetrics*, vol. 122 (1966), pp. 1084–1086.

D. A. Cooley, G. L. Hallman, and R. D. Bloodwell. "Definitive Surgical Treatment of Anomalous Origin of Left Coronary Artery from Pulmonary Artery: Indications and Results." *Journal of Thoracic and Cardiovascular Surgery*, vol. 52 (1966), pp. 798–808.

D. A. Cooley, G. L. Hallman, R. D. Bloodwell, and R. D. Leachman. "Two-Stage Surgical Treatment of Complete Transposition of the Great Vessels." *Archives of Surgery*, vol. 93 (1966), pp 704–714.

D. A. Cooley, G. L. Hallman, and R. D. Leachman. "Total Anomalous Pulmonary Venous Drainage: Correction with the Use of Cardiopulmonary Bypass in 62 Cases." *Journal of Thoracic and Cardiovascular Surgery*, vol. 51 (1966), pp. 88–102.

G. L. Hallman, D. A. Cooley, and D. B. Singer. "Congenital Anomalies of the Coronary Arteries: Anatomy, Pathology, and Surgical Treatment." *Surgery*, vol. 59 (1966), pp. 133–144.

D. A. Cooley, R. D. Bloodwell, G. L. Hallman, and J. A. Jacobey "Aneurysm of the Ascending Aorta Complicated by Aortic Valve Incompetence: Surgical Treatment." *The Journal of Cardiovascular Surgery*, vol. 8 (1967), pp. 1–15.

D. A. Cooley, R. D. Bloodwell, G. L. Hallman, A. F. LaSorte, R. D. Leachman, and D. W. Chapman. "Surgical Treatment of Muscular Subaortic Stenosis: Results from Septectomy in Twenty-Six Patients." *Circulation*, vol. 35 (1967), pp. I-124–I-132.

D. A. Cooley and G. L. Hallman. "Surgical Treatment of Congenital Heart Disease in Infancy: Results in 600 Cases." *AORN Journal*, vol. 26 (1967), pp. 67–72.

G. L. Hallman, J. J. Yashar, R. D. Bloodwell, and D. A. Cooley. "Intraperi-cardial Aortopulmonary Anastomosis for Tetralogy of Fallot: Clinical Experience." *Archives of Surgery*, vol. 95 (1967), pp. 709–716.

D. A. Cooley, R. D. Bloodwell, and G. L. Hallman. "Cardiac Transplanta-tion for Advanced Acquired Heart Disease." *The Journal of Cardiovascu-lar Surgery*, vol. 9 (1968), pp. 403–413.

D. A. Cooley, R. D. Bloodwell, G. L. Hallman, and J. J. Nora. "Transplan-tation of the Human Heart: Report of Four Cases." *The Journal of the American Medical Association*, vol. 205 (1968), pp. 479–486.

D. A. Cooley, G. L. Hallman, R. D. Bloodwell, J. J. Nora, and R. D. Leach-man. "Human Heart Transplantation: Experience with Twelve Cases." *The American Journal of Cardiology*, vol. 22 (1968), pp. 804–810.

D. A. Cooley, R. D. Bloodwell, G. L. Hallman, J. J. Nora, G. M. Harrison, and R. D. Leachman. "Organ Transplantation for Advanced Cardiopul-monary Disease." *The Annals of Thoracic Surgery*, vol. 8 (1969), pp. 30–46.

D. A. Cooley, D. Liotta, G. L. Hallman, R. D. Bloodwell, R. D. Leachman, and J. D. Milam. "Orthotopic Cardiac Prosthesis for Two-Staged Car-diac Replacement." *The American Journal of Cardiology*, vol. 24 (1969), pp. 723–730.

D. A. Cooley, D. Liotta, G. L. Hallman, W. Bloodwell, R. D. Leachman, and J. D. Milam. "First Human Implantation of Cardiac Prosthesis for Staged Total Replacement of the Heart." *Transactions of the American Society of Artificial Organs*, vol. 15 (1969), pp. 252–263.

B. J. Messmer, J. E. Okies, G. L. Hallman, R. D. Bloodwell, and D. A. Cooley. "Clinical Experience with a New Discoid Prosthesis for Mitral Valve Replacement." *Chest*, vol. 57 (1970), pp. 545–549.

C. W. Simmons Jr., B. J. Messmer, G. L. Hallman, and D. A. Cooley. "Vas-cular Surgery in Jehovah's Witnesses." *The Journal of the American Medi-cal Association*, vol. 213 (1970), pp. 1032–1034.

D. A. Cooley, R. D. Leachman, G. L. Hallman, S. Gerami, and R. J. Hall. "Idiopathic Hypertrophic Subaortic Stenosis: Surgical Treatment Includ-ing Mitral Valve Replacement." *Archives of Surgery*, vol. 103 (1971), pp. 606–609.

G. L. Hallman, J. J. Yashar, R. D. Bloodwell, and D. A. Cooley. "Correction of Double-Outlet Right Ventricle with Pulmonary Stenosis and Aortic Insufficiency in a Jehovah's Witness." *The Annals of Thoracic Surgery*, vol. 11 (1971), pp. 472–479.

D. A. Cooley, G. J. Reul, and D. C. Wukasch. "Ischemic Contracture of the Heart: Stone Heart." *The American Journal of Cardiology*, vol. 29 (1972), pp. 575–577.

J. R. Zaorski, G. L. Hallman, and D. A. Cooley. "Open Heart Surgery for Acquired Heart Disease in Jehovah's Witnesses. A Report of 42 Operations." *The American Journal of Cardiology*, vol. 29 (1972), pp. 186–189.

D. A. Cooley. "The First Implantation of an Artificial Heart: Reflections and Observations." *Transplantation Proceedings*, vol. 5 (1973), pp. 1135–1137.

D. A. Cooley, J. T. Dawson, G. L. Hallman, F. M. Sandiford, D. C. Wukasch, E. Garcia, and R. J. Hall. "Aortocoronary Saphenous Vein Bypass: Results in 1,492 Patients, with Particular Reference to Patients with Complicating Features." *The Annals of Thoracic Surgery*, vol. 16 (1973), pp. 380–390.

D. A. Cooley, R. D. Leachman, and D. C. Wukasch. "Diffuse Muscular Subaortic Stenosis: Surgical Treatment." *The American Journal of Cardiology*, vol. 31 (1973), pp. 1–6.

D. A. Cooley, J. E. Okies, D. C. Wukasch, F. M. Sandiford, and G. L. Hallman. "Ten-Year Experience with Cardiac Valve Replacement: Results with a New Mitral Prosthesis." *Annals of Surgery*, vol. 177 (1973), pp. 818–826.

D. A. Cooley, F. M. Sandiford, D. C. Wukasch, and G. J. Reul. "Mitral Valve Replacement with a New Prosthesis: Experience with 366 Patients." *Journal of Cardiovascular Surgery*, vol. 13 (1973), pp. 378–383.

D. A. Cooley, D. C. Wukasch, and F. M. Sandiford. "Contoured Knitted Dacron Baffle for Repair of Transposition of the Great Vessels." *The Annals of Thoracic Surgery*, vol. 15 (1973), pp. 620–623.

F. M. Sandiford, L. Chiariello, G. L. Hallman, and D. A. Cooley. "Aorto-Coronary Bypass in Jehovah's Witnesses: Report of 36 Patients." *The Journal of Thoracic and Cardiovascular Surgery*, vol. 68 (1974), pp. 1–7.

E. R. Kyger III, G. J. Reul Jr., F. M. Sandiford, D. C. Wukasch, G. L. Hallman, and D. A. Cooley. "Surgical Palliation of Tricuspid Atresia." *Circulation*, vol. 52 (1975), pp. 685–690.

J. Nef, J. Meyer, and D. A. Cooley. "Aneurysmal Dilatation of the Entire Aorta: Surgical Management of an Unusual Case." *Cardiovascular Diseases*, vol. 2 (1975), pp. 166–172.

G. J. Reul Jr., D. A. Cooley, D. C. Wukasch, E. R. Kyger III, F. M. Sandiford, G. L. Hallman, and J. C. Norman. "Long-Term Survival Following Coronary Artery Bypass: Analysis of 4,522 Consecutive Patients." *Archives of Surgery*, vol. 110 (1975), pp. 1419–1422.

D. A. Cooley. "Technical Considerations in Cardiovascular Surgery for Neonates." *The Journal of Thoracic and Cardiovascular Surgery*, vol. 71 (1976), pp. 551–553.

D. A. Cooley, P. Angelini, R. D. Leachman, and E. R. Kyger III. "Intraventricular Repair of Transposition Complexes with Ventricular Septal Defect." *The Journal of Thoracic and Cardiovascular Surgery*, vol. 71 (1976), pp. 461–464.

D. A. Cooley, J. C. Norman, G. J. Reul Jr., J. N. Kidd, and M. R. Nihill. "Surgical Treatment of Left Ventricular Outflow Tract Obstruction with Apico-Aortic Valved Conduit." *Surgery*, vol. 80 (1976), pp. 674–680.

D. A. Cooley, D. C. Wukasch, and R. D. Leachman. "Mitral Valve Replacement for Idiopathic Hypertrophic Subaortic Stenosis: Results in 27 Patients." *The Journal of Cardiovascular Surgery*, vol. 17 (1976), pp. 380–387.

D. A. Ott and D. A. Cooley. "Cardiovascular Surgery in Jehovah's Witnesses: Report of 542 Operations without Blood Transfusion." *The Journal of the American Medical Association*, vol. 238 (1977), pp. 1256–1258.

D. C. Wukasch, D. A. Cooley, F. M. Sandiford, G. Nappi, and G. J. Reul Jr. "Ascending Aorta-Abdominal Aorta Bypass: Indications, Technique, and Report of 12 Patients." *The Annals of Thoracic Surgery*, vol. 23 (1977), pp. 442–448.

D. A. Ott, D. A. Cooley, J. C. Norman, and F. M. Sandiford. "Delayed Sternal Closure: A Useful Technique to Prevent Tamponade or Compression of the Heart." *Cardiovascular Diseases*, vol. 5 (1978), pp. 15–18.

D. A. Ott, O. H. Frazier, and D. A. Cooley. "Resection of the Aortic Arch Using Deep Hypothermia and Temporary Circulatory Arrest." *Circulation*, vol. 58 (1978), pp. I-158-I-164.

D. C. Wukasch, D. A. Cooley, J. G. Bennett, B. Gontijo, and F. P. Bongiorno. "Results of a New Meadox-Cooley Double Velour Dacron Graft for Arterial Reconstruction." *The Journal of Cardiovascular Surgery*, vol. 20 (1979), pp. 249–260.

P. C. Gillette, A. Garson Jr., J. D. Kugler, D. A. Cooley, A. Zinner, and D. G. McNamara. "Surgical Treatment of Supraventricular Tachycardia in Infants and Children." *The American Journal of Cardiology*, vol. 46 (1980), pp. 281–284.

Z. Krajcer, R. Lufschanowski, P. Angelini, R. D. Leachman, and D. A. Cooley. "Septal Myomectomy and Mitral Valve Replacement for Idiopathic Hypertrophic Subaortic Stenosis: An Echocardiographic and Hemodynamic Study." *Circulation*, vol. 62 (1980), pp. I-158-I-164.

J. M. Smith III and D. A. Cooley. "Modified Procedure for Correction of Truncus Arteriosus." *The Annals of Thoracic Surgery*, vol. 29 (1980), pp. 387–389.

R. S. Bloss and D. A. Cooley. "Pancreaticojejunostomy for Fulminating Pancreatitis and Pancreatic Ascites in a Jehovah's Witness." *Journal of Pediatric Surgery*, vol. 16 (1981), pp. 79–81.

D. A. Cooley, T. Akutsu, J. C. Norman, M. A. Serrato, and O. H. Frazier.

"Total Artificial Heart in Two-Staged Cardiac Transplantation." *Cardiovascular Diseases*, vol. 8 (1981), pp. 305–319.

D. A. Cooley and J. J. Livesay. "Technique of 'Open' Distal Anastomosis for Ascending and Transverse Arch Resection." *Cardiovascular Diseases*, vol. 3 (1981), pp. 421–426.

D. A. Cooley, D. A. Ott, O. H. Frazier, and W. E. Walker. "Surgical Treatment of Aneurysms of the Transverse Aortic Arch: Experience with 25 Patients Using Hypothermic Techniques." *The Annals of Thoracic Surgery*, vol. 32 (1981), pp. 260–272.

D. A. Cooley, A. Romagnoli, J. D. Milam, and M. I. Bossart. "A Method of Preparing Woven Dacron Aortic Grafts to Prevent Interstitial Hemorrhage." *Cardiovascular Diseases*, vol. 8 (1981), pp. 48–52.

D. A. Cooley. "Staged Cardiac Transplantation: Report of Three Cases." *The Journal of Heart Transplantation*, vol. 1 (1982), pp. 145–153.

D. A. Cooley, O. H. Frazier, G. A. Painvin, L. Boldt, and B. D. Kahan. "Cardiac and Cardiopulmonary Transplantation Using Cyclosporine for Immunosuppression: Recent Texas Heart Institute Experience." *Transplantation Proceedings*, vol. 15 (1983), pp. 2567–2572.

M. J. Carmichael, D. A. Cooley, R. C. Kuykendall, and W. E. Walker. "Cardiac Surgery in Children of Jehovah's Witnesses." *Texas Heart Institute Journal*, vol. 12 (1985), pp. 57–63.

D. A. Cooley, M. J. Reardon, O. H. Frazier, and P. Angelini. "Human Cardiac Explantation and Autotransplantation: Application in a Patient with a Large Cardiac Pheochromocytoma." *Texas Heart Institute Journal*, vol. 12 (1985), pp. 171–176.

O. H. Frazier, D. A. Cooley, O. U. J. Okereke, C. T. VanBuren, and B. D Kahan. "Cardiac Transplantation at the Texas Heart Institute: Recent Experience." *Texas Medicine*, vol. 81 (1985), pp. 48–52.

C. E. Henling, M. J. Carmichael, A. S. Keats, D. A. Cooley. "Cardiac Operation for Congenital Heart Disease in Children of Jehovah's Witnesses." *The Journal of Thoracic and Cardiovascular Surgery*, vol. 89 (1985), pp. 914–920.

D. A. Cooley, O. H. Frazier, C. T. Van Buren, J. T. Bricker, and B. Radovancevic. "Cardiac Transplantation in an 8-Month-Old Female Infant with Subendocardial Fibroelastosis." *The Journal of the American Medical Association*, vol. 256 (1986), pp. 1326–1329.

R. K. Jarvik, W. C. DeVries, B. K. Semb, B. Koul, J. G. Copeland, M. M. Levinson, B. P. Griffith, L. D. Joyce, D. A. Cooley, and O. H. Frazier, "Surgical Positioning of the Jarvik-7 Artificial Heart." *The Journal of Heart Transplantation*, vol. 5 (1986), pp. 184–195.

R. Colon, O. H. Frazier, D. A. Cooley, and H. A. McAllister. "Hypothermic Regional Perfusion for Protection of the Spinal Cord During Periods of Ischemia." *The Annals of Thoracic Surgery*, vol. 43 (1987), pp. 639–643.

D. A. Cooley and M. T. Ingram. "Intravalvular Implantation of Mitral Valve Prostheses." *Texas Heart Institute Journal*, vol. 14 (1987), pp. 188–193.

O. H. Frazier, M. P. Macris, J. M. Duncan, C. T. Van Buren, and D. A. Cooley. "Cardiac Transplantation in Patients over 60 Years of Age." *The Annals of Thoracic Surgery*, vol. 45 (1988), pp. 129–132.

D. A. Cooley. "Ventricular Endoaneurysmorrhaphy: Results of an Improved Method of Repair." *Texas Heart Institute Journal*, vol. 16 (1989), pp. 72–75.

D. A. Cooley. "Surgical Treatment of Cardiac Neoplasms: 32-Year Experience." *The Thoracic and Cardiovascular Surgeon*, vol. 38 suppl. 2 (1990), pp. 176–182.

D. A. Cooley. "Repair of the Difficult Ventriculotomy." *The Annals of Thoracic Surgery*, vol. 49 (1990), pp. 150–151.

C. T. Lewis, M. C. Murphy, and D. A. Cooley. "Risk Factors for Cardiac Operations in Adult Jehovah's Witnesses." *The Annals of Thoracic Surgery*, vol. 51 (1991), pp. 448–450.

D. A. Cooley. "Simplified Techniques of Valve Replacement." *Journal of Cardiac Surgery*, vol. 7 (1992), pp. 357–362.

D. A. Cooley and R. T. Baldwin. "Technique of Open Distal Anastomosis for Repair of Descending Thoracic Aortic Aneurysms." *The Annals of Thoracic Surgery*, vol. 54 (1992), pp. 932–936.

D. A. Cooley and C. M. Burnett. "Considerations in the Surgical Treatment of Congenital Heart Disease in Children of Jehovah's Witnesses." *Texas Heart Institute Journal*, vol. 19 (1992), pp. 156–159.

D. A. Cooley, O. H. Frazier, J. M. Duncan, G. J. Reul, and Z. Krajcer. "Intracavitary Repair of Ventricular Aneurysm and Regional Dyskinesia." *Annals of Surgery*, vol. 215 (1992), pp. 417–424.

C. T. Lewis, D. A. Cooley, M. C. Murphy, O. Talledo, and D. Vega. "Surgical Repair of Aortic Root Aneurysms in 280 Patients." *The Annals of Thoracic Surgery*, vol. 53 (1992), pp. 38–46.

D. A. Cooley. "Myocardial Dysfunction and Mitral Valve Prolapse: A New Physiologic Concept." *Texas Heart Institute Journal*, vol. 20 (1993), pp. 69–70.

D. A. Cooley and L. R. Colosimo. "Eversion Technique for Carotid Endarterectomy." *Surgery, Gynecology and Obstetrics*, vol. 177 (1993), pp. 420–422.

D. A. Cooley. "Fifty Years of Cardiovascular Surgery." *The Annals of Thoracic Surgery*, vol. 57 (1994), pp. 1059–1063.

D. A. Cooley. "Repair of Postinfarction Ventricular Septal Defect." *Journal of Cardiac Surgery*, vol. 9 (1994), pp. 427–429.

D. A. Cooley. "Further Experience with Exsanguination for Descending Thoracic Aneurysms." *Journal of Cardiac Surgery*, vol. 9 (1994), pp. 625–630.

D. A. Cooley, O. H. Frazier, K. A. Kadipasaoglu, S. Pehlivanoglu, R. L. Shannon, and F. Angelini. "Transmyocardial Laser Revascularization: Anatomic Evidence of Long-Term Channel Patency." *Texas Heart Institute Journal*, vol. 21 (1994), pp. 220–224.

S. A. Scheinin and D. A. Cooley. "Graft Replacement of the Descending Thoracic Aorta: Results of 'Open' Distal Anastomosis." *The Annals of Thoracic Surgery* vol. 58 (1994), pp. 19–23.

D. A. Cooley. "Retrograde Replacement of the Thoracic Aorta." *Texas Heart Institute Journal*, vol. 22 (1995), pp. 162–165.

D. A. Cooley. "Acquiring and Improving Surgical Skills." *Current Surgery*, vol. 52 (1995), pp. 327–329.

D. A. Cooley. "Limited Access Myocardial Revascularization: A Preliminary Report." *Texas Heart Institute Journal*, vol. 23 (1996), pp. 81–84.

D. A. Cooley, O. H. Frazier, K. A. Kadipasaoglu, M. H. Lindenmeir, S. Pehlivanoglu, J. W. Kolff, S. Wilansky, and W. H. Moore. "Transmyocardial Laser Revascularization: Clinical Experience with Twelve-Month Follow-Up." *The Journal of Thoracic and Cardiovascular Surgery*, vol. 111 (1996), pp. 791–799.

D. A. Cooley. "Single-Clamp Repair of Aneurysms of the Descending Thoracic Aorta." *Seminars in Thoracic and Cardiovascular Surgery*, vol. 10 (1998), pp. 87–90

D. A. Cooley. "Postinfarction Ventricular Septal Rupture." *Seminars in Thoracic and Cardiovascular Surgery*, vol. 10 (1998), pp. 100–104.

O. H. Frazier, K. A. Kadipasaoglu, B. Radovancevic, H. B. Cihan, R. J. March, M. Mirheseini, and D. A. Cooley. "Transmyocardial Laser Revascularization in Allograft Coronary Artery Disease." *The Annals of Thoracic Surgery*, vol. 65 (1998), pp. 1138–1141.

D. A. Cooley and J. W. Boyer. "Selective Hypothermia in Repair of Aneurysms of the Descending Aorta." *Texas Heart Institute Journal*, vol. 26 (1999), pp. 103–105.

V. L. Gott, P. S. Greene, D. E. Alejo, D. E. Cameron, D. C. Naftel, D. C. Miller, A. M. Gillinov, J. C. Laschinger, H. G. Borst, C. E. A. Cabrol, D. A. Cooley, J. S. Coselli, T. E. David, R. B. Griepp, N. T. Kouchoukos, M. I. Turina, and R. E. Pyeritz. "Replacement of the Aortic Root in Patients with Marfan's Syndrome." *The New England Journal of Medicine*, vol. 340 (1999), pp. 1307–1313.

D. A. Cooley and O. H. Frazier. "The Past 50 Years of Cardiovascular Surgery." *Circulation*, vol. 102 (2000), pp. IV-87–IV-93.

D. A. Cooley, A. Golino, and O. H. Frazier. "Single-Clamp Technique for

Aneurysms of the Descending Thoracic Aorta: Report of 132 Consecutive Cases." *European Journal of Cardio-Thoracic Surgery*, vol. 18 (2000), pp. 162–167.

D. A. Cooley and B. A. Jones. "Use of Selective Hypothermia to Protect the Spinal Cord During Resection of Thoracoabdominal Aneurysms." *Texas Heart Institute Journal*, vol. 27 (2000), pp. 29–31.

D. A. Cooley, R. M. Lopez, and T. S. Absi. "Apicoaortic Conduit for Left Ventricular Outflow Tract Obstruction Revisited." *The Annals of Thoracic Surgery*, vol. 69 (2000), pp. 1511–1514.

D. A. Cooley. "The Total Artificial Heart as a Bridge to Cardiac Transplantation: Personal Recollections." *Texas Heart Institute Journal*, vol. 28 (2001), pp. 200–202.

D. A. Cooley. "Early Development of Surgical Treatment for Aortic Aneurysms: Personal Recollections." *Texas Heart Institute Journal*, vol. 28 (2001), pp. 197–199.

C. D. Fraser Jr., E. D. McKenzie, and D. A. Cooley. "Tetralogy of Fallot: Surgical Management Individualized to the Patient." *The Annals of Thoracic Surgery*, vol. 71 (2001), pp. 1556–1563.

D. A. Cooley. "Initial Clinical Experience with the Jarvik 2000 Implantable Axial-Flow Left Ventricular Assist System." *Circulation*, vol. 105 (2002), pp. 2808–2809.

R. M. Reul, D. A. Cooley, G. L. Hallman, and G. J. Reul. "Surgical Treatment of Coronary Artery Anomalies: Report of a 37½-Year Experience at the Texas Heart Institute." *Texas Heart Institute Journal*, vol. 29 (2002), pp. 299–307.

D. A. Cooley. "Early Experience with Cardiopulmonary Bypass: Reflections." *Journal of Cardiac Surgery*, vol. 18 (2003), pp. 265–267.

D. A. Cooley and J. W. Adams. "Package Pricing at the Texas Heart Institute," in *Consumer-Driven Health Care: Implications for Providers, Payers, and Policymakers*, edited by R. E. Herzlinger. San Francisco: Jossey-Bass, 2004, pp. 612–618.

D. A. Cooley. "Left Ventricular Aneurysm: Ventricular Endoaneurysmorrhaphy," in *Mastery of Cardiothoracic Surgery*, edited by L. R. Kaiser, I. L. Kron, and T. L. Spray. Philadelphia: Lippincott, Williams & Wilkins, 2007, pp. 430–437.

T. Z. Karas, G. J. Reul, and D. A. Cooley. "C-Ring Mitral Annuloplasty: 27-Year Follow-Up." *Texas Heart Institute Journal*, vol. 34 (2007), pp. 102–104.

D. A. Cooley. "A Brief History of the Texas Heart Institute." *Texas Heart Institute Journal*, vol. 35 (2008), pp. 235–239.

D. A. Cooley, O. V. Cabello, and F. M. Preciado. "Repair of Total Anomalous Pulmonary Venous Return: Results after 47 Years." *Texas Heart Institute Journal*, vol. 35 (2008), pp. 451–453.

D. A. Cooley. "Surgical Mentors: Blalock, Brock, and DeBakey." *Texas Heart Institute Journal*, vol. 36 (2009), pp. 433–434.

D. A. Cooley. "The First Blalock-Taussig Shunt." *The Journal of Thoracic and Cardiovascular Surgery*, vol. 140 (2010), pp. 750–751.

D. A. Cooley. "Recollections of the Early Years of Heart Transplantation and the Total Artificial Heart." *Artificial Organs*, vol. 35 (2011), pp. 353–357.

Books

D. A. Cooley and G. L. Hallman. *Surgical Treatment of Congenital Heart Disease*. 1st ed. Philadelphia: Lea & Febiger, 1966.

D. A. Cooley and J. C. Norman. *Techniques in Cardiac Surgery*. 1st ed. Houston: Texas Medical Press, 1975.

G. L. Hallman and D. A. Cooley. *Surgical Treatment of Congenital Heart Disease*. 2nd ed. Philadelphia: Lea & Febiger, 1975.

D. A. Cooley and D. C. Wukasch. *Techniques in Vascular Surgery*. Philadelphia: Saunders, 1979.

D. A. Cooley. *Reflections and Observations: Essays of Denton A. Cooley*. 1st ed. Austin: Eakin Press, 1984.

D. A. Cooley. *Techniques in Cardiac Surgery*. 2nd ed. Philadelphia: W. B. Saunders, 1984.

D. A. Cooley. *Surgical Treatment of Aortic Aneurysms*. Philadelphia: Saunders, 1986.

D. A. Cooley and C. E. Moore. *Eat Smart for a Healthy Heart Cookbook*. New York: Barron's, 1987.

G. L. Hallman, D. A. Cooley, and H. P. Gutgesell. *Surgical Treatment of Congenital Heart Disease*. 3rd ed. Philadelphia: Lea & Febiger, 1987.

D. A. Cooley and the Texas Heart Institute Foundation. *Twenty-Five Years of Excellence: A History of the Texas Heart Institute*. Houston: Texas Heart Institute Foundation, 1989.

D. A. Cooley. *Cardiac Surgery: Techniques for Treating Cardiovascular Disease*. How I Do It Series. Philadelphia: Hanley & Belfus, 1990.

D. A. Cooley and the Texas Heart Institute. *Heart Owner's Handbook*. New York: Wiley, 1996.

Denton A. Cooley Cardiovascular Surgical Society

International Meetings and Recipients, DACCVS Society
International Recognition Award

1972–
1978   Houston, Texas
        Award Not Given

1979   Monte Carlo, Monaco
        Award Not Given

1981   Rio de Janeiro, Brazil
        E. J. Zerbini, M.D.
        Sao Paolo, Brazil

1982   Athens, Greece
        Award Not Given

1984   London, United Kingdom
        Donald Ross, M.D.
        London, United Kingdom

1986   Maui, Hawaii
        Juro J. Wada, M.D.
        Tokyo, Japan

1988   Bermuda, United Kingdom
        C. Walton Lillehei, M.D.
        St. Paul, Minnesota

1990   Acapulco, Mexico
        Robert D. Leachman, M.D.
        Houston, Texas

1992   San Juan, Puerto Rico
        René G. Favaloro, M.D.
        Buenos Aires, Argentina

1994   Hilton Head, South
        Carolina
        Paul A. Ebert, M.D.
        Pebble Beach, California

1996   Sun Valley, Idaho
        Albert Starr, M.D.
        Portland, Oregon

1998   Colorado Springs,
        Colorado
        John L. Ochsner, M.D.
        New Orleans, Louisiana

2000   Coeur d'Alene, Idaho
        Jerome H. Kay, M.D.
        Los Angeles, California

2002   Carlsbad, California   2009   Galveston, Texas
         Bruce A. Reitz, M.D.   *George J. Reul, M.D.*
         Stanford, California   *Houston, Texas*

2004   Houston, Texas   2010   Austin, Texas[1]
         Stephen Westaby, M.D.   *Francisco Cigarroa, M.D.*
         Oxford, United Kingdom   *Austin, Texas*

2007   Houston, Texas
         Robert A. Guyton, M.D.
         Atlanta, Georgia

[1] First Joint Symposium of the Denton A. Cooley Cardiovascular Surgical Society and the Michael E. DeBakey International Surgical Society

Curriculum Vitae

Denton Arthur Cooley

ADDRESS	Texas Heart Institute
	P.O. Box 20345, 1101 Bates Avenue
	Houston, Texas 77225-0345
BIRTHDATE	August 22, 1920, Houston, Texas
MARRIED	Louise Goldsborough Thomas
CHILDREN	Mary, Susan, Louise, Florence, Helen

EDUCATION

Houston Public Schools

1931	Montrose Elementary School
1934	Sidney Lanier Junior High School
	American Legion Award
1937	San Jacinto High School
	All City Basketball Team
	Texas High School Basketball Hall of Honor

Undergraduate Education

1941 — B.A. University of Texas, Austin, Texas (zoology, highest honors)

Phi Eta Sigma freshman scholarship

Alpha Epsilon Delta premedical honor society

Phi Beta Kappa scholastic fraternity

Kappa Sigma social fraternity (National Man of the Year, 1964)

Texas Cowboys

Basketball: freshman team (1938), varsity letterman (1939–1940), Southwest Conference Champions (1939), Longhorn Hall of Honor (1967)

Graduate Education

1941–1942	University of Texas Medical Branch (Galveston, Texas)
1943–1944	M D. Johns Hopkins University School of Medicine, Baltimore, Maryland
	Alpha Omega Alpha scholastic fraternity

Postgraduate Training

1944–1945	Intern, Straight Surgery, Johns Hopkins University School of Medicine, Baltimore, Maryland
1945–1950	Resident, Surgery, Johns Hopkins University School of Medicine, Baltimore, Maryland
1950–1951	Senior Surgical Registrar, Thoracic Surgery, Brompton Hospital for Chest Diseases, London, England

MILITARY SERVICE

1946– 1948	Captain, Chief of Surgical Service, Army Medical Corps 124th Station Hospital, Linz, Austria (leave of absence from Hopkins Residency)

CERTIFICATIONS

1951	The American Board of Surgery
1952	The American Board of Thoracic Surgery

ACADEMIC APPOINTMENTS

1946–1950	Instructor of Surgery, Johns Hopkins University School of Medicine Baltimore, Maryland
1951–1959	Instructor of Surgery Associate Professor of Surgery Professor of Surgery Baylor University College of Medicine
1969	Resigned as Professor of Surgery, Baylor University College of Medicine
1975–Present	Clinical Professor of Surgery, University of Texas Medical School, Houston, Texas
2005– Present	Clinical Professor of Surgery, Baylor College of Medicine, Houston, Texas

HOSPITAL APPOINTMENTS

Texas Heart Institute
1962–Present   Surgeon-in-Chief

1995–2008   President

2008–Present   President Emeritus

St. Luke's Episcopal Hospital
1986–Present   Chief, Cardiovascular Surgery

Texas Children's Hospital
1956–Present   Consultant in Cardiovascular Surgery

SELECTED AFFILIATIONS

1969–1970   President, Johns Hopkins Medical & Surgical Association

1981–1987   Board of Trustees, The Johns Hopkins University

1995–Present   Development Board, The University of Texas, Austin

1995–Present   Board of Directors, The Texas Cowboys

PROFESSIONAL ORGANIZATIONS

American Association for Thoracic Surgery, American College of Chest
Physicians, American College of Cardiology, American College of Sur-
geons, American Heart Association, American Medical Association,
American Society of Artificial Organs, American Surgical Association,
Blalock "Old Hands" Club, Halsted Society, Harris County Medical Soci-
ety, Houston Academy of Medicine, Houston Heart Association, Houston
Surgical Society, International Cardiovascular Society, International Society
for Heart Transplantation, International Society of Surgery, Johns Hop-
kins Medical & Surgical Association, New York Academy of Sciences, Pan
Pacific Surgical Association, Society for Vascular Surgery, Society of Clini-
cal Surgery, Society of Thoracic Surgeons, Society of University Surgeons,
Southern Medical Association, Southern Surgical Association, Southern
Thoracic Surgical Association, Southwestern Surgical Association, Texas
Heart Association, Texas Medical Association, Texas Surgical Society,
Western Surgical Association

HONORARY MEMBERSHIPS IN PROFESSIONAL ORGANIZATIONS

Honorary memberships in thirty-nine professional organizations in countries throughout the world, including Argentina, Brazil, Bulgaria, Ecuador, France, Germany, Great Britain, Greece, Ireland, Israel, Italy, Japan, Mexico, Peru, Turkey, Ukraine, Venezuela, and Yugoslavia

Numerous honorary U.S. memberships, including one in the Michael E. DeBakey International Surgical Society

HONORARY FELLOWSHIPS

1980	Fellow, Royal College of Physicians and Surgeons of Glasgow
1982	Fellow, International College of Surgeons
1984	Fellow, Royal College of Surgeons in Ireland
1986	Fellow, Royal Australasian College of Surgeons
1988	Fellow, The Royal College of Surgeons of England
1994	Fellow, International College of Angiology
1994	Fellow, The Royal Society of Medicine, London, England
2007	Fellow, The Royal College of Surgeons, Edinburgh

HONORS AND AWARDS

1954	Hektoen Gold Medal for a Scientific Exhibit, American Medical Association
1954	Distinguished Service Award, Houston Junior Chamber of Commerce
1954	Five Outstanding Young Texans, Texas Junior Chamber of Commerce
1955	Ten Outstanding Young Men in the U.S., Junior Chamber of Commerce
1959	Distinguished Service Certificate, Houston Heart Association
1961	Silver Bucranium, Venice International Film Festival
1963	Grande Medaille, University of Ghent, Belgium
1963	Coronat Medal, St. Edward's University
1963	Humanitarian Award, Variety Clubs International

1964   Kappa Sigma Man of the Year, Kappa Sigma Fraternity

1965   Distinguished Citizen Award, Rotary Club of Houston

1966   Man of the Year, Tau Trustees of Kappa Sigma Fraternity

1966   Distinguished Alumnus Award, University of Texas

1967   Honor Award of the Year, National Jewish Hospital in Denver

1967   Longhorn Hall of Honor (Athletic), University of Texas

1967   René Leriche Prize (most significant contribution to cardiovascular surgery), International Surgical Society

1967   Billings Gold Medal, American Medical Association

1968   Distinguished Achievement Award, Modern Medicine

1968   Texas Man of the Year, United Press International

1968   Academic Grand Gold Collar, Accademia Internationale Di Pontzen

1969   Academy of Texas, Governor John Connally of Texas

1969   Samuel L. Siegler Foundation Award

1970   Dr. Eugene H. Drake Award, Maine Heart Association

1971   Distinguished Alumnus, Johns Hopkins University

1971   Vishnevsky Medal, Vishnevsky Institute, USSR

1972   Dr. Roswell Park Medal, Buffalo Surgical Society

1973   Wisdom Hall of Fame

1973   Semmelweis Medal, Semmelweis Medical Society

1973   Service to Mankind Award, Sertoma Clubs of Houston

1976   Souvenir Oration, V World Congress of Cardiology, Cardiological Society of India

1976   John H. Gibbon, M.D., Award (for outstanding contribution to perfusion technology), American Society of Extra-Corporeal Technology

1976   Meritorious Service Award, American Heart Association, Houston Chapter

1976   Presidential Citation, American College of Chest Physicians (in recognition of distinguished contributions to cardiovascular surgery)

1977   Distinguished Service Award, American Society of Abdominal Surgeons

1977	Commander, The Military and Hospitaller, Order of Saint Lazarus of Jerusalem, Grand Priory of America
1978	The Italian Historical Society of America Hall of Fame
1979	Founder's Recognition Award of the Morton F. Plant Hospital Foundation (First Annual)
1979	The National Society of the Sons of the American Revolution Good Citizenship Award
1980	National Collegiate Athletic Association, Theodore Roosevelt Award
1980	Distinguished Texan for Historic Preservation (Galvez Hotel)
1980	St. Frances Cabrini Gold Medal (Service to Humanity), First Recipient
1981	Distinguished Alumnus Award, Johns Hopkins University
1982	"Cavaliere dell'Umanità," The Societa Filantropica Internationale (Italy)
1982	Howard Miller Hour Glass Award
1984	Texas Heritage Award
1984	Presidential Medal of Freedom (Presented by President Ronald Reagan)
1984	Boehringer Ingelheim, Ltd. Award for World Leadership in Cardiovascular Surgery
1985	Dhanvantari Award (India)
1985	Houston Baptist University President's Council First Humanitarian Award
1985	Winston Churchill Medal of Wisdom (Wisdom Society and the Wisdom Hall of Fame)
1985	Ray C. Fish Award and the Texas Heart Institute Medal
1986	Houston Hall of Fame (Greater Houston Convention & Visitors Council)
1986	Knighthood, The Military and Hospitaller Order of St. Lazarus of Jerusalem
1986	Humana Heart Foundation Award
1986	Medal of the Social Welfare Society of Moschato (Athens, Greece)
1987	American College of Cardiology Gifted Teacher Award

1987 Johns Hopkins University Society of Scholars

1987 Silver Seal Award, City of Torino, Italy

1987 Profesor Honorario, Universidad de Buenos Aires Facultad de Medicina

1987 Profesor Extranjero de la Escuela de Graduado de la Asociación Médica (Argentina)

1987 The Father Flanagan Award for Service to Youth (Boystown, Nebraska)

1988 Personnalité de l'Année (Paris, France)

1991 Natural Sciences Hall of Honor Award, University of Texas, Austin

1992 President Elect, The Society of Thoracic Surgeons

1992 Distinguished Phi Beta Kappa Alumnus Award

1992 Cartier Pasha Award

1993 The Mended Hearts Dwight E. Harken Award

1993 Henry Renfert Award for Excellence in Medicine, Austin Diagnostic Clinic, Austin, Texas

1993 President, The Society of Thoracic Surgeons

1994 Honorary Member, The Romanian Medical Academy Praesidium

1994 Ashbel Smith Distinguished Alumnus Award, The University of Texas Medical Branch, Galveston

1994 Honorary Member, The Pennsylvania Association for Thoracic Surgery

1994 Honorary Fellow, Scientific Council, International College of Angiology

1994– President, Seniors Cardiovascular Surgical Society
1995

1995 Texas High School Basketball Hall of Fame

1995 Distinguished Surgeon, Alpha Omega Alpha

1995 Ukrainian Academy of Medical Sciences

1996 Grand Plaque of the University of Belgrade

1997 American Medical Association Distinguished Service Award

1998   Inventor of the Year Award, Houston Intellectual Property Law Association

1998   Admiral in the Texas Navy

1998   Association of Black Cardiologists Legends of Cardiology Award

1999   Association of Operating Room Nurses of Greater Houston Distinguished Surgeon Award

1999   National Medal of Technology (Presented by President William Clinton)

2000   Texas Science Hall of Fame (Charter Member)

2000   American Association of Thoracic Surgery Scientific Achievement Award

2000   Grand Hamdan International Award for Medical Science

2001   Johns Hopkins University School of Medicine Distinguished Medical Alumnus Award

2002   The Greats of Cardiac Surgery, University of Freiburg, Freiburg, Germany

2002   Houston Hall of Fame

2002   P. D. Chang Visiting Professor, The Chinese University of Hong Kong

2002   Visiting Professor, Shanghai 2nd Chinese Medical University, Shanghai

2003   John P. McGovern Compleat Physician Award, Harris County Medical Society

2003   Earl Bakken Scientific Achievement Award, The Society of Thoracic Surgeons

2003   The Woodrow Wilson Award for Public Service

2003   Eminent Churchill Fellow, Winston Churchill Medal of Wisdom Society

2003   Pioneer in Blood Management and Conservation by Society for Advancement in Blood Management

2003   Talal Zein Foundation Award, Mediterranean Association of Cardiology, Beirut, Lebanon

2005   Outstanding Surgical Patient Service Award (for Pioneering Cardiovascular Surgery), American College of Surgeons

2006	NCAA's 100 Most Influential Student Athletes
2006	Texas Surgical Society Distinguished Service Award
2006	World Society of Cardio-Thoracic Surgeons, Living Legends Award
2006	Finalist ACGME Parker J. Palmer "Courage to Teach" Award
2006	100 Tall Texans, George Bush Presidential Library
2006	Distinguished Scientist Award, St. Luke's Episcopal Hospital
2007	Legends in Medicine Award, University of Texas Medical Branch, Galveston, Texas
2007	Pro Bene Meritis Award, College of Liberal Arts, University of Texas, Austin
2007	BioLink USA/Ireland Life Science Award, New York, New York
2007	Kappa Sigma Hall of Honor (Greater Cause Distinguished Alumni Award)
2007	TIAA-CREF Distinguished Medical Educator Award
2007	People Helping People Foundation International (The Philippines), Helping Heart Award
2008	Dean, International Faculty for Medical Technologies (Houston, Texas)
2008	First Recipient of the Distinguished Texan Award, by Governor Rick Perry
2009	Galleria Chamber of Commerce Texas Legend Award (Houston, Texas)
2009	Houston Forum, Heart to Heart Award
2009	Men of Distinction Award
2009	Honorary Professor of Dental Sciences, University of Texas Health Science Center at Houston and University of Texas Dental Branch at Houston
2010	Dr. Barney Clark Award, Utah Artificial Heart Institute
2010	American Surgical Association Medallion of Scientific Achievement for Distinguished Service to Surgery
2010	National Marfan Foundation, Antoine Marfan Award
2010	Texas Cowboys Distinguished Alumnus Award
2011	Texas Lyceum Stewardship of Texas Values Award

2011 Texas State History Museum Foundation History-Making Texan Award

2011 Bakoulev Premium, Bakoulev Center for Cardiovascular Surgery, Russian Academy of Medical Science

DECORATIONS FROM FOREIGN COUNTRIES

Argentina

1974 Orden de Mayo al Mérito en el Grado de Gran Oficial (highest civil decoration)

1995 Dr. Luis Federico Leloir Medal for Science

1995 Medal for Scientific Achievement of the Twentieth Century

Ecuador

1961 Condecoración al Mérito

Greece

1982 The Golden Medal of Honor (City of Athens, Greece)

Italy

1970 Knight Commander in the Order of Merit of Italian Republic

1976 Cavaliere di Gran Croce, Order of Merit of the Italian Republic

Jordan

1975 Gran Cordon of the Order of Al-Kawakab Al-Urduni, Jordan

The Netherlands

1982 Order of Orange-Nassau

Panama

1967 Order de Vasco Nuñez de Balboa en el Grado de Caballero

Peru

1967 Order of the Sun

Philippines

1975 The Golden Heart Presidential Award

Spain

1969   Blue Cross Medal

1970   Grand Cross of the Civil Order of Alfonso X, The Wise

Venezuela

1977   La Condecoración General Francisco De Miranda (Primera Clase)

1993   Cruz Nacional de Sanidad de la Republica de Venezuela

1995   Orden de Andrés Bello

HONORARY DEGREES

1969   Doctor Honoris Causa, University of Turin, Italy

1984   Doctor of Humanities, Hellenic College and Holy Cross Greek Orthodox School of Theology, Brookline, Massachusetts

1985   Doctor of Humane Letters, Houston Baptist University, Houston, Texas

1987   Doctor of Science Honoris Causa, The College of William and Mary, Williamsburg, Virginia

1988   Doctor of Sport Sciences, United States Sports Academy, Daphne, Alabama

1993   Doctor of Medicine and Surgery, Honoris Causa, University Di Roma Tor Vergata, Rome, Italy

1993   Doctor Honoris Causa, Universidad Autonoma de Puebla, Puebla, Mexico

2002   Doctor Honoris Causa, Universidad de Morón, Buenos Aires, Argentina

Index

DAC in subheadings refers to Denton A. Cooley. Notes are indicated by 'n' following page number. Appendices and photos are not indexed.